The Communicative Grammar of English Workbook

The Communicative Grammar of English Workbook

Edward Woods and Rudy Coppieters

An imprint of **Pearson Education**

London · New York · Toronto · Sydney · Tokyo · Singapore · Hong Kong · Cape Town
Madrid · Paris · Amsterdam · Munich · Milan

PEARSON EDUCATION LIMITED

Head Office:
Edinburgh Gate
Harlow CM20 2JE
Tel: +44 (0)1279 623623
Fax: +44 (0)1279 431059

London Office:
128 Long Acre
London WC2E 9AN
Tel: +44 (0)20 7447 2000
Fax: +44 (0)20 7447 2170
Website: www.pearsoneduc.com

_____

First published in Great Britain 2002

© Pearson Education Limited 2002

The rights of Edward Woods and Rudy Coppieters
to be identified as Authors of this Work has been
asserted by them in accordance with the Copyright,
Designs and Patents Act 1988.

ISBN 0 582 38181 9

British Library Cataloguing in Publication Data
A CIP catalogue record for this book can be obtained from the British Library

Library of Congress Cataloging in Publication Data
A CIP catalog record for this book can be obtained from the Library of Congress

10 9 8 7 6 5 4 3 2 1

Typeset in 9/12pt Stone serif by Graphicraft Limited, Hong Kong
Printed in Malaysia

The Publishers' policy is to use paper manufactured from sustainable forests.

Contents

Acknowledgements

We are grateful to the following for permission to reproduce copyright material:

A. P. Watt Limited on behalf of Jan Morris for an extract from *Among the Cities* by Jan Morris; Cambridge University Press for extracts from *Exploring Spoken English* by R. Carter and M. McCarthy (1987); Her Majesty's Stationery Office for extracts from *The Highway Code*; The National Trust Magazine for an extract from *The National Trust Magazine* No. 95, Spring 2002; Ordnance Survey and Jarrold Publishing for an extract from *Pathfinder Guides: Dartmoor Walks* by Brian Conduit and John Brooks; Oxford University Press for extracts from *Britain* by James O'Driscoll © Oxford University Press 1995; Penguin Books Limited for extracts from *Pole to Pole* by Michael Palin, and *The Brimstone Wedding* by Barbara Vine; Saga Publishing Limited for an extract from *Saga Magazine* February 2002; and World Cancer Research Fund for an extract adapted from 'Losing weight and keeping it off' by Chris McLaughlin published in *World Cancer Research Fund Newsletter* Issue 45, Winter 2001.

Introduction

This is the workbook for *A Communicative Grammar of English* by Geoffrey Leech & Jan Svartvik (3rd edition, published by Pearson Education, 2002). As such, it should be used in conjunction with the grammar.

In this workbook, we have tried to combine the three parts of the grammar. While we have mainly drawn on Part 2 – Grammar in Use, we make reference to Part 1 and to Part 3. In some units, these parts are the main focus.

The workbook does not follow the order of the grammar, except insofar as the units follow the order of sections in Part One and Part Two. In general we have used the descriptions of the sections in the grammar as the headings for the sub-units here.

In the contents and at the beginning of each sub-unit, we list the sections referred to in the grammar. The main sections are those in bold at the beginning. The other sections mentioned indicate where reference is made to the topic.

At the beginning of each sub-unit, there is a brief explanation of how a particular structure is formed and/or when it is used, how certain meanings can be expressed, etc. This is based on the explanations in the grammar and users should refer to the main grammar for more detailed explanations and examples.

The nature of the grammar means that the length of the sub-units varies. In some cases there will be several tasks to demonstrate the variety of use, whereas in others there are only a few tasks or even just one.

Tasks vary in nature, ranging from traditional gap filling exercises to rewrite assignments and conversational passages in which the student is invited to participate in an interactive way.

Not all tasks are equally difficult. For the student's guidance, each task is followed by one, two or three asterisks, suggesting that it is relatively easy, moderately difficult or quite challenging.

At the end of the book there is an Answer Key. The nature of the grammar means that many tasks will have several possible answers. In these cases we have only suggested answers and others will be possible. Our answers should not be considered the best ones but are only there as a guide.

It is expected that students using this book will be advanced students with a good grounding in the grammar of the language. They now need the opportunity to perfect their skills in the language. They will find this book useful to work on their own and to practise the points raised in the descriptions in the main grammar. Where possible we have tried to use authentic material and to have a variety of different task types.

Teachers can use the book as a grammar course book to give students the extra practice they need. It will also be useful for homework tasks.

Finally, we would like to thank Professor Leech and Professor Svartvik for their support throughout this project. Their careful reading of the manu-script and the comments they made were invaluable and checked any misreading of the grammar we may have made in developing the tasks. We would also like to thank Professor Dr. Dieter Mindt of the Freie Universitat Berlin for making his corpus of the language in use freely available to Edward G. Woods during the semester he was there as a visiting lecturer.

Edward G. Woods and Rudy Coppieters

Spoken and written English

1.1. Informal spoken English

Sections 17–19

Informal spoken English has many features which, if written down, make it appear rambling and unstructured:

- **silent pauses**, often indicated by a dash (-) in transcription.
- **voice-filled pauses** (e.g. –erm) indicating hesitation.
- **repetition** (unplanned repeat, e.g. *I – I – I get*)
- **false starts** (e.g. *I mean, you know*, etc.)
- **discourse markers and fillers** (e.g. *well, you see*, etc.)
- **short forms and contractions** (e.g. *don't, we'll, gonna*)

Task one **

In the following text, underline the features, especially the features of grammar, that show it is spoken language.

I'll tell you a little tale. –er- When me mother was alive in Cambridge and -erm- we had some coal delivered – me mother was a terror if anything was wrong, you know – and –er- it got some rocks and bits of scale in it. And I was going. I was quite young then, and she said –er- get a, get a, we had a a bag. It was a, quite a strong bag. She said fill it up with some of the coal and stuff. And we got it on the bus and we went all the way to the bottom of Hills Road Bridge. Was –er- in fact the building's still there – the coal office. And inside was an old table, an oak –er- front. Was about as long as this room. And –er- I didn't know what she was going to do with it. Just take it back and probably tell them, you know, the coal's not very good. And as she went, she bent down and picked it up and WHOOSH! Straight across the counter. Dust coal everywhere. "Take it back," she said. "And come back and get the rest of it." They couldn't believe it. I can see their faces today.

> (from R. Carter & M. McCarthy,
> *Exploring Spoken English*, C.U.P. 1997, pp. 37–38)

Task two **

Rewrite task one as a written story.

Task three ***

Below are the instructions on how to vote in a British election. Each person receives a voting card with the instructions on. Rewrite the instructions as if you were explaining them orally to somebody. The first one has been done for you.

> Example: *This card is for information only. You can vote without it, but it will save time if you take it to the polling station and show it to the clerk there.*
>
> Answer: *The card tells you what to do. You don't need it when you go and vote. But take it to the polling station to show to the clerk. It'll save time.*

1. When you go to the polling station, tell the clerk your name and address as shown on the front of the card. The Presiding Officer will give you a ballot paper; see that (s)he stamps the official mark on it before (s)he gives it to you.

2. Go to one of the compartments. Mark only one cross (X) as stated in the polling booth in the box alongside the candidate you are voting for. Place only one mark on the ballot paper, or your vote will not be counted.

3. If by mistake you spoil a ballot paper, show it to the Presiding Officer and ask for another one.

4. Fold the ballot paper into two. Show the official mark to the Presiding Officer, but do not let anyone see your vote. Put the ballot paper in the ballot box and leave the polling station.

5. If you have appointed a proxy to vote in person for you, you may nevertheless vote at this election if you do so before the proxy has voted on your behalf.

6. If you have been granted a postal vote, you will not be entitled to vote in person at this election, so please ignore this poll card.

Task four ***

Underline grammatical features in the above text which show that it is probably a written text. Give reasons for your decisions.

1.2. Cooperation in conversation

Sections 21–23

A conversation is not just a matter of giving and receiving information. It is a form of social interaction and participant cooperation is a basic feature of conversation. There is a give-and-take process which is manifested in several ways:

- **turn-taking**, where the role of speaker is shared in a conversation. This is shown in the interplay of questions, answers and positive follow-up comments.
- **using fillers or discourse markers**. These usually add little information, but tell us something of the speaker's attitude to their audience and what they are saying.

Task ***

Look at the text below.

1. Comment on features of turn-taking.
2. Note the discourse items and indicate whether they are
   i. purely interactive, e.g. ah, aha, mhm, mmm, oh, yes, yeah, yup, uhuh
   ii. mainly interactive, e.g. no, please, I see, I mean, you know, you see, OK, that's OK, all right, thank you, that's right, that's all right, well, sure, right
   iii. also interactive, e.g. anyway, in fact, maybe, perhaps, probably, absolutely, of course, certainly, obviously, indeed, wasn't it (and other tags), really, honestly

EXTRACT

Speaker One who is a woman of 78 is telling speaker Two, a woman of 30, and speaker Three, a man of 47, about a plane journey she had.

S.1 .... somebody said to me the pilot says you can go in the cabin you see, well my mouth dropped open ....

S.2 (laughs)

S.1 No idea you see. Now I thought oh, I'd had a joke with one of the girls, you know ....

S.2 Yes

S.1 .... the stewardess girls, and –er- maybe it was her. Or there was a young man with us who had been in our hotel. Maybe he'd said something. Somebody had anyway. So they took me, and Jeanne went with me, of course, in case I fell ....

S.2 Yeah.

S.1 .... Right into where the two pilots were. It was absolutely fantastic.

S.3 Marvellous, wasn't it.

S.2 Was that the first time you've ever been ....

S.1 In the cabin?

S.2 Yeah.

S.1 Yeah.

S.3 Yeah. Normally they only take children and V.I ....

S.2 That's right.

S.3 And V.I.Ps

S.1 Yeah.

S.3 So I don't know which ....

S.1 Well, this was a V.I.P.

S.2 Yeah (laughs)

S.3 (laughs)

S.1 And –er- I went through this door and below was a city. All, all the lights and that. And it was fantastic.

S.2 What was the city?

S.1 Er – I was just, you know ....

S.2 Oh, you're coming to that.

S.1 And I kept thinking I wonder where we are now. Just, you know, and –er – one of the pilots said you're looking down on Budapest.

S.3 Mmm

S.1 He said the top side of that river is Buda and at this side is Pest. That's why it's called Budapest.

S.2 Oh, is it. I didn't know.

S.1 Well, I'd never heard that before.

S.3 Yeah, it is two ....

S.2 No, I hadn't.

S.3 .... two towns.

S.2 Oh.

S.1 I was absolutely transfixed with that.

S.2 Mmm

S.1 It was like looking on Fairyland.

S.3 Mmm. It was lovely, wasn't it?

(from R. Carter & M. McCarthy,
Exploring Spoken English, C.U.P. 1997, pp. 32, 33)

1.3. Tag questions and ellipsis

Sections 24–25; 245; 384; 684

With **tag questions** the speaker asserts something and then invites the listener's response. Initial ellipsis is a characterisation of informal talk. It creates the sort of relaxed atmosphere that we try to achieve in a cooperative social situation.

Task one *

Complete the statements below by adding tag questions.

1. You saw Anne last week, ...?

2. I was sorry for you on your holiday. It rained every day, ...?

3. I'd like to be back in England now. The Spring flowers are out, ...?

4. They're very young, so we won't tell them about Uncle David, ...?

5. I know they were late, but the car broke down, ...?

6. He hasn't failed the exam again, ...?

7. I can see it in your face. You don't remember meeting me, ...?

8. The bank wouldn't lend them the money, ...?

9. I am coming with you, ...?

10. We'll meet again next week to discuss this further, ...?

Task two *

Complete the sentences below by adding what has been omitted through initial ellipsis.

1. Quite a comic, isn't he?

2. Sound like my mother, don't I?

3. Very difficult, isn't it?

4. Something to do with a strike, wasn't it?

5. Not coming with us, are you?

6. Didn't believe all that nonsense, did you?

7. Couldn't tell him that, could I?

8. Solve the problem, won't he?

9. Get the money, won't you?

10. Seen that before, haven't we?

Task three *

Complete the sentences below by adding what has been omitted through initial ellipsis.

1. Thought it was a good film.

2. Mind coming a bit earlier, say 5.30?

3. Had a good day in Siena.

4. Bought some good local wine.

5. Hope you had a good holiday.

6. Tell me where Elizabeth Street is, please?

7. Wasn't me! I wasn't there.

8. Can't help you! Sorry!

9. Really think it was me? I can't believe that.

10. Gotta be off now, haven't we?

Task four **

Rewrite the following sentences, omitting part of the sentences.

1. I hope you don't mind my asking, but did you really threaten to resign?
2. You can't believe a word he says.
3. I saw them out together again last night. They're getting on very well, aren't they!?
4. It didn't help that you were half-an-hour late.
5. I've gotta get this in the post by tonight.
6. It doesn't matter if you don't get the best grades.
7. I don't know why he thought we weren't coming.
8. There's no problem about leaving so early.
9. You didn't bother to let him know, did you?
10. I can't help thinking we should have done more to help her.

1.4. Coordination

Section 26

A preference for coordination of clauses, rather than subordination of clauses, is often a characteristic of speech. Phrasal coordination, on the other hand, is a characteristic of writing.

Task one **

Rewrite the sentences below using clause-level coordination rather than subordination or phrasal coordination.

1. If you are late again, you'll be fired.
2. Now that he's been to Italy, he wants to live there.
3. Neither John nor Mary can answer the question.
4. You'll meet Sally if you go to the new coffee bar.
5. Now that you've been paid, you should be happy.
6. Neither Irene nor I can understand this tax form, although we're both accountants.
7. When that tree grows higher, it will damage the telephone lines.
8. If you stop eating so late, you'll sleep better.
9. Both the Wilsons and the Brooks went to Egypt for their holiday.
10. Because he upset the old lady, I don't want to meet him.

Task two **

Rewrite the sentences below using subordination rather than coordination.

1. Finish that work tonight and you can take the rest of the week off.
2. He's got the manager's job and won't speak to his old friends.
3. They've got a new car and will be telling everyone how much it cost.
4. I don't like that house. It's too dark and miserable.
5. He's been all over the world and thinks he knows everything.
6. We've changed our money from Francs to Euros and everything costs more.
7. The fire spread quickly and the whole factory was destroyed.
8. The crowds were waiting patiently at the side of the road. Then suddenly it began to rain.
9. Get there early or they won't let you in.
10. Get the early train and you'll have a good day in the city.

1.5. Finite clauses in spoken English

Section 27; 360–374

In written English, we often use non-finite and verbless clauses as adverbials and modifiers. Such constructions would be highly unlikely in speech, where finite clauses and coordination are preferred.

Task one **

The sentences below are more likely to be formal, written English. Rewrite them in a form more likely in spoken English.

1. After winning the race, he enjoyed the prize money.
2. Having been in trouble in school before, the boy was afraid to tell his mother why he was home so late.
3. Having missed the last train, he stayed at his sister's overnight.
4. Feeling ill, he decided not to go to work that day.
5. Built in 1903, the theatre was too big for small, contemporary plays.
6. Of all the mothers interviewed not in paid work, the majority intended to return to work when their children were older.
7. Given the steepness of the stairs, it was an accident waiting to happen.
8. Taking the dog for a walk across the fields, he realised that the new road they were going to build would go very near his own house.

9. On reading the biography of Sophia Loren, she determined to become an actress.

10. Getting home late, he found everyone had gone to bed.

Task two ***

The sentences below are more likely to be informal, spoken English. Rewrite them in a form more suitable for formal, written English.

1. Pete reminded her about the visit and hoped she would come.

2. They reorganised the shop but still didn't get a lot of customers.

3. I saw her in the street and told her the good news.

4. They bought an old house, modernised it and made a lot of money when they resold it.

5. When you get to the top of the hill, you get a good view over the plain.

6. I didn't like that stuff they gave us to eat last night. I left most of it on my plate.

7. He went to a lot of trouble to get the picture and so expected they would pay him a good price.

8. They felt very depressed – their team had lost for the third time.

9. I haven't been to Mexico before so I don't know what to expect.

10. We yelled at the top of our voices, but nobody took any notice.

1.6. Stress

Sections 33–35; 633; 743–745

The rhythm of spoken English can be felt in the sequence of stressed syllables. Between one stressed syllable and another there may occur one or more unstressed syllables.

Stressed syllables:	(i) one-syllable words belonging to one of the major word-classes
	(ii) accented syllables of words of more than one syllable of major word-classes.
Unstressed syllables:	(i) one-syllable words belonging to one of the minor word-classes
	(ii) unaccented syllables of words of more than one syllable.

In most contexts, prepositional adverbs are normally stressed while one-syllable prepositions are usually unstressed.

Task one *

Put stress marks in front of stressed syllables in the following sentences.

1. The rain in Spain stays mainly in the plain.
2. The tourist forgot to buy a ticket at the counter.
3. Janet is throwing a party for her twentieth birthday.
4. We met in Rome, visited the sights and then flew home.
5. John is fond of chocolate but Mary thoroughly dislikes it.
6. I was admiring the landscape that unfolded in front of my eyes.
7. This unexpected encounter with my worst enemy really upset me.
8. Do you remember the dramatic events of September the eleventh?
9. The United Nations decided to lift the embargo imposed on military equipment.
10. As a true democrat, I sincerely hope that democracy will always prevail over tyranny.
11. Slow progress has been made to persuade the warring factions to accept a compromise.
12. The photographer had taken a dozen pictures, all of which appeared in glossy magazines.

Task two **

Specify whether the underlined words in the following text are stressed or not.

Many people tend to be put <u>off</u> learning foreign languages as it also means taking <u>in</u> a lot <u>of</u> foreign grammar and vocabulary. Having attended two or three classes, they simply give <u>up</u> and put the whole thing <u>on</u> the backburner.

As time goes <u>by</u>, however, those who dropped <u>out</u> are beginning to wonder how they will be getting <u>on</u> <u>in</u> the country they've chosen to go <u>to</u> <u>for</u> their next holiday. So they happily turn <u>to</u> a popular phrasebook written <u>for</u> the average tourist, convinced that they will easily get <u>by</u> <u>under</u> foreign skies.

After their plane has touched <u>down</u>, these tourists cheerfully get <u>through</u> customs control, where the stock phrases come <u>out</u> all right. Then they set <u>off</u> <u>in</u> a hired car, driving <u>on</u> and <u>on</u> . . . until they run <u>out</u> <u>of</u> petrol or the car breaks <u>down</u>, leaving them stranded <u>on</u> a lonely road. The nearest farm is miles <u>away</u> but, fortunately, a local person happens to drive <u>by</u>, slow <u>down</u> and back <u>up</u> their car. Now the poor tourists are <u>in</u> <u>for</u> a nasty surprise: no more stock phrases but sentences they've never heard or used before. So the conversation virtually breaks <u>down</u> and all <u>of</u> a sudden the tourists remember their language classes, making a silent vow to pick <u>up</u> again where they left <u>off</u>.

Task three **

    (a) Arrange the underlined words in two groups depending on which word-class they belong to.

    (b) Check whether there is a match between stress and word-class.

1.7. Nucleus and tone units

Sections 36–37

Some stressed syllables have greater prominence than others and form the nucleus, or focal point, of an intonation pattern.

    The basic unit of intonation is the tone unit, a stretch of speech which contains one such nucleus. A sentence contains one or more tone units, depending on its length and the degree of emphasis given to its various parts.

Task **

Mark any tone unit boundaries in the following sentences with vertical bars, underlining the syllables which would normally form the nucleus of the respective tone units.

1. My only sister is married to an accountant.
2. Would you give me the bottle opener, please.
3. Shirley was watching a film by Alfred Hitchcock, the master of suspense.
4. Hurricane Freddy swept across Indonesia last night and is now heading for Japan.
5. Although the war has been over for years, there are still occasional clashes along the border.
6. The new car model comes in four colours: red, dark blue, grey and white.
7. Driving on the left-hand side is something most people get used to in no time at all.
8. I haven't got the faintest idea if the evidence given by Karen will prove her innocence.
9. Either your informant is completely ignorant of the facts or he is deliberately deceiving us, which is even worse.
10. In contrast with conventional wisdom, forests in northern countries are expanding rather than shrinking.
11. The politician said he wasn't involved in the cover-up but he was, as appeared from an incriminating document found in the flat of his former mistress.
12. For Christ's sake, why couldn't you behave properly in the company of such distinguished guests, whose only fault was that their English sounded slightly pompous?

1.8. Tones

Sections 38–42

Tone is the type of pitch change which takes place on the nucleus. There are three basic types of tone in English, each of which tends to express a number of related meanings:

  (i) **falling tone**: certainty, completeness, independence (esp. straight-forward statements, *wh*-questions)

 (ii) **rising tone**: uncertainty, incompleteness, dependence (esp. *yes-no* questions, subsidiary information)

(iii) **fall-rise**: combines the meaning of 'certainty, assertion' with that of 'incompleteness, dependence' (esp. reservation, implied contrast, etc.).

Task one **

Assign one of the three basic tones to each tone unit in the following sentences, underlining the nuclear syllable on which the pitch change takes place.

1. Are any of these titles still available?
2. Don't lean too far out of the window.
3. I don't want to spend ALL my dollars.
4. How many passengers survived the plane crash?
5. You've seen some of these films before?
6. George Stephenson was the inventor of the steam engine.
7. In terms of profitability, the current year has been quite exceptional.
8. Why didn't you turn up at the meeting, because you had overslept again?
9. Technically speaking, these devices are extremely sophisticated.
10. If you haven't got enough time now, you can write those letters tomorrow.
11. Edith may not be a very good cook, she knows at least how to appreciate good food.
12. There's a wide choice of cheese here: Cheddar, Stilton, Camembert, Gorgonzola and Danish blue.

Task two ***

For each sentence, first mark tone unit boundaries with vertical bars. Second, underline the nuclear syllable on which the pitch change takes place. Third, assign one of the three basic tones to each tone unit. (cf Section 42 in *CGE*)

1. Members of the jury, I thank you for your attention during this trial. Please pay attention to the instructions I am about to give you.

   Henry Johnson, the defendant in this case, has been accused of the crimes of First Degree Murder with a Firearm and Aggravated Assault with a Firearm.
   In this case Henry Johnson is accused of First Degree Murder with a Firearm.
   Murder in the First Degree includes the lesser crimes of Murder in the Second Degree, Murder in the Third Degree and Manslaughter, all of which are unlawful.
   If you find Mr. Peter Smith was killed by Henry Johnson, you will then consider the circumstances surrounding the killing in deciding if the killing was First Degree Murder, Second Degree Murder, Third Degree Murder or Manslaughter.

   (slightly adapted from *www.pbcountyclerk.com*)

2. Ruth: Steve, where's my handbag?
   Steve: Over there, on the windowsill. You're not going out shopping, are you?
   Ruth: Of course I am. How else am I to prepare dinner tonight?
   Steve: Oh, I thought we were going to a restaurant.
   Ruth: The last time we went to a restaurant you kept complaining about the food.
   Steve: It was one of those very exotic places. You know I don't like them.
   Ruth: What would you suggest then? As long as it isn't fish and chips, of course.
   Steve: Well, shall we go to an Italian restaurant? That's not too exotic as far as I am concerned.
   Ruth: All right. You still remember the terms of the agreement we made last time?
   Steve: I don't, quite frankly.
   Ruth: In that case, let me just refresh your memory. Whoever chooses the restaurant pays the bill for the two of us.
   Steve: You will have your revenge, won't you.

Emotion

2.1. Emotive emphasis in speech 1

Sections 298–301; 528

Emotive emphasis can be given in a variety of ways:

- **interjections**: words like *oh, ah, wow, ouch*, etc.
- **exclamations** beginning with *what-* and *how-*phrases which do not cause subject-operator inversion
- **emphatic** *so* and *such*
- **repetition** (which also denotes degree)
- **stress on the operator**
- **nuclear stress on other words**
- **intensifying adverbs and modifiers**

Task one *

Identify the various emotive features that you can find in the following extracts.

1. 'Well!' thought Alice to herself. 'After such a fall as this, I shall think nothing of tumbling down stairs! How brave they'll all think me at home! Why, I wouldn't say anything about it, even if I fell off the top of the house!' (Which was very likely true.)

    Down, down, down. Would the fall *never* come to an end?

    (from Lewis Carroll, *Alice's Adventures in Wonderland* and *Through the Looking-glass*, p. 13)

2. "You know something, Maria? We fought."

    "Fought?"

    "We were in the goddamned jungle . . . and we were attacked . . . and we fought our way out." Now he sounded as if the dawn were breaking wider and wider. "Christ, I don't know when the last time was I was in a fight, an actual fight. Maybe I was twelve, thirteen. You know something, babe? You were great. You were fantastic. You really were. When I saw you behind the wheel – I didn't even know if you could drive the car!" He was elated. *She* was driving. "But you drove the hell out of it! You were great!" Oh, the dawn had broken. The world glowed with its radiance.

(from Tom Wolfe, *The Bonfire of the Vanities*, pp. 98–99)

Task two *

Give emotive emphasis by adding the kind of element suggested by the 'prompt' in brackets, changing the sentence structure where necessary.

1. John Thaw was a brilliant actor. (emphatic *so/such*)
2. You're wearing a beautiful tie. (exclamation)
3. That was an awful thing to say. (repetition)
4. It was stupid of you to insult the ambassador like that. (exclamation)
5. I'm really disappointed now. (repetition)
6. The lounge is elegantly decorated. (emphatic *so/such*)
7. It would be far better to ignore that man altogether. (repetition)
8. When I came back, I felt exhausted. (emphatic *so/such*)
9. Joan's mood changed suddenly again. (exclamation)
10. The Wilsons are nice people. (emphatic *so/such*)
11. Olive can be a charming hostess. (exclamation)
12. A bedbug is a tiny creature. (repetition)

Task three **

Underline the operators, modifiers, etc. which are likely to receive nuclear stress in the sentences making up the following dialogue. Add the dummy auxiliary *do* where it makes sense.

Helen: George, what are you doing so early in the morning?
George: I'm awfully sorry, but I had to get out of bed.
Helen: Tell me what's the matter with you, then.
George: Well, I had the most horrifying nightmare.
Helen: You will have to calm down, you know. This isn't an isolated thing. Something must be bothering you.
George: I can't deny that. I've been terribly worked up lately.
Helen: I wish you'd tell me more. I have a right to know.
George: If I told you, you'd be incredibly angry.
Helen: You owe me an explanation. I am your wife, after all.
George: I decided to buy a hugely expensive car and it could ruin us.

Task four **

Complete the following sentences, using the most appropriate of the intensifying adjectives or adverbs in brackets. Use each word just once.

| absolute | definitely | gorgeous | great | horrendous | indeed |
| literally | raving | really | terribly | tremendous | utterly |

1. Most of the relatives were _____ devastated by the terrible news.

2. The fact that I knew the local culture so well turned out to be a _____ asset.

3. Yet another country in this volatile region is descending into _____ chaos.

4. The evidence _____ proves that the victim was killed with a blunt instrument.

5. We enjoyed two weeks of _____ weather while we were cruising in the Pacific.

6. The stock market guru was _____ knocked off his pedestal.

7. Five-star hotels are often associated with luxury and _____ bills.

8. Jennifer was described by some experts as a _____ beauty.

9. To be quite honest, I'm not _____ impressed with Jim's performance.

10. Are you _____ going to get married to this unscrupulous person?

11. It was a _____ idea to cut bus and tram fares in big cities.

12. The documentaries broadcast by *National Geographic Channel* are very interesting _____.

2.2. Emotive emphasis in speech 2

Sections 302–305; 417

- **The emotive force** of a *wh*-question can be strengthened by adding *ever*, *on earth*, etc. to the *wh*-word.

- **Negative sentences** can be intensified by adding *at all*, *a bit*, *whatever*, *a thing*, etc. or by putting *not a* before a noun. The negative element can also be placed at the beginning of a clause, which normally causes subject-operator inversion.

- **An exclamatory question** is a *yes-no* question spoken with an emphatic falling tone. It often has a negative form.

- **A rhetorical question** is more like a forceful statement and can have a positive or negative form. There are also rhetorical *wh*-questions.

Task one **

Intensify the emotive force of the underlined parts by adding one of the phrases below. Use each of these phrases only once, some of them being interchangeable.

| a bit | a fig | a thing | a wink | at all |
| by any means | ever | in heaven's name | on earth | whatever |

1. I didn't have any money.
2. Why are you going to sell such a unique painting?
3. I wasn't surprised that things had got out of hand.
4. There was so much noise that night that I didn't sleep.
5. How did the serial killer manage to escape from prison?
6. What have you been doing to your hair?
7. There is no reason to be so upset about Erica's sudden departure.
8. Without light, no one could see in that dark cave.
9. It is not true that the whale is a type of fish.
10. Gary was severely reprimanded but he doesn't care.

Task two *

Put the negative element in front position to make the sentence sound more rhetorical, using the appropriate word order.

1. I had never met the Sultan of Brunei before.
2. It is by no means clear that the United States will sign the agreement.
3. These magnificent flowers are nowhere else to be found.
4. The harsh ruler spared not a single insurgent's life.
5. We should in no way lend credibility to the witness's account of the facts.
6. I will support Mr Barlow under no circumstances whatsoever.
7. British women did not get the vote until after the First World War.
8. This evil man not only murdered his wife, he also mutilated her body.

Task three ***

Rewrite the following dialogue by turning the sentences into exclamatory OR rhetorical questions, as indicated in brackets.

Dick: Oh boy, I'm tired. (exclamatory positive)
Emma: You've been overdoing it again. (rhetorical negative)
Dick: I haven't got an alternative. (rhetorical wh-question)
Emma: You could ask me to lend you a hand from time to time. (rhetorical negative)
Dick: That's a most generous offer. (exclamatory negative)
Emma: I detect some irony in your voice. (rhetorical positive)
Dick: I've asked you many times in the past. (rhetorical wh-question)
Emma: I was suffering from depression then. (rhetorical negative)
Dick: Hard work is the best antidote to depression. (rhetorical negative)

Emma: Oh, but I felt sleepy all the time, taking those pills. (exclamatory positive)

Dick: I would have been a far better doctor for you, then. (rhetorical negative)

Emma: Oh Dick, you are hopeless. (exclamatory positive)

2.3. Describing emotions 1

Sections 306–308; 499

The cause of an emotive reaction to something can be expressed by:

- **prepositions**: *at* (events), *with* (persons and objects), *about* and *of*
- *to*-**infinitive clause** or *that*-**clause** (with or without *should*)
- **subject** (active constructions) **or** *by*-**agent** (passive constructions).
- **more impersonal constructions**: the person affected by the emotion can be identified by a phrase introduced by *to* or *for*.

Some sentence adverbials, including comment clauses, can express an emotional reaction or judgement.

Task one *

Match the clauses in the left-hand column with the structures in the right-hand one.

1. It's a shame	a. about the possible outbreak of cholera.
2. Caroline was angry	b. at what they found in the basement.
3. The proliferation of biological weapons	c. with their status because they felt exploited.
4. The authorities are concerned	d. at my naïve belief in a better world.
5. We were overjoyed	e. that we were not informed earlier.
6. The investigators were astonished	f. to learn that he had been turned down.
7. Some secretaries were dissatisfied	g. is really frightening.
8. To some observers, it was surprising	h. that I should feel perfectly at home.
9. The philosopher smiled	i. with me for not having invited her.
10. Paul was disappointed	j. of their outrageous behaviour at the party.
11. Aunt Rebecca was anxious	k. that so many people had cast their votes.
12. The twins were ashamed	l. to meet again after so many years.

Task two **

Rewrite the following sentences, using sentence adverbials corresponding to the underlined adjectives and verbs.

Example: *It is surprising that nobody complained about what had happened.*
   ⇒ *Surprisingly, nobody complained about what had happened.*

1. It was amazing that most passengers of the crashed airliner escaped unhurt.
2. I would like to buy a flat, and would prefer to have one with a good view.
3. It is tragic that five skiers died in the avalanche.
4. Barbara was foolish to carry thousands of dollars in her handbag.
5. It is unfortunate that too little is being done to protect the environment.
6. I regretted that some people failed to appreciate my point of view.
7. I was lucky not to be at home when the gas explosion occurred.
8. It was quite sensible of the government to launch a new campaign against drink-driving.
9. It is to be hoped that the economy will pick up again later this year.
10. We had not expected the minister to hand in his resignation.

Task three **

Complete the sentences in the following dialogue, adding the most appropriate of the comment clauses listed below. Use each clause just once.

I believe   I'm afraid   I'm sure   I see   putting it more bluntly
so to speak   to be honest   what's more   you bet   you see

Max: Nora, we can no longer afford to stay in this lavish apartment, _____. _____, we'll have to move to a cheaper place.
Nora: I don't know what to say, _____.
Max: I may soon be made redundant, _____. _____, I lost a considerable amount of money in a risky project a few weeks ago.
Nora: Erm . . . there is a way out, _____, if at least you are prepared to listen to me first.
Max: _____ I will listen to you.
Nora: Well, there is this dear cousin of mine who was born with, _____, a silver spoon in his mouth. He will help us out, _____.
Max: Oh, _____. That would be wonderful, of course.

2.4. Describing emotions 2

Sections **309–318**; **722–723**

The verbs *like, love, hate* and *prefer* can be followed by a noun phrase object, a *to*-infinitive clause or an *-ing* clause. The infinitive clause tends to express an 'idea' and is also used when the main verb is hypothetical, while the *-ing* clause rather expresses a 'fact'.

The verbs *enjoy, dislike* and *loathe* take only *-ing* clauses.

The rejected alternative following the object of *prefer* is introduced by a *to*-phrase, by an infinitive clause introduced by *rather than* or by an *-ing* clause.

Other emotions can be expressed in a large variety of structural and lexical ways and can range in tone from more to less tentative, tactful, enthusiastic, etc.

Task one **

Complete the following sentences, using the infinitive OR *-ing* form of the verb in brackets.

1. I dislike (sit) _____ in overcrowded trains.
2. I wouldn't like (drive) _____ a thousand miles all on my own.
3. On the whole, I prefer (walk) _____ to (cycle) _____ .
4. We both enjoyed (cook) _____ dinner for our newly arrived guests.
5. The traditional housewife likes everything (be) _____ neat and tidy.
6. Margaret is an actress who has always loved (perform) _____ on the stage.
7. Rather than (sack) _____ part of the workforce, the management preferred (introduce) _____ part-time work.
8. I hate (say) _____ this, but you keep giving us the wrong signal.
9. Arthur tells me he loathes (go) _____ to these conferences.
10. Would you really love (work) _____ with autistic children?
11. I like (be) _____ with Jerry because he is so entertaining.
12. We have always preferred (travel) _____ abroad, rather than (stay) _____ close to home.

Task two **

(a) What is the basic emotion expressed by each of the following pairs of sentences? Choose the appropriate label from the following list of seven: (A) hope, (B) anticipation of pleasure, (C) disappointment or regret, (D) approval, (E) disapproval, (F) surprise, (G) concern or worry.

(b) Which of the two versions expresses the stronger emotion, i.e. sounds more direct, more emphatic, less tentative, etc.?

1a. You handled the situation very clumsily.

  b. Couldn't you have handled the situation a little more carefully?

2a. I'm a bit worried about these new developments.

  b. I find these new developments very alarming indeed.

3a. What a strange way of dealing with young children.

  b. I thought it a rather strange way of dealing with young children.

4a. I'm looking forward to participating in this new venture.

  b. I'm very eager to participate in this new venture.

5a. I was hoping we could discuss some of the remaining problems.

  b. I hope to discuss some of the remaining problems with you.

6a. How unfortunate that so few people turned up in the end.

  b. Unfortunately, not many people turned up in the end.

7a. The food on board the plane wasn't too bad, was it?

  b. I really liked the food on board the plane, didn't you?

8a. Don't you agree that an alternative approach might have been more appropriate?

  b. I don't think this was the appropriate approach, you know.

9a. The news coming from the Middle East is most disturbing.

  b. There is growing concern over the news coming from the Middle East.

10a. If only solar energy could be used on a much wider scale!

  b. It's a bit of a pity that solar energy can't be used on a wider scale yet.

Task three ***

Rewrite the following dialogue by adding the emotional meanings in brackets to the sentences as they stand. Give for each sentence two 'expanded' versions, which differ in form and possibly also in terms of emotive strength.

Example: *We couldn't go cycling this afternoon.* (disappointment)

    ⇒ *What a pity we couldn't go cycling this afternoon.*

      It would have been more fun if we had been able to go cycling this afternoon.

Walt: Viv, I'm going to indulge in a five-course dinner this evening. (anticipation of pleasure)

Viv: You'll be stuffing yourself with fattening food again. (disapproval)

Walt: You envy people who like a hearty meal from time to time. (surprise)

Viv: More and more of those people are becoming overweight these days. (concern)

Walt: That's not going to happen to me. (hope)

Viv: You don't seem to realize that too much food is bad for your health. (regret)

Walt: YOU don't seem to realize that I'm taking a lot of exercise now. (surprise)

Viv: You've at least changed that part of your lifestyle. (approval)

Walt: Some of the physical activities make me feel exhausted. (disappointment)

Viv: As you lose weight, the activities will seem lighter too. (hope)

Structure

3.1. Clauses

Sections **486–495**; 151; 170; 198; 202–204; 207; 211; 499; 573–577; 588; 613; 686; 718; 724; 727; 737; 739

There are five different clause elements:

S–subject; V–verb; O–object; C–complement; A–adverbial.

There are six basic verb patterns: SVC/SVA; SVO; SVOV ....; SVOO; SVOC; SV.

There are three types of clauses: finite; non-finite; verbless

There are two clause functions: main clause; subclause

There are various types of subclauses: nominal; relative; comment; comparative; adverbial

Task one **

Identify the organisation of the clauses below – SVC, SVA, SVO, SVOO, SVOC, SVOV ...., SV. Identify optional adverbials as [A].

1. I did it without his help.
2. Manchester United lost!
3. The earthquake destroyed hundreds of homes.
4. The government gave the poorest people a tax cut.
5. His mother told the child a story every night at bedtime.
6. He became leader of the party after a bitter battle.
7. The 18th century was an age of reason.
8. Eleven hundred years ago, the Hungarian tribal alliance arrived in the Carpathian Basin.
9. The humiliating defeat of the government served the progressive forces.
10. Foreign Affairs is not all fun and games.

Task two *

State what types of subclauses there are in each of the items below: finite; non-finite; verbless. Identify each subclause by underlining.

1. Bring me a cup of coffee when you've finished.
2. Ignoring the accident is not an option.
3. Many children were left orphans in the war, babies among them.
4. He gave up a very good job to work for the charity.
5. Covered in mud, the boy proudly showed his father the athletics prize.
6. Angered by the manager's attitude, she decided to resign her job.
7. Happy with the result, the barrister congratulated his client.
8. Is sending lots of Christmas cards only a British habit?
9. They didn't want him to leave.
10. Opening an art gallery in such a small town was a very brave thing to do.

Task three **

Identify the functions of the clauses underlined as nominal, relative, adverbial, comparative or comment clauses. Also identify the clause patterns (SVC, SVA, SVO, SVOO, SVOC, SVOV ...., SV) and, where these begin with a conjunction, show this by putting 'conj' in front of the pattern-type.

1. In the new job, he's earning twice as much <u>as he used to</u>.
2. <u>To be fair</u>, I don't think it was really Joan's fault alone.
3. <u>That he's now having to do so much extra work</u> shows he's borrowed too much for the new apartment.
4. I take the dog with me <u>wherever I go</u>.
5. The 'Titanic', <u>which was the most advanced passenger ship of its day</u>, was not properly equipped for an emergency.
6. House prices in the North of England are much lower <u>than they are in the South</u>.
7. <u>To be cruel</u>, I think Martin deserved to fail.
8. The couple, <u>who are both aged 102</u>, have been married for 77 years.
9. They moved to Kendal <u>because they wanted to be near their friends</u>.
10. <u>That it's rained so much this winter</u> doesn't mean we'll have a dry summer.

3.2. Combinations of verbs

Section 739; 735–737

When a verb phrase consists of more than one verb, there are certain rules about how the verbs can be combined. There are four basic verb combinations:

A – **modal** – a modal auxiliary followed by a verb in the infinitive;

B – **perfect** – a form of *have* followed by a verb in the *-ed* participle form;

C – **progressive** – a form of *be* followed by a verb in the *-ing* form;

D – **passive** – a form of *be* followed by a verb in the *-ed* participle form.

Task one *

Put the verbs and adverbials in the correct order in the verb phrases below.

1. I do can nothing for you.
2. I have been could here before, but I don't remember.
3. They never going are to tell him the truth about the accident. It's too terrible.
4. That house built must been have at the end of the nineteenth century.
5. The work completed is being as we speak.
6. He working been has on that project for two years now.
7. She already seen has the film.
8. Surely he be can't going to waste all that money on a car he never uses.
9. They have might gone to the meeting. I just don't know.
10. That made hasn't things difficult for you, has it?

Task two **

In the story below, the verb phrases have been omitted. Complete the story, by putting one of the verb phrases here as indicated by the alphabetical order shown where the verbs should be. *couldn't believe; couldn't do; had been intending; had been locked away; had been losing; had been made; had lost; hadn't arrived; hadn't done; must have got up; should have remembered; was only just getting; were still locked; would only be opened*

I ....(1 – A+B).................. very early that morning because the morning newspaper ....(2 – B).................., and, when I left the house, it ....(3 – C).................. light. I ....(4 – B+C).................. to get to work early for some time as I had a large backlog of work to catch up with. The night security guard ....(5 – A)................... it when I arrived and the doors ....(6 – D)................... He let me into my office. I was ready for work. Now came the problem. I ....(7 – A+B)...................! The files I wanted ....(8 – B+D)................... for security reasons. The room where they were ....(9 – A+D)................... when the day-time security guard came on duty at 8.30. Arrangements ....(10 – B+D)................... beforehand. In the past weeks, I ....(11 – B+C)................... sleep because I ....(12 – B)................... the work. Now I ....(13 – B)................... sleep because I wanted to do the work, but ....(14 – A)...................

Determiners

4.1. Count and non-count nouns

Sections **57–69**; 510; 597–601

> **Count nouns** are so called because they can be counted individually, e.g. house, pen, etc.
>
> **Non-count nouns** refer to things which cannot be counted individually, e.g. water, wood, etc.
>
> **Group nouns** refer to a set or collection of count nouns, e.g. a *set* of tools.
>
> **Unit nouns** subdivide non-count nouns into separate pieces, e.g. a *piece* of paper.

Task one **

Match the group nouns in column A with the objects in column B, e.g. a gang of thieves

A	B
set	wolves
clump	fish
herd	sheep
crowd	keys
pack	chairs
swarm	cows
flock	trees
stack	clothes
bundle	people
shoal	bees

Task two **

Match the unit nouns in column A with the appropriate objects in column B, e.g. a bowl of rice

A	B
blade	bread
lump	wine
cup	hay
sheet	sugar
slice	string
load	grass
block	cake
pile	paper
length	tea
bottle	dust
piece	ice

Task three **

Decide which of the following are count nouns and which are non-count nouns. There are some which can be either. So make three columns.

advice	education	money
bank	engineer	news
behaviour	fruit	night
book	furniture	progress
butter	group	quarrel
carrot	homework	scenery
ceramic	industry	shopping
cheese	information	variety
clothing	joke	work
conduct	language	year

Task four **

Complete the following texts with an appropriate group or unit noun.

1. The room was a mess. There was a (1) of paper on the floor, some empty (2) of wine by the desk and (3) of food scattered all over the room.

2. The picture shows a (4) of sheep sheltering from the storm by a (5) of trees. In the distance the storm is clearing and the sun is shining through a (6) of clouds.

3. "Tea or coffee?"
   "Oh, a (7) of tea, please."
   "And a (8) of cake?
   "No, thank you."

4. Foot and mouth disease has meant that (9) of cattle and many (10) of sheep have had to be destroyed. This is especially so in the Lake District in the north-west of England. Many farmers have seen years of hard work destroyed overnight.

Task five **

Complete the text by selecting an appropriate noun from those below. Decide whether it should be singular or plural and whether the verb in brackets should be singular or plural.

advice, education, engineer, experience, help, information, language, management, method, situation, skill, transportation, variety, weather, work

The (1) we have at the moment (2. Be) very unclear. We know that the (3) that (4. Need) to be done will require a (5) of (6) which (7. Need) to come from many sources. We require (8) who (9. Have) worked in developing countries, people with (10) skills and people with (11) in (12).

The (13) for recruiting we have received (14. Have) so far been of little (15). It goes without saying that working in developing countries requires people who are able to take on board cultural differences and accept (16) that often (17. Seem) bizarre.

For our part, we must be able to tell people:

What the (18) (19. Be) like. How the seasons are defined.

What (20) (21. Be) like, road, rail and telephone.

What the level of (22) (23. Be), so we can use the appropriate teaching (24).

(adapted from memo on recruiting for World Bank contracts in Indonesia)

Task six **

Read through the following paragraphs and decide whether the nouns are countable or uncountable as they are used. Then make a list of those that can be used as both.

Vienna feeds upon its past, a fond and sustaining diet, varied with chocolate cake or boiled beef with potatoes (Franz Josef's favourite dish), washed down with the young white wine of the Vienna Woods, digested and re-digested, and ordered once more, over, and over, and over again . . . If it reminds me sometimes of Beijing, sometimes it suggests to me the sensations of apartheid in South Africa. The city is obsessed and obsessive. Every conversation returns to its lost greatness, every reference somehow finds its way to questions of rank, or status, or historical influence. Viennese romantics still love to wallow in the tragic story of Crown Prince Rudolf and his eighteen-year-old mistress Marie Vetsera, 'the little Baroness', who died apparently in a suicide pact in the country house of Mayerling in 1889. The tale precisely fits the popular predilections of the city, being snobbish, nostalgic, maudlin and rather cheap. I went out one Sunday to visit the grave of the little Baroness, who was buried obscurely in a village churchyard by the command of Franz Josef, and was just in time to hear a Viennese lady of a certain age explaining the affair to her American guests. 'But in any case,' I heard her say without a trace of irony, 'in any case, she was only the daughter of a bourgeois . . .'

I often saw that same lady waiting for a tram, for she is a familiar of Vienna. She often wears a brown tweed suit, and is rather tightly clamped around the middle, and pearled very likely, and she never seems to be encumbranced, as most of us sometimes are, with shopping bags, umbrellas or toasters she has just picked up from the electrician's. If you smile at her, she responds with a frosty stare, as though she suspects you might put ketchup on your Tafelspitz, but if you speak to her she lights up with a flowery charm. Inextricably linked with the social absurdity of Vienna is its famous *Gemütlichkeit*, its ordered cosiness, which is enough to make a Welsh anarchist's flesh creep: the one goes with the other, and just as it made the people of old Vienna one and all the children of their kind father His Imperial, Royal and Apostolic Majesty, still to this day it seems to fix the attitudes of this city as with a scented glue – sweetly if synthetically scented, like flavours you sometimes taste upon licking the adhesives of American envelopes.

(Jan Morris, *Among the Cities*, Penguin Books, 1985, pp. 383–384)

4.2. Amount and quantity

Sections 70–81; 675–680; 697–699

Amount words like *all, some, none* can be used with both count and mass nouns. Amount words can specify more precisely the meaning such as *a large quantity, a small quantity* and *not a large quantity*.

Words like *all, both, every, each* and sometimes *any* carry a general or inclusive meaning.

Task one **

Consider the scale of amounts where *all* is the most inclusive and *no(ne)* is the most negative and organise the statements below so that 1 is the most inclusive and the highest figure is the most negative. Some items will have the same score. Also indicate whether they show whether the amount word is a determiner (D) or a pronoun (P).

1. There are some great artisan ateliers hidden in Treviso's backstreets.
2. All the candidates spent the day hustling for votes.
3. I'd like to welcome everyone here and thank you all for giving up your time.
4. Anyone you ask is bound to know the way.
5. Nothing I said could tempt her to tell us what she knew about the candidates.

6. There are few things more tedious than hearing other people blaring into their mobiles.

7. He read every scientific paper he could find on cheese, immersing himself in the finer points of microbiology.

8. Although many of us stay fit and healthy well into our eighties and nineties, the risk of suffering some sort of health problem increases with age.

9. This booklet aims to answer most of your questions about Capital Bonds.

10. Each of the so-called multi-modal studies are "looking at some of the severe transport problems around the country".

Task two **

Explain the (possible) difference of meaning in the pairs of sentences below. Say if two sentences have the same basic meaning.

1. The manager gave all the staff a week's holiday.

   The manager gave each of the staff a week's holiday.

2. Some of the students could easily pass the exam.

   Any of the students could easily pass the exam.

3. Either date will be all right.

   Neither date will be all right.

4. Either date will be suitable.

   Both dates will be suitable.

5. He couldn't remember some of their names.

   He couldn't remember any of their names.

6. There are few books I'd like to read again.

   There are a few books I'd like to read again.

7. Speak to each of my parents about it.

   Speak to either of my parents about it.

8. Will he tell us whether he agrees with everything he said 17 years ago?

   Or indeed whether he agrees with anything he said 17 years ago?

9. Neither of us could help him.

   None of us could help him.

10. You can see him any Sunday morning walking by the canal.

    You can see him every Sunday morning walking by the canal.

Task three **

Households with selected consumer durables: by type of household, 1999–00 (percentages) – *National Statistics – Social Trends* – 2001 ed.

	One adult	One adult with children	Two adults no children	Two adults with children	Two or more adults	Overall
Television	97	100	99	99	99	99
Telephone	91	86	98	96	98	95
Deep freeze fridge freezer	81	96	95	96	95	91
Washing machine	78	97	96	99	97	91
Video recorder	67	94	91	97	92	86
Microwave	67	86	82	90	83	80
CD player	49	84	72	93	76	72
Tumble dryer	33	54	55	68	57	52
Home computer	19	33	35	62	39	38
Satellite TV	18	32	30	47	33	32
Dishwasher	7	16	26	38	26	23

With reference to the chart above complete the sentences below with the most suitable *amount* expressions: *all, few, a few, half, little, a little, the majority of, majority of, many, most, much, none, several, some*

1. .... homes with one adult with children had television.

2. .... homes with one adult had a dishwasher.

3. .... homes with two or more adults had a computer, but not all.

4. Only .... households had a dishwasher.

5. Not .... households with one adult had satellite TV.

6. A large .... households with two or more adults had a video recorder.

7. .... families of two adults with children have a video recorder.

8. Just over .... the households of one adult with children have a tumble dryer.

9. A .... households of two adults have a microwave.

10. Overall .... households were without a telephone.

Task four ***

Television viewing and radio listening by age and gender, 1999 (hours per week) –
National Statistics – Social Trends – 2001 ed.

	Television viewing		Radio listening	
	Males	Females	Males	Females
4–15	18.6	17.9	8.4	9.2
16–24	17.7	22.8	19.8	18.4
25–34	21.6	26.5	22.1	17.4
35–44	22.5	25.4	22.6	18
45–54	25.3	26.9	23.7	20.3
55–64	28.8	32.1	23.3	22
65 and over	36.4	36.5	20.9	20.4
all aged 4 and over	24.1	26.9	19.9	17.9

With reference to the chart above and the chart in Task three complete the text below with appropriate *amount* words.

The figures show the number of hours per person by age and gender per week spent watching television and listening to the radio. As you can see ....(1)........ time among 4–15 year olds of both genders was spent listening to the radio. A ....(2)........ time was spent watching television by older people which reflects the fact that a ....(3)........ older people own a television. However, a ....(4)........ the television watched by those over 65 consisted of news programmes, whereas only a ....(5)........ of those under 15 watched these. A ....(6)........ of time was spent watching TV by women between the ages of 45 and 54.

The survey also showed the variations across the country. ....(7)........ time spent watching television was in the Scotland BBC region. This was almost five hours more than the time spent by those in the South of England. Generally men spent ....(8)........ their time listening to the radio. This was possibly because they did so in the car on their way to and from work.

Overall, there was ....(9)........ of difference between the age groups at either end of the scale, but among those between the ages of 25 and 54, there was only ....(10)........ difference.

4.3. The use of the article

Sections **82–90**; 448; 475; 579; 597; 641; 747

Task one ***

Underline the definite articles, the indefinite articles and the places where zero article has been used in the texts opposite. Then list rules for their use in the table opposite. Ignore proper nouns.

1. The owner of a pet shop in Leeds saved the life of a lizard by giving it mouth-to-mouth resuscitation after it choked on a locust. (*Metro*, 21 June 2001)

2. Stolen property recovered by police in Sandwell, West Midlands, is to be sold on the internet to raise money to increase the number of bobbies on the beat. (*Sandwell Chronicle*, 15 June 2001)

3. The outbreak of foot and mouth disease was detected in England on February 20. Since then the disease has spread in the U.K. in an explosive manner. By March 2, the disease had been found in England, Wales, Scotland and Northern Ireland. The virus causes foot and mouth disease only in hoofed animals, but may cause a transient infection in horses and people. Hoofed animal species include cattle, pigs, sheep, goats, deer, reindeer and elks. The disease causes no risk for humans. (Finland: Ministry of Agriculture and Forestry, Food and Health Department – Press release, 5 March 2001)

4. With Special Delivery we give you a guarantee that, if we fail to deliver by the guaranteed time, we will refund your money within five days. In cases of lost or damaged items, compensation is based on the loss suffered up to the market value of the item or the compensation level paid for up to £2,500), whichever is the lower. (Royal Mail's *Code of Practice*, August 2000)

5. Demos, the independent think tank, is looking for imaginative, experienced and forward looking people to join a growing team and broad-ranging work programme. (Ad. For Demos in *New Statesman*, 25 June 2001)

DEFINITE ARTICLE	INDEFINITE ARTICLE	ZERO ARTICLE

Task two***

Add any other uses not included in the texts above.

Task three **

Select from the list below the use of the definite article in the following texts.

A: When the person or thing is generally known.

B: When the person or thing has been mentioned in the text before.

C: When the person or thing is defined later.

D: When the person or thing is unique.

E: For countries which are a federation of states.

F: For names of rivers and ranges of mountains.

1. We are boosting pensioner incomes and meeting *the* concerns of motorists and hauliers.

2. Victory for *the* Queen and Prince Philip!

3. Turner's painting "*The* Crook o'Lune near Lancaster" frames a famous view of *the* river Lune.

4. *The* sun was shining on *the* sea,
   Shining with all his might:
   He did his very best to make
   The billows smooth and bright –
   And this was odd, because it was
   The middle of the night.

5. After a fortnight of glorious indolence staying with friends in a diplomatic suburb of Damascus, I was woken this morning by *the* sound of Bing, their Filipino manservant, blow-drying my now spotlessly clean rucksack. (W. Dalrymple, *From the Holy Mountain*, Harper Collins, 1997)

6. On a hill overlooking *the* Lune, stands Lancaster Castle. *The* castle has always been a prison. *The* prison now houses grade C prisoners.

Task four **

In the following text, all the articles (definite and indefinite) have been removed. Rewrite the text with the appropriate articles. The first one is done for you.

I'd bought *the* revolver on impulse from morose, tubby man who said he went by name of 'Lefty'. I gave him story about needing to defend my home from scum who were running around these days. He nodded in sympathetic but slightly bored way. He didn't care what I was going to do with gun any more than car salesman cares where you plan to drive. All Lefty wanted to do was make sale. He proceeded to describe technical virtues and drawbacks of various models he had on sale. As he talked me through each one, he picked it up and put it in my hand. It was odd feeling. I realised that I had never before touched something which was solely and specifically designed to kill.

(M. Dibdin, *Thanksgiving*, Faber & Faber, 2000)

Task five **

1. Give reasons for your choice of articles in Task Four.
2. Give reasons for leaving some words governed by zero articles.

Task six ***

In the following text, underline the generic uses of the article (definite article, indefinite article and zero article). Then rewrite the text with alternative articles where possible, if necessary changing the noun from singular to plural or from plural to singular.

Lions, tigers and other big cats

Few creatures are held in such awe as lions, tigers, cheetahs and leopards, which we often call the big cats. These agile predators have strong, razor-sharp teeth and claws, muscular bodies and excellent senses. Their beautiful striped and dappled fur camouflages among the trees, allowing them to leap from the shadows to ambush unwary zebras, giraffes and other prey. There are seven kinds of big cats. The tiger is the largest. A fully-grown tiger may measure more than three metres from nose to tail; a fully-grown lion is almost as big.

The first large cats lived 45 million years ago. Many, including the lion, cheetah and leopard still inhabit parts of Africa. Snow leopards dwell in the mountains of Asia. Jaguars are the largest of the big cats in North and South America. They are equally at home swimming in lakes or climbing in trees.

Lions are the only big cats that live in groups, called prides, which may be up to thirty strong. The pride roams over an area of 100 sq. km. or more, depending on the abundance of prey in that area. The large male lion protects the pride's territory against other prides. The lion also defends the female against other males.

Lions, tigers and other big cats are true carnivores (flesh eaters). Lions usually eat large prey such as antelopes and zebras. One giraffe is often enough to feed a whole pride of lions.

4.4. Other words of definite meaning

Sections 91–101; 521; 619; 667

Other words which signal definite meaning are:

- **proper nouns** – *Susan, Chicago, Tuesday*, etc.
- **personal pronouns** – *I, we, he, she, it, they, you*, etc.
- **pointer words or demonstratives** – *this, that, these, those*

Task one *

Complete the following sentences with an article (*the*, *a*, *an*) where necessary.

1. .... Tom I'm talking about is the person you met last week, not .... one who used to be at school with us.

2. .... Tokyo of today is very different from .... one I knew in the seventies.

3. .... San Juan is an old market town.

4. I'm talking about .... San Juan in Puerto Rico not .... one in Argentina.

5. He intended at one time to marry .... Jenny.

6. .... Jenny? Which one? He knew two Jennys. There was .... Jenny from Australia and then there was .... one from Scotland.

7. Oh, I think it was .... Scottish Jenny.

8. Can you tell me the way to .... Brook Street?

9. Which one? There are three Brook Streets in this area.

10. Oh dear. Is there .... Brook Street by the river?

11. Yes.

12. That's .... one I want.

Task two **

Complete the sentences below with an appropriate third person pronoun. Rewrite the sentence where necessary to avoid gender discrimination.

Example: *A bank manager has a lot of responsibility. On the one hand .... has to be careful with money, but on the other hand, ... needs to be flexible enough to help people, especially those with small businesses.*

Here, in order to avoid gender discrimination, i.e. a bank manager may be male or female, it is necessary to make the subject plural.

Answer: *Bank managers have a lot of responsibility. On the one hand they have to be careful with money, but on the other hand, they need to be flexible enough to help people, especially those with small businesses.*

1. .... adopted the cat of a dying friend and it soon settled in her home.

2. A doctor in the emergency department of a hospital sometimes has to deal with violent patients so .... needs police support.

3. His colleagues were very supportive and .... helped ....
through a difficult period.

4. These days a teacher isn't paid enough money and .... often
leaves the profession after a few years.

5. .... was a beautiful yacht and .... was very fast.
.... was expected to win the challenge cup race.

6. Her life was essentially unfulfilled and .... crammed it with
trivia.

7. Ming, the panda, used to sulk in his cage and .... refused to
meet his intended wife.

8. .... were always together in a group known as the clan and
.... was thought .... would never break up.

9. Patrick saw the two children trying to get into the house. ....
shouted at .... and they ran away.

10. Last year Britain lost a lot of tourists. So this year, ... is
making a big effort to attract them back.

Task three *

In the sentences below, mark those E if the use of the first person pronoun
is exclusive and I if it is inclusive.

1. We saw a very good play last night. It was a pity you couldn't come. ☐

2. We've discussed this problem already, when you were here last week. ☐

3. We should all support him. He has a difficult job. ☐

4. We did enjoy meeting them. You would have liked them as well. ☐

5. He's never been very friendly with us. So don't worry. ☐

6. I suggest we take a vote on that. ☐

Task four *

Rewrite the following passage in an informal manner, avoiding the passive, and using *they*, *you*, *people* and contractions such as *it's*, *isn't*.

One shouldn't take it for granted that one will be admitted to a top
university simply because one has been to the right school. It is said that,
on occasion, one can be rather disadvantaged if one has been to certain
schools. It is said that colleges like to have a balance of scholars from
different backgrounds. So if one's background group is full, nothing can
be done.

Task five **

Indicate whether the pointer words (*this, that, these, those, here, now, then, there*) are forward (F) or backward (B) pointing or (S) situational.

1. I want you to listen to this. It's very important. ☐

2. I quite agree. That goes without saying. ☐

3. I tried to explain, but that was a mistake. ☐

4. Here is an important announcement. Will Dr Keiko Suzuki please call at the information desk immediately? ☐

5. John: There'll be trouble if they don't get home early. ☐

   Mary: I've already told them that. ☐

6. These are the rules here. First no lights on after 11 p.m.; second everyone ready for a run round the park at 7 a.m.; third no eating anything except at meal times. ☐

7. He will be doing that exam now. The one that's important for promotion. ☐

8. Come and have a look at my garden. Now, these tulips are my favourites. ☐

9. That was the bad news. Now for the good news. ☐

10. Those were not good annual results after the business expanded last year. ☐

4.5. Expressions using 'of' and the genitive

Sections 102–107; 530–535

'Of' is used to indicate various relations between two nouns.

A genitive can often be used with the same meaning as an 'of' phrase, especially where the genitive has human reference. Some of these relations are:

'*Have*' relation; subject-verb relation; verb-object relation; subject complement relation.

A genitive can be a noun phrase containing more than one word and ending with the genitive ending '*s or s*' (see 532).

The genitive is more commonly used for an *origin* relation or for a *classifying* relation. There are special cases where *time* and *place* nouns frequently use the genitive. It is especially the case when the place noun is followed by a superlative.

In some cases, the uses of the '*of*' phrase can suggest a different meaning from the genitive use.

Task one *

Underline the genitive and *of*-phrases in the passage below.

The art gallery's next exhibition will be a retrospective of the early drawings of Keith Mason. Mason was an East Anglian artist whose interest lay in capturing the atmosphere of the region. When he was in East Anglia, he often stayed at the Shearers'. He had become a friend of David Shearer's when, as teenagers, they had gone each week to the local school's evening art classes. Mason showed early signs of a very individual talent and was encouraged to apply for a scholarship to the Cambridge art school. After studying there, he travelled a lot through Europe but always returned to his beloved East Anglia and became one of the Cambridge college's regular visiting lecturers. He became a friend of several galleries in the region and donated several of his paintings to each gallery. Mason's death in 1993 left a gap in the region's art scene. While the region has always produced interesting painters whose work created interest in the region, Mason's created a national interest for the region.

Task two **

Show where the apostrophe should be in the following genitive phrases. In some cases, it is possible to omit the apostrophe.

1. A teachers work
2. The writers circle
3. The over-fifties club
4. Shakespeares plays
5. Bruce Willis early films
6. The United States economic policies.
7. The governments performance
8. The Managing Directors car
9. Yesterdays news
10. An old boys network

Task three **

Rewrite the following '*of*' phrases to show the relation between the two nouns.

Example: *the envy of the world* – THE WORLD ENVIES ...

The penguins of Antarctica – THE PENGUINS LIVE IN ANTARCTICA

1. people of Africa
2. the main entrance of the building

3. the concern of the workers

4. the dishonesty of some journalists

5. a lack of ideas

6. the courage of ordinary people

7. a bottle of wine

8. the causes of the economic crash

9. the result of his complaint

10. the postponement of the meeting.

Task four **

State the relation between the nouns in the following phrases: 'have' relation; subject-verb relation; verb-object relation; subject complement relation.
Rewrite them as 'of' phrases.

1. his mother's despair

2. the sovereign's rights

3. the actor's charm

4. the town's traffic problems

5. the government's downfall

6. the killer's arrest

7. the child's murder

8. the moon's effect on the tides

9. the father's anger

10. the orchestra's performance

Task five ***

Show how the meaning may differ in the pairs of phrases below.

1. The girl's story.	The story of the girl.
2. Scott's discovery.	The discovery of Scott.
3. The examination of a doctor.	A doctor's examination.
4. His life's dream.	His dream of life.
5. A lifetime's award.	The award of a lifetime.
6. Manet's portrait.	The portrait of Manet.
7. Peter's friend.	A friend of Peter's.
8. Mary's story is interesting.	The story of Mary is interesting.
9. The time of the month.	A month's time.
10. An actor's role.	The role of an actor.

Task six *

Rewrite the following phrases using the genitive.

1. The meeting taking place today.
2. The most successful airline in the world.
3. A wait for an hour.
4. The oldest married couple in Britain.
5. The highest mountain in Scotland.
6. A delay lasting a month.
7. A pause for a minute.
8. The favourite son of Liverpool.
9. The worst-kept secret in London.
10. The bush fires which took place last year.

Time, tense and aspect

5.1. Auxiliary verbs

Sections 477–478; 582; 735

Auxiliary verbs, or auxiliaries, are verbs which help to make up a verb phrase in combination with a main verb. The verbs *do*, *have* and *be* can be used as primary auxiliaries, while *can*, *could*, *will*, etc. are used as modal auxiliaries.

Auxiliaries only occur by themselves if the main verb is supplied by the earlier context. They can be placed before *not* and also before the subject in questions.

Contracted forms of auxiliaries are typical of spoken and informal English. Most auxiliaries also have contracted negative forms.

Task one *

Identify the auxiliary verbs in the following text, underlining the <u>primary auxiliaries</u> once and the <u>modal auxiliaries</u> twice.

> Ruth watched him as he dropped his bag down on the sofa, felt in his pocket and carefully laid fifteen brand new fifty-pound notes on the table.
> Ruth was impressed. 'Great-grandmother's legacy? Bank raid?'
>   Martin was biting his lip hard. 'It's all there. You can count it.'
> Ruth fingered the money. The new logs that Mr Wellbeing had cut for her hissed and spat from the fire.
> 'You're serious.'
> 'I had more money in my account than I thought.'
>   Martin began to hum as he pulled at the zip of his anorak. It was an odd, uneasy sound and Ruth had never heard it before. For the first time since she had met him, Ruth sensed that he might not be telling the truth and she was intrigued. 'You mean you cashed in your life savings for a one-legged chair?' Ruth did laugh then. 'I think Papa would have appreciated that.'
> 'Don't mock.'
> 'I wasn't mocking, Martin. Hemingway had a sense of humour. You must know that.'
> 'Not about himself. He didn't like to be laughed at.'
>   (from Michael Palin, *Hemingway's Chair*, pp. 159–160)

Task two *

Rewrite the verb phrases in the following sentences by replacing the full forms with contracted ones where possible.

1. It is going to be hard to get away with this but I will do my best.
2. Although I had made an awful mistake, Marjorie did not notice.
3. You need not worry if I have not come back by midnight.
4. Jim has been in trouble before, so he had better watch out.
5. We are getting complaints from people who have been treated unfairly.
6. Do you mind if we suspend these talks until everybody is listening again?
7. We must not condemn others as long as we are not setting an example ourselves.
8. I do not approve of what you have done but I will not tell anyone.
9. I would be prepared to lend a hand this afternoon but I am afraid I cannot come.
10. Should the Robinsons not have told us they were not going to share the costs after all?

5.2. The auxiliary verbs *do*, *have* and *be*

Sections 479–482; 736

The verbs *do*, *have* and *be* are used both as auxiliaries and as main verbs:

- **The auxiliary *do*** helps to form the *do*-construction, also called *do*-support. When used as a main verb or a substitute verb *do* has the full range of forms, including non-finite ones.
- **The auxiliary *have*** helps to form the perfect aspect. When used as a main verb meaning *possess*, *have* is sometimes constructed as an auxiliary in British English but the form *have got* can be used instead.
- **The auxiliary *be*** helps to form the progressive aspect and the passive. When used as a main verb *be* is constructed as an auxiliary, except with imperatives needing *do*-support.

Task one *

Specify for each of the underlined verbs whether it is used as an auxiliary (A) or as a main verb (M).

1. It is true that we were trying to help people in need.
2. Karen does realize that I did her a favour by also inviting her boyfriend.

3. Those who <u>had</u> dinner with Mr Partridge <u>have</u> been told about his latest project.

4. Brian <u>is</u> a long-distance commuter, so he <u>has</u> a car of his own.

5. <u>Do</u> come over to see us if you <u>have</u> enough time to spare.

6. Mark <u>was</u> appointed for the job because he <u>had</u> good references.

7. <u>Be</u> silent about the points you <u>do</u> want to remain secret.

8. The fact that you <u>have</u> reported these incidents to the police <u>does</u> you credit.

9. We <u>were</u> convinced that the door <u>had</u> been forced open before.

10. I <u>did</u> all the exercises as I <u>was</u> preparing for an important exam.

Task two *

Make the above sentences negative, using contracted forms where possible.

5.3. The modal auxiliaries

Sections 483–485; 736

The modal auxiliaries do not have -s forms, -ing forms or -ed participles. *Can, may, shall* and *will* have corresponding past forms, while the other modals have only one form.

Dare and *need* can be constructed either as main verbs followed by a *to*-infinitive or as modal auxiliaries followed by a bare infinitive.

The modal auxiliary *used* is a past form which is always followed by a *to*-infinitive. This auxiliary often takes the *do*-construction, in which case the spellings *use* and *used* both occur.

Task **

Complete the following sentences, giving two grammatically acceptable versions where possible. N stands for 'negative' and Q for 'yes–no question'.

1. (you / need) _____ come back until the end of this week. (N)

2. (Sandra / used) _____ send postcards when she was abroad. (N)

3. (you / dare) _____ call me a selfish person? (Q)

4. (I / dare) _____ think how disastrous such a policy might be. (N)

5. (Mrs Barnes / used) _____ give money to charity? (Q)

6. (I / need) _____ write more than thirty lines, sir? (Q)

7. (the PM / dare) _____ call an election yet. (N)
8. (we / used) _____ condemn such eccentric behaviour.
   (N)
9. (John / need) _____ have his passport renewed? (N/Q)
10. (people / used) _____ be afraid of ghosts in those days?
    (N/Q)

5.4. Meanings and forms

Sections **113–115**; 573–578; 740–741

Verbs can refer to:

● **an event**, i.e. a happening thought of as a single occurrence with
clearly defined limits

● **a state**, i.e. a state of affairs continuing over a period with or without
clearly defined limits

● **a habit**, i.e. a state consisting of a series of events.

All three meanings are normally expressed by simple, i.e. non-progressive
forms of the verb (simple present, simple past, present perfect and past
perfect).
   A fourth type of meaning is the temporary meaning expressed by the
progressive aspect (present progressive, past progressive, present perfect
progressive and past perfect progressive).

Task one **

Identify the (non-modal) finite verb phrases in the text below, specifying
for each

(a) which of the four above meanings it expresses

(b) which of the eight verb forms mentioned in brackets is used.

> The argument for a Slow Europe is not only that slow is good, but also that it
> can *work*. In 1999 Slow Food gave birth to the Slow City movement, which
> started in the tiny Tuscan town of Greve and has since spread throughout
> Italy. The organization has turned around local economies by promoting local
> goods and tourism, and now has a waiting list of cities hoping to copy the
> success of its members. Young Italians are moving from larger cities to Bra,
> where unemployment is only 5 per cent, about half the nationwide rate. Slow
> food and wine festivals draw thousands of tourists every year. Shops are thriv-
> ing, many with sales rising at a rate of 15 per cent per year. "This is our answer
> to globalization," says Paolo Saturnini, the founder of Slow Cities and mayor of
> Greve.
>
> (from *Newsweek*, 2 July 2001, p. 21)

Task two ***

Convert the following sentences expressing state meaning into corresponding sentences expressing <u>habit meaning</u>.

> Example: *Basil is a teetotaller* ⇒ *Basil <u>doesn't drink</u> alcohol. / Basil never <u>drinks</u> alcohol.*

1. Fiona is a vegetarian.
2. Sibyl is a pianist.
3. Winston Churchill was a cigar smoker.
4. We were regular churchgoers in those days.
5. Mr Hazelhurst was a Russian teacher for twenty years.
6. Dr Winter is a brain surgeon.
7. Davy is a beggar.
8. Ms Booth is a barrister.
9. Alan Sparke is an arsonist.
10. My cousin is a conscientious objector.
11. This convict is a serial killer.
12. Ben Jonson was an actor and a playwright.

5.5. Present time

Sections 116–121

Present states, present (complete) events and present habits are all referred to by verbs in the simple present tense.

Temporary present events, and temporary and persistent habits, are referred to by verbs in the present progressive.

Occasionally, the simple past is used with verbs like '*want*' and '*wonder*' as a more tactful alternative to the simple present.

Task one **

Specify which of the above basic meanings is expressed by the underlined verb phrases in the following sentences.

1. I<u>'m</u> not <u>drinking</u> any alcohol this week as I<u>'m</u> on antibiotics.
2. My adoptive mother <u>cooks</u> for my father and for any relatives who <u>drop in</u>.
3. Rare properties <u>are</u> already <u>being snapped up</u> by western tourists who <u>visit</u> the Dalmatian coast each summer.
4. The patients <u>pay</u> according to means and some of them <u>are sent</u> here under contractual arrangements.

5. Why <u>are</u> you always <u>asking</u> if Uncle Toby really <u>owns</u> three Jaguars?

6. I <u>don't belong</u> to a secret organization, I <u>swear</u> it.

7. I'<u>m</u> just <u>showing</u> the kids how to fly a kite and . . . look, up it <u>goes</u>.

8. Charles <u>doesn't live</u> at the cottage, but he and his wife <u>do come</u> almost every weekend.

9. Mr Duisenberg <u>hails</u> from Friesland, a Dutch province where people <u>are known</u> for their patience.

10. <u>Did</u> you <u>want</u> to see the doctor, Mrs Hopkins?

Task two **

Complete the following sentences using the most appropriate (active or passive) form of the verb in brackets.

1. My car (still repair) _____ so I (commute) _____ by train this week.

2. I (assure) _____ you the situation (get) _____ out of hand very quickly.

3. Lions (hunt) _____ by night and (feed) _____ on any animals they can pull down.

4. Bob, you (be) _____ very rude again to the very person who (love) _____ you most.

5. It (say) _____ in the newspaper that new measures (consider) _____ to fight organized crime.

6. Why (you continually interrupt) _____ the speaker? He (deserve) _____ your undivided attention, you (know) _____.

7. I (wonder) _____ if you could possibly help me. I (try) _____ to fix the ventilator but it (not work) _____ yet.

8. Millions of people in Britain (get) _____ their paper early in the morning because many newsagents (organize) _____ 'paper rounds'.

9. I (make) _____ a mess of this job but I (promise) _____ to do better next time.

10. (you still think) _____ of moving to the Seychelles or (you prefer) _____ to stay in our northern hemisphere after all?

11. Dad (keep) _____ telling me that the early bird (catch) _____ the worm.

12. This tropical disease (spread) _____ fast in Central Africa, where people (not earn) _____ enough to buy expensive medicines.

5.6. Past time 1

Sections **122–127**; **550–572**

Past-time meanings are similar to present-time meanings and can be expressed in various ways:

- **the (simple) past tense** refers to a definite time in the past and is identified by a past-time adverbial, the preceding language context or the context outside language.

- **the past progressive** refers to a past activity in progress or a state with limited duration.

- **the (simple) present perfect** refers to a past happening in relation to a later event or time. It is used for past events with results in the present time and for past indefinite events, past habits and past states (in a period) leading up to the present time.

- **the present perfect progressive** stresses the idea of limited duration and/or continuation of an activity up to the recent past or into the present.

- **the past perfect** refers to a time in the past as seen from a definite time in the past (= 'past in the past'). It can be the past equivalent of both the past tense and the present perfect.

Task one **

Identify the verb phrases which refer to past time in the following texts, specifying for each

(a) which of the above <u>meanings</u> is expressed

(b) which <u>verb form</u> is used (in terms of tense and aspect).

> Example: *I have visited Canada.* ⇒ <u>*have visited*</u>*: past indefinite event –*
> *simple present perfect*

> A former teacher from Coventry, who was shot in the stomach at point blank range while on holiday in Turkey, has been awarded £495,000 compensation.
> Mick Botterill was seriously injured when he disturbed a burglar at the holiday apartment in the resort of Side where he was staying with his wife and two teenage daughters in August 1996.
> Mr Botterill, from Stoke Park, lost two litres of blood and needed two operations to remove the bullet, which had perforated his intestine and nicked his spinal cord.
> (from the *Coventry Evening Telegraph*, 13 November 2001, p. 5)

Task two **

Use a simple past or a present perfect form (active or passive) in the following sentences.

1. TV and stage actress Peggy Mount (die) _____ aged 86. The star (become) _____ known to millions in the early ITV sitcom *The Larkins*.

2. Scotland (elect) _____ its first Parliament in May 1999 while it (have) _____ its own legal system for centuries.

3. Salman Rushdie (be) _____ born in India but (spend) _____ most of his life in Britain.

4. The Ramblers' Association (found) _____ in 1935 and (help) _____ to develop the footpath network ever since.

5. Alcohol-related deaths (rise) _____ by nearly half over the past five years, a report (warn) _____ yesterday.

6. The ancient Greeks (think) _____ pearls (create) _____ when lightning (strike) _____ the sea.

7. Environmentalists (make) _____ significant progress in recent years: they (even succeed) _____ in preventing further destruction of the coral reefs.

8. People (know) _____ to die as a result of the fever they (contract) _____ while travelling in the tropics.

9. Some artists (escape) _____ the Soviet Union while others (send) _____ to one of the gulags.

10. The current year (be) _____ a bad one for the economy: one airline alone (shed) _____ thousands of jobs and many other industries (have) _____ to sack workers too.

Task three **

All three (slightly adapted) extracts below are from articles which appeared in various issues of *The Independent* in mid-2001. Rewrite them as if you were a journalist reporting in 2010 about states and events at the beginning of the decade.

Example:

Local chiefs <u>stress</u> that more food aid <u>may</u> be needed <u>this</u> winter to stave off famine.

⇒ *Local chiefs <u>stressed</u> that more food <u>might</u> be needed <u>that</u> winter to stave off famine.*

1. Rural communities feel their traditions are threatened as English people buy property at prices that are out of the reach of locals.

2. Police officers approaching retirement are to be offered more money to stay on for a further five years under new Home Office plans to retain experienced staff.

Supporters of the proposals hope they will encourage long-serving constables and sergeants in their 50s to stay on. Under existing rules, police in the lower ranks must retire at 55, and many choose to take their pension after 30 years' service. As a result, forces across the country are facing a retirement "timebomb", with many officers due to leave this decade.

3. Top scientists believe that global warming has caused an unexpected collapse in the number of the world's most hunted whale.

They think that a sharp contraction in sea ice in the Antarctic is the likeliest explanation behind new findings, which suggest that the numbers of minke whales in the surrounding seas has fallen by half in less than a decade. The findings have greatly strengthened the arguments of conservationists who are resisting moves to lift a 15-year-old official ban on the hunt. (. . .)

Commercial whaling has been banned officially since 1986, but Japan and Norway each continue to kill about 500 minke whales a year. Japan does so under the guise of "scientific research", allowed under the IWC's treaty; Norway by exempting itself from the ban, which is also permitted under the agreement.

Task four *

Complete the following sentences, using a simple or progressive present perfect.

1. It (rain) _____ cats and dogs again.
2. (you see) _____ any films directed by Stanley Kubrick?
3. I (write) _____ at least five letters to complain about the infernal noise next door.
4. (you drink) _____ , I can smell it!
5. Liz and I (know) _____ each other for only a few days.
6. Tell me, how long (you wait) _____ here?
7. We (study) _____ your report but (not draw) _____ any conclusions yet.
8. The refugee camp (become) _____ quite crowded as people (cross) _____ the border in ever greater numbers.
9. I (never witness) _____ a hijacking although I (fly) _____ across the oceans dozens of times.
10. Boris (cheat) _____ on his live-in girlfriend for months, so she (decide) _____ to leave him at last.
11. Somebody (just tell) _____ me that Fred and Wilma (constantly argue) _____ about trivial things lately.
12. Pat (work) _____ flat out all morning but (still not finish) _____ the repair job.

Task five ***

Rewrite the following text using direct instead of indirect speech. Replace the past perfect forms by corresponding simple past or present perfect forms.

Example:

Stella Soames often said that she had experienced an unhappy childhood but had always been a very happy adult. ⇒

Stella: "I experienced an unhappy childhood but have always been a very happy adult."

Stella Soames phoned last night to tell me that her husband Kevin had just died in hospital. He had fallen off his horse a week before and broken a leg and several ribs. Instead of recovering after the operation, however, he had suffered a stroke and lain in a coma for three or four days, from which he had not woken up again.

Stella told me she had already fixed a date for the funeral but hadn't contacted her husband's brother and sister yet as she had been out of touch with them for years. She added that Kevin had been a wonderful man and she had never regretted marrying him.

She also asked me if I knew about Kevin's recent conversion to Buddhism. I said I had heard some rumours about it at the local pub and had considered converting to it myself lately. I told Stella I had always believed in an afterlife but had kept it to myself until then. Upon which she thanked me, saying I had at least offered her the prospect of one day meeting Kevin again.

5.7. Past time 2

Sections 128–131

The difference between past tense and perfect aspect cannot be expressed by infinitives or -*ing* constructions. Instead, the perfect expresses general past meaning: It seems that John (*has*) *missed* the point ⇒ John seems *to have missed* the point.

Adverbials referring to a point or period of time which finished in the past go with the past tense, while those referring to a period leading up to present or recent past time go with the present perfect. Adverbials such as *this morning*, *today* and *recently* can go with either verb form.

The auxiliary *used to* can express state or habit in the past as contrasted with the present, while *would* stresses the idea of characteristic behaviour in the past.

Task one ***

Rephrase the following sentences, replacing the finite verb phrase of the subclause by the perfect infinitive or perfect *-ing* form as in the example above.

1. It is suspected that Harry Trotter killed his aunt.
2. It appears that 60 per cent of viewers watched the Cup Final yesterday.
3. Edith is very pleased that she has been given a second chance.
4. It is rumoured that millions of euros were stolen from a local bank last night.
5. It is unlikely that the police have identified the culprits.
6. I'm so sorry I drew everyone's attention to the flaws in your project.
7. We are very much aware that the authorities were forced to accept this questionable deal.
8. It is certain that all three candidates have been screened.
9. Some people are worried about the fact that they have not been informed at all.
10. Mr Bunker is the first man who swam across the lake in winter.
11. It is alleged that some politicians accepted bribes from lobbyists in the early 90s.
12. Dozens of drivers were fined because they had exceeded the speed limit.

Task two **

Complete the following sentences, using the simple past or present perfect form.

1. A small number of tourists (catch) _____ malaria in Africa last summer.
2. Humphrey (lie) _____ in bed until a quarter to nine.
3. (you teach) _____ any of the third formers lately?
4. The mugger apparently (creep) _____ up from behind before attacking his victim.
5. I (spend) _____ two hours marking exams up until now.
6. The number of people below the poverty line (not rise) _____ any more since 1998.
7. The town council (choose) _____ to renovate the opera house half a decade ago.
8. I (tear up) _____ the receipt after leaving the shop.

9. A major earthquake (strike) _____ eastern Iran on Monday.

10. The main waterpipe (burst) _____ early this morning but we (have) _____ a regular supply for about half an hour now.

11. – (you feed) _____ the parrot yet?

   – Oh, (it already eat) _____ more than its daily ration!

12. Arthur (bear) _____ me a grudge ever since I (beat) _____ him at chess.

Task three **

Replace the underlined verb phrases, using either *used to* or *would* in order to express the idea of past state or habit.

1. Bouncy castles <u>were</u> an attraction at fair grounds, pubs and school fêtes – now you can <u>hire</u> one for your own back garden.

2. As I entered Grandma's shop, a brass bell <u>tinkled</u> and the smell of putty filled my nostrils. Then I <u>opened</u> the door marked *Private*, leading to the dining room where Grandma was sitting. She always had a welcoming smile and I <u>kissed</u> her soft cheek.

3. The chief child-eating troll in Iceland, Gryla, <u>sent</u> her 13 sons out every year to catch bad children for her table. But the violent figure has softened and now gives children presents when they come back to her home.

      (1,2 and 3: adapted from various articles in *Woman's Weekly*)

4. Kate Simpson <u>hated</u> exercise, but when Mom took it up, she did, too, and slimmed down.

      (*Newsweek*, 3 July 2000, p. 58)

5. When I went into the studio as a young boy, 5 or 6, my father <u>did not stop</u> as he was working. I <u>did not ask</u> for the attention. Later on, when I was a little older, sometimes I <u>worked</u> side by side with my father, with my sister present, too. We <u>were working</u> at the same table, we <u>were doing</u> something, he <u>was doing</u> something else. Sometimes he <u>asked</u> me to help prop something up or hold something. He worked with plaster, and the plaster <u>had to set</u>. I could see he was always trying to do something a little bit different.

      (*Newsweek*, 19 July 1999, p. 58)

5.8. The progressive aspect

Sections 132–139

The progressive aspect refers to activity in progress and therefore suggests that the activity is of limited duration and that it need not be complete.

The verbs which typically take the progressive are verbs denoting activities or processes. With verbs denoting momentary events the progressive suggests repetition.

State verbs often cannot be used with the progressive at all and include verbs of perceiving, verbs referring to a state of mind or feeling, and verbs referring to a relationship or a state of being.

Verbs referring to an internal sensation can be used with either the progressive or the simple form with little difference of effect. Some state verbs can also refer to an active form of behaviour and be used with the progressive.

Task one **

Use the most appropriate simple or progressive form (present, past or perfect) of the verb in brackets.

1. We (have) _____ dinner last night when Alice (burst in) _____ to tell us about her latest conquest.

2. I (search) _____ for the missing documents all day . . . and look: I (only find) _____ this draft contract.

3. (you still consider) _____ sacking your secretary or (you want) _____ to give her a second chance?

4. When I (come in) _____ a few minutes ago the two little boys (punch) _____ each other in the face.

5. More and more people (get) _____ tired of the way the government (handle) _____ the country's economic problems these days.

6. How (you normally react) _____ when someone (call) _____ you an incompetent teacher?

7. What (you whisper) _____ into Amanda's ear when I (see) _____ you in that dark alley the other day?

8. A: (you finish) _____ those two book reviews yet?

   B: No, I (work) _____ on various other things lately.

9. Why (you complain) _____ about the food all the time? You (eat) _____ five big meals today.

10. After conquering Mount Everest the mountaineers (fast run) _____ out of oxygen but fortunately a helicopter (come) _____ to their rescue.

11. We (send) _____ an urgent message but (still wait) _____ for a response.

12. The prison population (rise) _____ by more than 2,000 in the five months since Mr Blunkett (take over) _____ at the Home Office after three years during which it (stabilise) _____ at around 66,000. (*The Guardian*, 15 November 2001, p. 12)

Task two **

Rewrite the following text, replacing the underlined parts by one of the state verbs listed below and making any other changes which are necessary.

believe	*belong to*	*consist of*	*contain*	*depend*
know	*lack*	*love*	*look like*	*owe*
remain	*remember*	*require*	*resemble*	*understand*

Not many people <u>are acquainted with</u> the name of William Campbell, but I still <u>have a vivid memory of</u> reading his biography. The book <u>is divided into</u> five chapters, <u>in</u> the first of which <u>there are</u> a lot of anecdotes about William's early years at Moorcock Manor. This <u>had been in the possession of</u> the Campbell family for centuries.

William <u>was</u> really <u>fond of</u> life in the open and at the age of 18 <u>had the appearance of</u> a young country squire. However, as a result of some very risky investments, his father one day <u>was in debt to</u> the local bank <u>for</u> a huge amount of money. After the sale of vast tracts of land, little <u>was left</u> of the original estate.

It was <u>clear to William</u> that his future <u>was</u> now <u>dependent</u> on his own resourcefulness. Fortunately, he <u>was like</u> the very first Campbell in many ways: he <u>had faith</u> in himself and <u>was</u> never <u>without</u> the resolve to do what the situation <u>made necessary</u>.

Task three **

Complete the following sentences, using both the simple and the progressive form of each of the verbs listed below at least once. Also pay attention to tense.

be   feel   hear   see   smell   taste

1. We _____ rumours about a possible coup for quite some time now.

2. A: It's hard to say what this cake _____ like.

   B: Well, I would say it _____ like cardboard.

3. Karen hadn't been in the job long and (still) _____ her way.

4. I _____ no reason why you _____ such a nuisance again!

5. The dog _____ the lamppost and when I bent down I _____ a half-eaten hamburger, which really _____ awful.

6. The chef _____ the sauce when I entered the kitchen.

7. I _____ you _____ no longer interested in buying a second home.

8. Stop it, Billy, you _____ very unpleasant to me. I really _____ like throwing you out.

9. Carol and David _____ a lot of each other lately.

10. When he slipped into the pantry Andy _____ a piercing scream, followed by a thud. Seconds later he _____ a droplet of sweat trickling down his neck.

5.9. Future time 1

Sections 140–146

There are five chief ways of expressing future time in the English verb phrase:

(i) **will/shall + infinitive**: neutral future of prediction (often element of intention with personal subjects)

(ii) **be going to + infinitive**: future resulting from present intention or from present cause

(iii) **progressive aspect**: future event arising from a present plan, programme or arrangement

(iv) **simple present tense**:
– future in adverbial clauses (of time and condition) and after *hope*, *assume*, etc.
– future event in main clauses which is seen as absolutely certain

(v) **will/shall + progressive aspect**:
– future + temporary meaning
– future event which will take place 'as a matter of course'.

Some less common ways of expressing the future: *be to + infinitive, be about to + infinitive, be on the point of + -ing form*.

Task one *

Identify the verb phrases referring to future time, specifying which of the above types of future meaning is involved.

1. Alan tried to start the car and failed as she had failed. (. . .) Alan got out of the car.
   "It's not going to start," he said. "I'll drive you home and we'll phone someone to see to your car."
   (from Barbara Vine, *The Brimstone Wedding*, p. 283)

2. Her mother accepted the lie. She said:
   "I shall be an embarrassing flat mate. How will you explain me to your friends?"

"We shan't be seeing my friends. If we do run into them, I shall explain that you're my mother."

(from P.D. James, Innocent Blood, p. 85)

3. It's ten o'clock on a Friday morning, and Helen is about to celebrate her seventeenth wedding anniversary with a visit to the hairdresser's. She and Daniel will, as usual, be going out tonight and she wants to look her best.

4. Sagittarius: Encouraging news will reach you soon but not before you've been through a period of anxious anticipation. Don't over-react to this week's drama and it will soon pass.

5. "Penny and I have lived with my parents since the divorce," she said. "I left her with them this week as it was half-term but she's starting at the village school tomorrow."
Again I nodded. "What will she do when school finishes?"
Marietta smiled. "Mrs Jones in the village has offered to look after her. I finish work at five, so we're well organized."

(3–4–5: from various issues of Woman's Weekly)

Task two **

Complete the following sentences using the most appropriate form to express the future.

1. Our neighbours' silver wedding anniversary (be) _____ on 1 April.

2. (you stay) _____ here for another day, sir?

3. If Barbara (not take) _____ her pills, she (get) _____ very ill.

4. I've had far too much whisky, I (throw up) _____ .

5. I (see) _____ a specialist tomorrow to discuss my backache.

6. The Joneses (cruise) _____ in the Mediterranean this time next week.

7. We (win) _____ this election: we are already 7 per cent ahead in the polls.

8. The conference (begin) _____ at 10 a.m. tomorrow.

9. (you buy) _____ a new video recorder after all?

10. We (leave) _____ for the States in a few hours and (probably return) _____ at the end of summer.

11. I hope this war (not last) _____ too long, otherwise it (take) _____ ages to rebuild the country.

12. Stay away from that landmine! It (blow up) _____ !

13. Dan and Ruth (come) _____ over for Christmas Eve, so we (be) _____ able to tell them the great news at last.

14. When the ship (enter) _____ the harbour, you (see) _____ the old customs house on your left.

15. Politicians (complain) _____ about the low turn-out again but they only have themselves to blame for it.

Task three **

Use an appropriate form of the verb in brackets to refer to future time in the following dialogue.

Sue: Hello! Is that you, Pat? It's just to tell you that we've packed all our stuff and Randy and I (leave) _____ for the airport. The taxi we called (be) _____ here any minute now. Our plane (take off) _____ at 10.30, so there's not much time left.

Pat: Where (spend) _____ your holidays? I hope you (not get) _____ as much rain as you did last year.

Sue: Oh, no chance of that at all! We (fly) _____ to Crete this time, so we (get) _____ plenty of sunshine, I'm sure.

Pat: (you lie) _____ on the beach all day or have you got other plans?

Sue: Oh, no, we both hate crowded beaches, and Randy is an art historian, so we (tour) _____ the island instead and we (definitely visit) _____ the main archaeological sites. Of course, I expect we (also go) _____ for a swim in the evening now and then.

Pat: Well, you (enjoy) _____ yourselves again, you lucky people. Anyway, have a safe trip and do send me a card or you (never get) _____ one from **me** when **I** (go) _____ on holiday.

5.10. Future time 2

Sections 147–148

The 'future in the past' is the future seen from a viewpoint in the past. It is expressed by future constructions whose first verbal element is a past tense:

- **was going to** and **was about to** usually suggest that the anticipated happening did not take place
- **was/were to** and **would** are rather literary in style and can refer to the fulfilled future in the past.

The 'past in the future' is expressed by *will + perfect infinitive*. In subordinate clauses it is often replaced by the ordinary *present perfect*.

Task **

Use one of the above constructions with the verb in brackets to express future in the past or past in the future as required by the context.

1. If we don't reach an agreement soon, all our efforts (be) _____ in vain.

2. We thought they (not cancel) _____ the fireworks but in the end they did.

3. Firefighters continued to work frantically and (rescue) _____ two more trapped residents later that afternoon.

4. All the letters (be delivered) _____ by the end of this week.

5. Robin (jump) _____, but Alice tried to stop him, so he didn't.

6. Indiana Jones's best partner had died and (never see) _____ those he cherished dearly.

7. Richard (come) _____ but he fell asleep while Clare was taking a shower.

8. It had been a dreadful experience, which _____ haunt the victims for the rest of their lives.

9. By the time you (read) _____ this sentence, someone (die) _____ somewhere.

10. The little boy looked as though he (cry) _____, but when I picked him up he smiled at me.

11. The disgruntled lawyer wrote a vicious letter, which he (regret) _____ for the rest of his life.

12. We (just leave) _____ the building when it began to rain.

5.11. Summary

Sections 149–150

At least 26 common meanings can be expressed through tense and aspect. They relate to:

- **time:** (a) present – (b) past – (c) future
- **type of 'happening':** (1) single event – (2) state – (3) habit – (4) temporary state or event – (5) temporary habit
- **a variety of other factors** such as definiteness, anteriority, anticipation, etc.

Task one **

Identify the (non-modal) finite verb phrases in the following text, specifying

(a) which combination of tense and aspect category they exemplify

(b) which of the 26 meanings listed in *CGE* section 150 they express.

> Example: *Despite the recession, Americans <u>have been spending</u> lots of money.*
>
> ⇒ *(a) present perfect progressive*
>
> *(b) 6 (= temporary habit up to present time)*

CHINESE EXPORTS

During holidays or on weekends, the Lo Wu border crossing between Hong Kong and the mainland Chinese city of Shenzen resembles a churning ocean, with stranded travellers milling together in queues that stretch to the horizon. Hong Kong officials are hoping the lines will soon grow even longer. Beginning this week, the border will stay open another half hour, until midnight each night. "We're getting complaints," says a senior Hong Kong security official. "The guards are saying they don't even have time to eat their meals." (. . .)

For years Beijing imposed strict restrictions on travel outside its borders. Into the early 1970s, until the Cultural Revolution ended, China was virtually sealed off from the rest of the world. (. . .) But as levels of affluence have risen – especially in the south, where GDP levels more than doubled between 1993 and 1998 – ordinary Chinese can now afford overseas trips, at the moment the country itself is seeking a greater role in the world. Having effectively abandoned its communist identity, Beijing is encouraging its newly affluent citizens to travel abroad. (. . .)

Asian countries have long seen China's 1.4 billion people as a major potential source of tourist revenues. Now they are expected to pick up the slack from more traditional moneymakers. In the last two months, Japanese tourists have virtually stopped travelling outside their country. European and American arrivals are down by almost half in some places. At the same time, in Hong Kong the number of arrivals from China has risen more than 25 per cent. That represents more than chump change: mainland Chinese spend only slightly less per day ($625) than their American counterparts ($680).

(from Newsweek, 10 December 2001, pp. 42–43)

Task two ***

Complete the sentences in the following extracts, using the most appropriate combination of tense, aspect and voice (active vs passive).

1. "When (you tell) _____ Mike you (leave) _____ him?" Philippa asked.
   "Next week," I said. "When he (get) _____ back from Yorkshire. You can keep it dark till then."

"You (bet) _____ ," she said. "By the way, there (be) _____ one of your Gilda Brent's films on tomorrow, two p.m., you (be) _____ at work, so (you want) _____ me to video it for you?"

(adapted from Barbara Vine, *The Brimstone Wedding*, p. 209)

2. Acid rain, one of the greatest pollution scourges of the last decade, (rapidly reduce) _____ across Britain and Europe, a new official report (reveal) _____. It (conclude) _____ that the acidity of rainfall in Britain (cut) _____ in half over the past 15 years and that acidified lakes in Scandinavia (begin) _____ to recover in what (promise) _____ to be one of the most remarkable environmental success stories on record.

(from *The Independent*, 30 December 2001)

3. Why (the natives of the Amazon Rainforest live) _____ so long? The entire world (discover) _____ the life extending and healing power of the Rainforest. Find out how you can too.

For thousands of years, the natives of the South American Rainforests (traditionally rely) _____ on flowers, leaves, stems, barks and roots of various plant species. Many of these botanicals (use) _____ to maintain and optimize health. (. . .)

"After a few months on the Amazon Rainforest herbs I (start) _____ to feel the vitality of the Rainforest working in my body. I (not be) _____ sick since, not even a sniffle in well over a year. I (be) _____ a believer." (K.C.)

(adapted from *www. rainforest.amazon.net*)

4. I (be) _____ born in 1948 to parents who (be) _____ absolutely devoted to each other. My sister, Janet, (be) _____ two, and three more siblings (follow) _____ me in quick succession – the last arriving just in time to be held by my father before he (pass) _____ away. (. . .)

My father (be) _____ a successful and talented musician, but he (spend) _____ as much as he (earn) _____ , so as a family we (be) _____ totally unprepared for his death. It (be) _____ a non-stop struggle for my mother, who (love) _____ him so very much that, to this day, no other man (ever feature) _____ in her life. (. . .)

The loss of my father, coupled with the problems I (experience) _____ at school, (turn) _____ me into somewhat of a rebel. I couldn't understand why I (struggle) _____ to read and write, while it (appear) _____ to come naturally to everybody else. (. . .)

(from *Woman's Weekly*, 23 October 2001, p. 12)

5. The golden age of ocean travel is back and a cruise (constitute) _____ a great holiday by itself. For those who (already travel) _____ extensively it (be) _____ a novel and exciting experience.

Our staff (recognize) _____ that cruise travel management (require) _____ exceptional product knowledge. Our cruise manager Alison S. (be) _____ in the travel industry for 15 years and cruising (be) _____ her special interest. Please email Alison and she (put) _____ together something that you (never forget) _____.

We (list) _____ a small sample of the products available through CRUISE TRAVELLER. Please do not hesitate to let us know what your experience of cruises (be) _____ . This way we can ensure that we (provide) _____ our clients with the best products.

(adapted from *www.sydneyexpresstravel.com.au*)

Task three ***

Rewrite the following text, turning the dialogue into **indirect speech** as in the following exchange:

Ronald: "How long have you been working on this building site?"
Chris: "Well, I started here two years ago but with some luck, I hope I'll be able to move to another job in a couple of months."   ⇒
Ronald asked Chris how long he had been working on that building site. Chris replied that he had started there two years before but that, with some luck, he hoped he would be able to move to another job a few months later.

Vivien: Pearl, you are a social worker running a project for single mothers. Is it possible for them to keep their babies?

Pearl: Well, in some parts of my country these women are still experiencing problems. The family often can't feed an extra mouth, but I have found that if the woman and her baby get some support they are accepted into the family.

Vivien: What if they are not?

Pearl: The less fortunate women are told that there are support services at several refuges. Over two hundred single mothers have passed through them since 1998 and most are coping quite well on their own now.

Vivien: I imagine that in spite of all your efforts you don't always reach those who need to be helped most.

Pearl: Oh, you're absolutely right. I know dozens of women who have given up their babies but I feel sure their numbers will keep going down, as they have over the past few years.

Adjectives

6.1. Adjectives

Sections **440–444**

Here are four features of adjectives:

(i) Most adjectives can be used attributively (before nouns) and predicatively (as complements of linking verbs)

(ii) Most adjectives can be modified by degree adverbs

(iii) Most adjectives have comparative and superlative forms

(iv) Many adjectives are derived from nouns and can be recognized by their endings.

Task one **

Some of the adjectives in the following texts are used attributively, some are used predicatively. Arrange them in three groups according to whether they are normally used

(a) attributively only

(b) predicatively only

(c) both attributively and predicatively.

1. It is quite obvious, according to the medical profession, that vegetable oil should be one of the chief ingredients of a healthy diet.

2. Most people would consider Brian extremely lazy, but I think that's sheer nonsense. The main thing about him is that he is a little clumsy at times and he is afraid to make an utter fool of himself.

3. Tomorrow will be a mainly bright day, with skies over Scotland becoming cloudier in the afternoon and perhaps the odd shower mixed in towards late evening.

4. Sandra had been feeling really ill for a week or so. Being a mere child, the girl feared she might be suffering from a deadly disease, but in the

end she made a complete recovery and now she is alive and kicking again.

5. I thought Linda had already fallen asleep but in fact she was still wide awake, trying to come to terms with the shocking events of the day. The live pictures on TV had made it abundantly clear to her that the heinous crimes perpetrated by evil minds should not go unpunished.

Task two *

Underline in the above texts any degree adverbs premodifying an attributive or a predicative adjective.

Task three ***

State the difference in meaning between the two versions of the following sentences, using synonymous expressions or paraphrases.

1. Social workers had to counsel

   (a) the concerned parents

   (b) the parents concerned.

2. I want you to meet

   (a) the present members of the board

   (b) the members of the board present.

3. The bathroom is

   (a) five square metres

   (b) five metres square.

4. Several mathematicians offered to deal with

   (a) the involved calculations

   (b) the calculations involved.

5. (a) Everything is still in its proper place.

   (b) Some Londoners do not live in London proper.

Task four ***

Determine whether the -ing and -ed forms in the following sentences are (a) adjectives or (b) participles, justifying your decision.

Examples: *We were very pleased to be invited by the Lord Mayor.*

⇒ (participial) adjective, cf premodifying degree adverb

Although admired by many, the author does not give interviews.

⇒ (past) participle, cf the by-agent (= signals the passive).

1. I don't want you <u>worrying</u> about me all the time.
2. We were rather <u>amused</u> to hear that Ms Upstart had been demoted.
3. I shall always be grateful to my truly <u>devoted</u> parents.
4. The story of the Holy Grail is still <u>fascinating</u> people all over the world.
5. I was terrified to go there and also very <u>ashamed</u> of myself.
6. *The Little Mermaid* turned out to be quite a <u>moving</u> film.
7. The signals coming from Brussels are <u>encouraging</u>.
8. If you're that <u>worried</u> about your health, go and see a doctor.
9. You will be <u>astonished</u> by the detail and depth of our reports <u>describing</u> access to the site.
10. The purchase of new computer hardware is always a <u>daunting</u> task, with so many guides and experts <u>bewildering</u> us with technical jargon.
11. I was <u>informed</u> of Ms Dando's murder by my mother, and was absolutely <u>flabbergasted</u> as to why such a thing could happen.
12. The Education Secretary became <u>incensed</u> when he read the <u>scathing</u> criticism <u>voiced</u> by a number of headmasters in *The Times*.

Task five **

Restore the following extract to its original form by filling the blanks with one of the adjectives listed below. Each adjective should be used only once.

dressed	*former*	*oily*	*plastic*	*prickly*	*rear*	*sharp*
spongy	*squeaky*	*sure*	*towering*	*useful*	*wiry*	*working*

ALASKA: OIL'S GROUND ZERO

If you want somebody to fly you over the _____ peaks of the Brooks Range and drop you onto the _____ tundra of the Arctic National Wildlife Refuge, Dirk Nickisch is your man. Dirk is a _____ rodeo rider and crop-duster, a _____ fellow with _____ eyes and _____ whiskers whom some in his home state of North Dakota have likened to a coyote. He meets clients at a gravel airstrip in a Gwich'in Indian village just south of the range. _____ in _____ pants and a baseball cap, he kicks the tires on his 1952 single-prop de Havilland Beaver, shoulders the _____ rudder back and forth to be _____ it's still in _____ order and tells you, if you ask him, that he reckons his Pratt & Whitney engine has been overhauled "a few times". He doesn't have much time for people who stand around asking questions without making themselves _____ , however. So he rolls four _____ barrels of fuel under the plane and puts you to work with a hose and a _____ hand pump.

(from *Newsweek*, 13 August 2001, p. 38)

6.2. Adjective or adverb?

Sections 445–447

Most adverbs in English are derived from adjectives by the addition of -ly, but there are some which do not end in -ly. These words can be used both as adjectives and adverbs.

An adjective is used after verbs of the senses. Here we consider the adjective to be a complement, not an adverbial.

The difference between an adverb form and an adjective form does not always involve a difference in meaning. The form without -ly tends to be more informal and is especially common in comparative and superlative constructions.

Task one **

Complete the following sentences, using an <u>adjective</u> OR a <u>corresponding adverb ending in -ly</u> related to the noun or verb in brackets.

1. Stung by so much criticism, the PM reacted very (anger) _____.

2. After the confrontation the headmaster felt extremely (anger) _____.

3. Most of the young recruits looked very (courage) _____.

4. The two frail women had behaved (courage) _____.

5. It all sounds (marvel) _____, doesn't it?

6. This (marvel) _____ executed story captures the spirit of the series perfectly.

7. It was a (delicacy) _____ creamy soup.

8. The local food tastes (delicacy) _____.

9. That type of weakness is considered (fate) _____ by most neutral observers.

10. Two firefighters were (fate) _____ injured in the explosion.

11. Later that afternoon the sky turned (haze) _____.

12. The victim remembered the events only (haze) _____.

Task two **

Add the most appropriate of the adverbs listed below, using the base form OR the form ending in -ly. Each form should be used only once.

bare(ly)	close(ly)	direct(ly)	hard(ly)	high(ly)
late(ly)	loud(ly) and clear(ly)	right(ly)	short(ly)	strong(ly)

1. Does this train go to London _____ or via Canterbury?

2. The Queen praised _____ what had already been achieved.

3. With your help, one day I might come _____ to being 'perfect'.

4. The landscape was stripped _____ after the civil war.

5. Professor Appleby's untimely death cut _____ his brilliant career.

6. There have been more and more signs of unrest _____.

7. Due to fog I could _____ make out the contours of the ferry.

8. Mrs Curry is in her late eighties and still going _____.

9. Regular troops were involved _____ in the attack.

10. Captain Cook, I have received your message _____.

11. I'm not in town now but I will be _____.

12. The eagle was flying _____ over the mountains.

13. Having worked _____ all his life, the builder decided to retire at last.

14. There is no question: the chairman expressed himself _____.

15. We are already behind schedule, so we will arrive _____.

16. The two brothers _____ resembled each other.

17. The two rapists have _____ been punished for what they did.

18. The football fans are so disciplined that there is _____ any need for a police presence.

19. The redecorated rooms smelled _____ of paint.

20. The Internet Keyword brings you _____ back here.

6.3. Adjectives as heads

Section **448**; 90; 579–580

Some adjectives can be heads of noun phrases and have generic reference:

- **adjectives denoting a class of people,** including some nationality adjectives (plural): *the English*

- **adjectives denoting an abstract quality (singular):** *the symbolical*

Task one *

Use adjectives acting as heads of noun phrases to refer to the following classes of people.

1. people who are out of work:
2. people who have a physical handicap:
3. people who are well-off:
4. people who have great faith in God:
5. people who are victims of oppression:
6. people who have nowhere to live:
7. inhabitants of Great Britain:
8. inhabitants of Wales:
9. inhabitants of Ireland:
10. inhabitants of Spain:
11. inhabitants of France:
12. inhabitants of the Netherlands:

Task two ***

Complete the following sentences, using adjectives acting as heads of noun phrases to refer to the abstract qualities referred to by the phrases in brackets.

1. Some people believe in _____.
   (= things that are impossible to explain by natural causes)
2. Why do some politicians keep stating _____?
   (= things that are already clear to everyone)
3. The name of Samuel Beckett is associated with the theatre of

   _____.
   (= things that do not make sense at all)
4. Police officers and firefighters did _____.
   (= succeed in doing what an ordinary person cannot achieve)
5. This type of extreme behaviour borders on _____.
   (= typical of people who belong in a mental hospital)
6. Leave everything to me – I'll do _____.
   (= whatever is required under the circumstances)
7. _____ has captivated me over _____ as

   long as I can recall.
   (= things that endure for ever vs things that do not)
8. On 11 September 2001 _____ happened.
   (= something that nobody can accept or even imagine)

6.4. Adjective patterns

Sections 436–438

Adjectives can have different types of complement, such as

- **a prepositional phrase**: I feel very sorry *for her*
- **a *that*-clause:**   Everybody's pleased *that she is making such good progress*
- **a *to*-infinitive:**   I'm glad *to hear she is recovering.*

Task one **

Complete the following sentences, adding the appropriate prepositions.

1. Most of Europe is still dependent _____ oil from the Middle East.
2. More and more women are financially independent _____ their husbands.
3. The starving stowaway was impatient _____ his first meal in five days.
4. Teachers are very impatient _____ students who don't understand the basics of mathematics.
5. Kenneth has been deeply involved _____ a younger colleague for some time.
6. Several companies are involved _____ producing the Airbus.
7. Even in the face of adversity most of the aid workers remained true _____ their ideals.
8. What you were saying about Germany is also true _____ Austria.
9. General Swordfish was furious _____ his chief-of-staff because of his improper behaviour.
10. Karen was furious _____ being told she might be sacked.
11. Some emancipated men are still not very keen _____ cooking.
12. People eager _____ a quick cure are likely to be disappointed.

Task two **

Expand each of the following sentences by adding an introductory clause such as *I am/was + adjective* or *it is/was + adjective*, using an adjective related to the noun or verb in brackets. In some cases both patterns are possible, as in

The watch continued to work without any problems. (amaze)

⇒ (a) <u>I was amazed</u> *that the watch continued to work without any problems.*

(b) <u>It was amazing</u> *that the watch continued / should continue to work without any problems.*

1. So many people are using drugs these days. (shock)

2. The government should form a Royal Commission. (essence)

3. You are offering me this unique opportunity. (gratitude)

4. I had helped in the attempt to fight poverty. (pride)

5. We have not learned any lessons from this bloody conflict. (shame)

6. *Titanic* beat *Star Wars* at the box office. (outrage)

7. The scheme will be very successful. (confidence)

8. Mr Welsh offers useful advice on how to deal with the war on drugs. (no surprise)

9. Peter tried to deny the gravity of the problem. (alarm)

10. I was watching another movie altogether. (convince)

11. We should move forward in positive and productive ways. (evidence)

12. I will begin to get some real answers at last. (hope)

6.5. Adjective patterns with a *to-infinitive*

Section 439

There are at least four different types of adjectives which have a construction with *to*-infinitive:

(i) She's wrong *to say a thing like that.* (= It's wrong of her to say a thing like that.)

(ii) Such people are hard *to find nowadays.* (= It's hard to find such people nowadays.)

(iii) I was delighted *to make that personal contact.* (= It made me delighted to make that contact.)

(iv) Many dealers were quick *to buy the new shares.* (= Many dealers quickly bought the new shares.)

Some adjectives do not belong to any of these four types:

(v) I might be able *to afford it.*

Task one **

Paraphrase the following sentences by turning the adjective patterns with a *to*-infinitive into alternative structures.

1. The doctor was <u>slow</u> to realize the seriousness of his patient's condition.

2. Susan was <u>wise</u> to ditch her boyfriend.

3. Manual typewriters are almost <u>impossible</u> to come by these days.

4. The Queen was <u>astonished</u> to see so many well-wishers.

5. Such vicious attacks are <u>likely</u> to recur in the next few months.

6. Sixteen-year-olds can be very <u>pleasant</u> to teach.

7. The 6 o'clock plane for Tokyo is <u>certain</u> to arrive on time.

8. You were <u>foolish</u> to accept a bribe from that man.

9. Some species of fish are increasingly <u>hard</u> to catch.

10. The couple next door were <u>relieved</u> to get news from their son.

11. Bob was <u>clever</u> to write a letter of apology to the headmaster.

12. I was <u>happy</u> to be invited to the Prime Minister's birthday party.

Task two **

Arrange the above adjectives in groups according to type, adding to each group one synonym OR antonym of your own which patterns in the same way.

Adverbs, adverbials and prepositions

7.1. Adverbs

Sections 464–469

Most adverbs are formed from adjectives by adding the suffix *-ly:* complete ⇒ completely.

Adverbs can function as

- **adverbials in sentences:**
  Everything was *carefully* planned/planned *carefully*.
- **pre-modifiers of**
  – adjectives and other adverbs:
  John was *extremely* angry/He reacted *extremely* angrily.
  This is *too* weak an argument to convince anybody./*How* painful a reminder it was!
  – prepositions, determiners, numerals and pronouns:
  The pub is *just* round the corner/It is *just* two hundred yards away.
  – nouns or noun phrases:
  It was *rather* a disappointment./*What* a painful reminder it was!
- **post-modifiers of**
  – adjectives and other adverbs:
  That's not good *enough*./Oddly *enough*, he didn't turn up.
  – certain quantifiers, pronouns and interrogatives:
  I met somebody *else*./Who *else* was there?
  – nouns or noun phrases:
  Our journey *home* was uneventful./We had left the day *before*.
- **complements of prepositions:**
  Keep all that stuff for *later*./The snake was in *there*.

Task one *

Identify the adverbs (12 in all) in the following text.

> Saying Tajikistan's borders are "soft" would be too kind. Foreign diplomats and local journalists say the place is effectively run by a coalition of feudal warlords largely financed, directly or otherwise, by the drug trade. The country derives fully a third of its GDP from the heroin industry, according to U.N. estimates. Even so, Tajikistan's senior narcotics officer must be doing something right. Why else would a gang of gunmen have attacked his apartment in Dushanbe back in March?
>
> (from *Newsweek*, 17 September 2001, p. 22)

Task two **

Classify the above adverbs on the basis of their function, i.e. in terms of the elements they modify.

Example: *I knew pretty well what I was doing.*

⇒ *(pretty) well:* adverbial in sentence

⇒ *pretty:*   premodifier (of adverb)

Task three **

Fill the gaps in the following text, using one of the adverbs below:

ago	*almost*	*beautifully*	*certainly*	*far*
however	*just*	*mainly*	*more*	*nearly*
never	*normally*	*only*	*still*	*well*

Note: *never* and *still* are to be used twice

> As _____ as roles are concerned, most people assume that a family's financial situation is not _____ the responsibility of the man. On the other hand, they would _____ _____ compliment the woman, not the man, on a _____ decorated or _____-kept house. Every-day care of the children is _____ seen as _____ the woman's responsibility. Although _____ as many women have jobs as men, _____ half of the jobs done by women are part-time. In fact, the majority of mothers with children under the age of twelve either have no job or work _____ during school hours. Men _____ take a _____ active domestic role than they did forty years _____. Some things, _____, _____ seem to change. A comparison of child-rearing habits of the 1950s and the 1980s showed that the proportion of men who _____ changed a baby's nappy had remained the same (40 per cent)!
>
> (from James O'Driscoll, *Britain*, p. 51)

Task four *

Replace the underlined parts by alternative collocations (with adverbs) which are equivalent in meaning.

Example: *We had <u>very little</u> time to make up our minds.*
⇒ *We had <u>hardly any</u> time to make up our minds.*

1. I want to spend my holidays <u>at some other place</u> this year.
2. The organization was <u>sufficiently powerful</u> to strike back again.
3. <u>What an impertinent</u> young man Tony is!
4. There were <u>very few</u> people around at that moment.
5. I was <u>familiar enough</u> with local customs to appreciate their importance.
6. <u>How ludicrous an</u> idea it was!
7. Surprisingly, there was <u>hardly any</u> food left in the refrigerator.
8. Under the circumstances there was <u>no other person</u> I could turn to.
9. Wilma was <u>too inexperienced a</u> pilot to fly a jumbo jet.
10. Ronald is <u>an honest stockbroker and would never cheat</u> you out of your money.

7.2. Adverbials – Introduction

Sections 449–452

Adverbials give extra information about an action, happening or state as described by the rest of the sentence.

Adverbials have a number of different forms:

- adverbs, adverb phrases, noun phrases, prepositional phrases
- finite clauses, non-finite clauses (infinitives, *-ing* and *-ed* participles), verbless clauses.

Most adverbials are mobile, so that they can occur in different places in the sentence:

- front-position (FP): before the subject
- mid-position (MP): before the main verb occurring on its own, after an unstressed operator, before a stressed operator
- end-position (EP): after the verb (and its object and/or complement, if present).

Long adverbials normally occur in end-position, while short ones usually occur in mid-position. Front-position gives contrast or provides the background or setting for what follows.

Task one **

Underline the adverbials in the following text.

> In the last 50 years mining and forest industries have taken a larger place in Newfoundland economics. Although the fishing industries are still the largest employers, the province no longer depends upon them exclusively for its livelihood. In recent years gas and oil reserves to rival those in the North Sea have been discovered off the coast of the island and off Labrador. The federal government has given the go-ahead to a $5.2 billion project known as the Hibernia Oil Fields just off the east coast of St John's. If plans are realized, oil could flow by the millennium.
>
> (from *Insight Guide: Canada*, p. 232)

Task two **

(a) Arrange the above adverbials in groups on the basis of form categories, while adding FP, MP or EP in brackets to designate their position in the sentence.

(b) How does length affect these positions?

Task three **

Insert the adverbials (presented in alphabetical order) in the most appropriate position. Only the underlined sentences should be considered.

1. General elections take place.
   (*always; on a Thursday*)
      They are not public holidays. People have to work, polling stations are open.
   (*from seven in the morning; in the normal way; so; till ten at night; to give everybody the opportunity to vote*)

   (from James O'Driscoll, *Britain*, p. 101)

2. Andrew Nugée would pack an SLR film camera and about 30 rolls of film.
   (*not long ago; when he went on vacation*)
      He takes a digital camcorder.
   (*for capturing both moving and still images; now; simply*)
      Nugée is just one of many who have been bitten by the digital-imaging bug: "It's changed my approach to photography. I take my camcorder," he says.
   (*completely; everywhere*)   (from *Newsweek*, 3 September 2001, p.16)

7.3. Time-when 1

Sections **151–155; 455–456**

Time-when is often expressed by adverbials having end-position.

The commonest type of adverbial is the prepositional phrase, used especially to refer to points and periods of time:

- *at* 6.30 p.m.; *at* noon (= clock-time)
- *on* Sunday; (*on*) the next day (= day periods)
- *in/during* the morning; *in/during* April (= shorter or longer than day periods)
- *between* 1990 and 2000 (= periods with clearly defined limits)
- *by* night; *by* day (= idioms).

Noun phrases and adverbs are used in adverbials such as:

- last Saturday; this year; yesterday; tomorrow.

Task one *

Add time-when adverbials to the sentences below, giving them end-position and using the most appropriate connecting preposition where necessary.

1. Western society changed profoundly. (the 1960s)
2. British-born actor Sir Alec Guinness died. (2000; 5 August)
3. Two people were killed in an accident on the nearby motorway. (last Friday)
4. A system of voluntary schools developed. (the 19th century)
5. Have you ever visited Paris? (night)
6. I heard the clock strike twelve. (midnight)
7. People tend to spend less money. (a recession)
8. We are leaving for the Seychelles. (next week)
9. The inter-city bound for Bristol was derailed. (10.54 a.m.)
10. Most schools are open again. (early autumn)
11. The operation is due to take place. (Tuesday morning)
12. World War One ended. (1918; 11 a.m.; 11 November)

Task two **

Complete the following sentences by adding time-when adverbials at the end. Use a variety of adverbials.

1. I was born ....
2. I went to school for the first time ....
3. The last time I was abroad was ....
4. The happiest time in my life was ....
5. I usually get up .... and go to bed ....
6. I'm in the right mood for working ....
7. I often feel frightened ....
8. I can relax best ....
9. I intend to visit my dentist ....
10. I would like to go on holiday ....

Task three **

Complete the following sentences, using the most appropriate of the time-when adverbials listed below. Any missing prepositions are still to be added.

again	*August*	*half-past nine*	*July*
this autumn	*three years later*	*when I get back indoors*	
3.30 a.m.	*11 May 1926*	*14 May*	

1. The midnight sun is shining brightly when I climb into a bunk _____, and equally brightly when I wake _____.

2. I ask Jack if the snow ever disappears.
   'Oh yes,' he assures me, 'it melts _____. And starts snowing

   _____ _____.

3. Roald Amundsen's airship *Norge* left Ny Alesund _____ and landed in North America _____, after a journey of over 3000 miles. _____ Amundsen died in the Arctic attempting to rescue his friend Nobile.

4. I stumble outside clutching my toothbrush (. . .). _____ Harald is off the phone and preparing coffee. _____, he tells me, he will be celebrating fifteen years at Kap Wik.

   (adapted from Michael Palin, *Pole to Pole*, pp. 4–12)

7.4. Time-when 2

Sections 156–160

Time relationships can be indicated by a variety of prepositions, adverbs and conjunctions:

- *before/after* the war; *by* Friday; *before(hand)/afterwards; before/after/when/ as* it happened

- *already; still; yet; any more.*

Time measurement expressions include phrases such as:

● *three years ago; (in) three years from now; in three years; in three years' time.*

Time-when adverbs like *again, now, today,* etc. identify a point or period of time directly, while adverbs like *afterwards, later, next,* etc. do so indirectly.

Time-when clauses are introduced by conjunctions like *when, after, as, before,* etc.

Task one **

Complete the following sentences by inserting one or two of the time–when adverbials listed below. In most cases a pair of (correlating) adverbials are to be added.

a few years from now	*after the collapse of communism*
already; by the end of 1999	*before he was succeeded by Bill Clinton*
earlier that month; after a while	*first; afterwards*
hours ago; by now	*soon; previously*
still; yet	*two weeks ago; since*

1. I decided to talk to my wife and see my solicitor.
2. Over 170 nations had signed the non-proliferation treaty.
3. The European Union may well consist of about twenty-five member states.
4. George Bush Sr. was President of the United States.
5. The missing girl left home and has not been seen.
6. The Boeing 747 took off from Dubai Airport, so it should have landed in Delhi.
7. The situation in Eastern Europe began to change very fast.
8. I don't know whether a solution has been found.
9. Hostilities had resumed, but fortunately things quietened down.
10. We were to learn that the suspect had been convicted of drugs trafficking.

Task two **

Combine the following pairs of sentences, turning the second sentence into an adverbial clause and using each of the conjunctions listed below just once. The sentence parts in square brackets are NOT to be included.

after   as   as soon as   before   now that   once   since   until   when   while

> Example: *I went to see several specialists [last month].*
>
> > *I decided to have a pacemaker implanted [early this week].*
> >
> > ⇒ *I went to see several specialists <u>before</u> I decided to have a pacemaker implanted.*

1. I met Sheila [three years ago].

   I was 17 years old [then].

2. The tourists picnicked in the city's main park [at noon].

   They visited a local museum [at 2 p.m.].

3. Two wings of the castle were destroyed by fire [early this morning].

   It was struck by lightning [around midnight].

4. I will phone you [soon].

   I [have to] finish this repair work [first].

5. The car crash happened [on Sunday evening].

   It was raining heavily [all evening].

6. We can all heave a sigh of relief [now].

   The worst of the storm is over [now].

7. Steering a canoe is relatively easy.

   You [should] get the hang of it [first].

8. The patient's condition seemed to stabilize [gradually].

   Time passed [gradually].

9. I do not want to fly to Canada [in the next few weeks].

   The international situation [should] have improved [first].

10. There has only been one single burglary [lately].

    A security camera was installed [some time ago].

7.5. Duration

Sections 161–165; 457

Duration is normally expressed by adverbials occurring in end-position, though short adverbials can also occur in mid-position.

The commonest time duration adverbials are prepositional phrases, especially those introduced by the preposition *for*: stay *for* the summer/*for* two years (but: all day). Other common prepositions are *over*, *until/till*, *up to* and *from . . . to/until*.

Adverbial clauses of duration can be introduced by the conjunctions *while*, *since* and *until/till*.

Task one **

Complete the following sentences, using one of the time duration adverbials listed below:

all winter long　　　　　　　　　　　　　　　　　*briefly*
ever since I've known about the health risks involved　*for ever*
for millennia　　　　　　　　　　　　　　　　　*for several years now*
from 1837 to 1901　　　　　　　　　　　　　　*temporarily*
until his grasp loosened　　　　　　　　　　　　*up to now*

1. In Australia time stood still _____, then the country suddenly became part of the modern world.

2. The promise of more food aid _____ raised hopes among the starving population.

3. Fortunately, the world has been spared a major nuclear conflict _____.

4. The cold spell that began in December 1962 lasted _____.

5. The failure of living in flats has been generally recognized _____.

6. Lisa let Simon hold her hand _____.

7. I've abstained from smoking _____.

8. The present income disparities cannot go on _____.

9. Queen Victoria reigned _____.

10. Two lanes are _____ closed for resurfacing purposes.

Task two **

Replace the underlined part in each of the following sentences by an adverbial of duration expressing (roughly) the same meaning. Sentences 9 and 10 should be slightly changed in other ways as well.

Example: *I stayed in Scotland from Monday morning to Sunday evening.*
　　⇒ *I stayed in Scotland for a week.*

1. The First World War lasted from 1914 to 1918.

2. Humans may not be able to live on another planet before the beginning of the next century.

3. It was quite obvious that we couldn't wait eternally.

4. I haven't been feeling too well in the past few weeks.

5. We stayed on the Bahamas until the day before Easter.

6. Fighting in the area has been going on all day long.

7. We've been receiving nuisance calls since a short time ago.

8. The Olympic team did a lot of training on Saturday and Sunday.

9. The heatwave began on 21 June and ended around 20 September.

10. Several reporters were present and police officers were combing the woods for the missing girl at the same time.

7.6. Frequency

Sections 166–169; 458

Frequency, both indefinite and definite, is expressed by adverbials, which normally occur in mid- and end-position respectively.

- Most **indefinite frequency adverbials** are adverbs, ranging in meaning from an upper to a lower limit of frequency:

  – We *always/sometimes/never* drink wine.

  – We eat meat *on numerous/some/few occasions*.

- **Definite frequency adverbials** usually take one of the following (equivalent) forms:

  – I visit the local bar *once a week/every week/weekly*.

Task one **

Replace the expressions of frequency in the following sentences by alternative adverbials having more or less the same meaning.

1. I've met this famous comedian several times.
2. I used to see Mum every two days.
3. Even hardened soldiers sometimes become sentimental.
4. I go to the sauna once a month.
5. I've been to the United States many times.
6. Our neighbours have a barbecue most weekends.
7. Mr Sweethome travels abroad on very few occasions.
8. Some people go for a walk every day of the year.
9. We usually have breakfast at 7.30.
10. My elder brother is almost never at home.
11. I borrow books from the library every other week.
12. Bossy people are often difficult to communicate with.

Task two ***

Complete the following sentences by adding a frequency adverbial which makes sense in the context.

Example: *Labour delegates meet at their party conference.*

⇒ *Labour delegates meet annually at their party conference.*

Labour delegates meet at their party conference once a year.

1. True vegetarians eat meat.
2. A footballer performing a hat-trick is a player who scores.
3. Gypsies are people who are on the move.
4. Bill Clinton was elected President of the United States.
5. Drunk-driving is a serious offence.
6. The Olympic Games take place.
7. Even the best actors forget their lines.
8. A bimonthly journal is published.
9. Most adults go to bed between 10 p.m. and midnight.
10. Astronauts have orbited our planet.
11. People aged over 100 live on their own.
12. Commuters travel to work.

7.7. Place, direction and distance

Section 170; 454

Expressions of place and direction are chiefly adverbials and post-modifiers. Place adverbials usually have end-position. When there are two adverbials in this position, the smaller location normally comes first: Many people eat *in Chinese restaurants in London.*

The range of grammatical structures includes adverbs and adverb phrases, prepositional phrases, noun phrases followed by *away, back* etc., and adverbial clauses.

Task one **

Underline the expressions of place, direction and distance in the following texts.

1. Nowhere in Chester is the delightful impact of the River Dee so evident than when strolling on the north bank and enjoying the splendid sight of the many boats which can always be found there. Indeed, regattas have been held on the Dee since the early nineteenth century. It is also possible to hire boats from various companies situated on the Groves and there are some cruises which sail past Eaton Estate, home of the Duke of Westminster.

   (from *Chester, Cathedral and City*, p. 20)

2. Having crossed Australia from north to south we must now head east again, back to the Pacific coast and on to New Zealand, the most southerly landfall on this side of the Rim. There is a train, suitably called the 'Indian Pacific' which winds its way in leisurely fashion across flat plains, past Broken Hill, where an Aboriginal by the name of Charlie Rasp came across one of the richest seams of silver, lead and zinc found anywhere in the world, through the Blue Mountains and into Sydney twenty-four and a half hours later.

   (from Michael Palin, *Full Circle*, p. 195)

Task two **

(a) Which of these place expressions are NOT adverbials?

(b) Classify the adverbials on the basis of grammatical structure.

7.8. Prepositions of place

Sections 171–178

The most important words for indicating place are prepositions.

- **'at -type' prepositions** indicate a point in space:
  to, at, from, away from such a remote spot

- **'on -type' prepositions** indicate a line or a surface:
  on, on to, off, across, over, along, through the river

- **'in -type' prepositions** indicate an area or a volume:
  in, into, out of, through, inside, outside, within the prison compound.

Task one **

Complete the following sentences and text, using each of the above prepositions at least once.

1. The discredited politician lived _____ Grantchester, a small village just _____ Cambridge.

2. The pilot came aboard three miles _____ Vancouver Island and steered the freighter safely _____ the harbour.

3. The high road _____ Kingsbridge _____ Plymouth passes _____ three small villages.

4. Today we are trekking _____ dense forests _____ the island of Mindanao.

5. It was in 1799 that Wordsworth moved _____ Dove Cottage with his sister Dorothy, but lack of space caused them to move _____ it again in 1808 _____ larger premises.

6. _____ the parliament building, gazing out _____ the Ottawa River, one has a fine view of the twin city _____ the far shore – Hull.

7. Walk straight _____ the field, go _____ a gate and continue _____ the edge of the next field.

8. Very little is known about what is going on _____ the country, except that most civilians are staying well _____ war zones.

9. As soon as I had arrived _____ Axminster railway station, I stepped _____ the train _____ the platform, got _____ my car and drove off _____ Charmouth _____ the coast of Dorset.

10. On Tuesday 15 August, Scase was _____ York Station beginning his watch by half-past eight in the morning. He had travelled _____ York the previous evening and had taken a room _____ a dull commercial hotel close _____ the station. He could have been lodged _____ any provincial city. It never occurred to him to visit the Minster or to stroll _____ the cobbled streets _____ the city walls.

(from P.D. James, *Innocent Blood*, p. 123)

Task two *

Complete the following sentences, using prepositional phrases which act as acceptable place adverbials in the context.

1. One of the rodeo riders lost his balance and fell ....
2. Two people escaped from the burning building by jumping ....
3. The commuters were relieved to see that the London train was at last pulling ....
4. Looking outside, I could see two pigeons perched ....
5. To get to the other side of the river you only have to walk ....
6. Firefighters had already rescued the driver but two passengers were still trapped ....
7. It is safer to sail .... than to go further out to sea.
8. Billy wanted to play in the neighbours' garden, so he simply climbed ....
9. Instead of visiting the old town centre we just drove ....
10. Eastern Docks have been blockaded, so ferries will have to leave .... Docks this time.
11. I thought Barbara was married because she was wearing a ring ....
12. People who want to socialize often have some drinks ....

7.9. Overlap between types of prepositions

Sections 179–183

The preposition '*at*' is preferred to the preposition '*in*'

● for smaller towns or villages when they are seen as places on the map: live *at* Chatham.

● for buildings when they are thought of as institutions: be *at* school.

The preposition '*at*' is preferred to the prepositon '*to*' with verbs such as *aim, throw, point, shout,* etc. when the following noun phrase indicates a target: shout *at* the intruder.

The preposition '*on*' is preferred to the preposition '*in*' when a surface is meant, rather than an area or a volume: to sit *on* the grass.

Task *

Fill the gaps with one of the following prepositions: *at, in, into, on, to.*

1. Cornelius Vanderbilt was born _____ Staten Island in 1794.

2. Would you please stop yelling _____ me like that?

3. Jack the Ripper killed at least seven prostitutes _____ the East End.

4. Do you still have an account _____ Barclays Bank?

5. Local youths were playing football _____ the freshly mown grass.

6. After taking a degree _____ Oxford, Thomas Hughes trained as a barrister.

7. The orangutan still lives in the wild _____ Borneo.

8. The PM and the Home Secretary are meeting _____ No.10, Downing Street.

9. One tourist threw a bath-towel _____ the girl who was scrambling up the embankment.

10. Thousands of troops are pouring _____ eastern Congo again.

11. The ferry had to dock _____ Plymouth for urgent repair work.

12. Several bodies were found _____ the collapsed building.

7.10. Various positions

Sections 184–186

Position is a relation between two objects and can be indicated by a range of prepositions, including the following pairs: *in front of ~ behind; above ~ below; over ~ under; on top of ~ underneath.*

The prepositions *by* and *beside* can be synonymous with *at the side of* or *near.* Other sets of prepositions which are related in meaning are [a] *between, among* and *amid,* and [b] *about* and *(a)round.* The preposition *opposite* means *facing.*

There are corresponding prepositional adverbs which are identical or related in form: *in front ~ behind; above ~ below; overhead ~ beneath; on top ~ underneath.*

Task one ***

Complete the following sentences, using a phrase beginning with one of the above prepositions.

Example: *Secret meetings normally take place ....*

⇒ *Secret meetings normally take place behind closed doors.*

1. An eyebrow is a line of hair ....
2. A basement is a room or area ....
3. If you want to get warm again, just sit ....
4. A national border is a dividing line ....
5. Nobody could see the bullet-proof vest the officer was wearing ....
6. The passage was so narrow that the candidates had to line up and stand ....
7. If you do not know the itinerary, just follow the vehicle ....
8. A party of tourists accompanied by a guide would tend to trail .... after some time.
9. When somebody lives right across the street, they occupy the house ....
10. When you are surrounded by professionals doing the same work, you are ....
11. When a town is besieged, there are enemy soldiers all ....
12. When piling up things, you normally put the last object ....

Task two **

Add the most appropriate prepositional adverb where necessary, using each adverb just once:

above	*around*	*behind*	*below*	*in between*
in front	*on top*	*opposite*	*overhead*	*underneath*

1. Most of the divers had resurfaced but one or two were still trapped.
2. During the occupation of the area only the old and sick stayed.
3. Dozens of B-52s and other warplanes were flying that morning.
4. Young children travelling in cars are not normally allowed to sit.
5. I was awakened by a persistent stamping of feet produced by the people living.
6. Before putting the pizza in the oven just sprinkle some Parmesan.
7. The man sitting leaned forward and suddenly grabbed me by the shoulders.
8. I lifted the carpet to find out what had been hidden.
9. Hours after the tragedy groups of relatives and friends were still standing.
10. On this side of the road are several detached houses, with a few remaining plots of land.

7.11. Motion

Sections 187–189

Many prepositions of place indicate different aspects of motion:

- **motion towards**: *into, onto, to, towards,* etc.
- **motion away from**: *away from, out of,* etc.
- **passage and direction**: *across, along, down, over, past, through, up,* etc.
- **circular motion**: *about, around.*

Task ***

Replace the transitive verbs in the following sentences by 'simple' verbs followed by a preposition indicating motion.

Example: *The host preceded his guests while showing them around.*

⇒ *The host went/walked in front of his guests while showing them around.*

1. Several people I did not know entered the room.
2. Lady Snodgrass slowly descended the stairs.
3. The plane circled the church spire several times.
4. Hundreds of troops were approaching the garrison town.
5. Aid workers wanted to leave the area as fast as they could.
6. The lorry passed the local supermarket.
7. Two elderly tourists were climbing the hill.
8. Small groups of infantrymen had already penetrated enemy lines.
9. On their way back the hikers followed the river.
10. It took me less than a minute to cross the Golden Gate Bridge.
11. People were allowed to board the high-speed train at 8.45.
12. The crippled man was unable to negotiate the stile leading to the next field.

7.12. Space and motion

Sections 190–192

The meanings of space and motion can be combined in various ways:

- **viewpoint** (speaker's position) often expressed by prepositional phrases used as post-modifiers: the town *beyond* the lake, the garage *past* the stadium

● **place meaning resulting from motion**: The horses are *over* the fence.

● **pervasive meaning**: all *over/through* the building/*throughout* Germany.

Place prepositions are often used in more abstract, metaphorical senses: *out of* danger, *under* suspicion, *over* ten miles, *beyond* recognition, etc.

Most place prepositions correspond in form and meaning to prepositional adverbs: We stopped the bus and got *off*. Some prepositional adverbs have special uses: They travelled *on*.

Task one **

Replace all of the underlined part by the most appropriate preposition in sentences 1–7. Use alternative expressions in sentences 8–10.

> Examples: *One suspect was seen in the vicinity of the water tower.*
>
> ⇒ *One suspect was seen near the water tower.*
>
> *Two burglars had already got into the vault.*
>
> ⇒ *Two burglars were already inside the vault.*

1. Who is the man standing on that ladder?
2. Jane was phoning a woman who lived on the other side of the Atlantic.
3. It would be nice to see the vineyards on the other side of those hills.
4. I could just make out the shed which was partly hidden by the shrubs.
5. The petrol station is just at the bottom of the road.
6. You can get a beer at the pub when you turn the corner.
7. Hurricane Hugo caused extensive damage in all the countries of Central America.
8. There was a strong police presence in every single place.
9. Some of the terrorists have left the country already.
10. Susan will have left home for good next week.

Task two **

Complete the following sentences, using one of the prepositions listed below:

along	*amid*	*behind*	*below*	*beneath*	*beyond*
into	*on top of*	*out of*	*over*	*past*	*under*

1. Don't criticize the PM: his behaviour was _____ reproach.
2. It is morally indefensible to drive _____ the influence.
3. Whoever was _____ the bombing should get a life sentence.

4. Sadly, education in some developing countries is still _____ standard.

5. I looked up all the unfamiliar words _____ curiosity.

6. Susan's silly remarks made me fly _____ a temper.

7. We should aim for some uniformity and therefore work _____ the same lines.

8. Ms Owen may be _____ her prime but she is still very attractive.

9. After all his recent successes Basil felt _____ the world.

10. Essential duties were neglected _____ all the confusion.

11. Some people were so angry that they lost control _____ their feelings.

12. Tristan considered such a menial job _____ his dignity.

Task three ***

Replace the verb and its object by an alternative verb followed by a prepositional adverb.

> Example: *The strikers left the workplace.*
>
> ⇒ *The strikers walked out.*

1. We all entered the house.

2. Our yacht crossed the lake.

3. The truck left the car park.

4. A stranger approached me all of a sudden.

5. Several people left their flats to live somewhere else.

6. We continued our cycle tour.

7. Richard paid a casual visit this afternoon.

8. The couple ended their relationship after ten years of marriage.

7.13. Distance

Section 193

Distance can be expressed by noun phrases of measure such as *a foot* and *a long way*. These phrases can modify a verb of motion (He ran *several kilometres*) or precede and modify an adverbial of place (they live *a long way away*).

Task *

Complete the following sentences by adding the most appropriate noun phrase:

about two hundred yards from here   *a few hundred yards*
a hundred feet above our heads   *five thousand feet below*
just inches from my head   *miles away*
six hundred miles   *thousands of miles*
thousands of miles away   *two inches*

1. My parents live near Manchester and my sisters in Canada, which is
   _____.

2. Most aeroplanes can fly _____ without needing to refuel.

3. The newsagent's is further down the road, _____.

4. From the summit of Mont Blanc, I gazed into the valley
   _____.

5. Last summer I cycled _____ in ten days.

6. I had been walking uphill only _____ when I was already out of breath.

7. Two bullets perforated the windscreen of my car, _____.

8. A kite was flying _____.

9. The explosion at the steel works could be heard _____.

10. Water levels have dropped _____ since it stopped raining.

7.14. Manner, means and instrument

Sections 194–197; 453

Adverbials of manner, means and instrument specify how an action is performed or how an event takes place. They usually have end-position, but in passive sentences mid-position is also possible: The point was put *well*./The point was *well* put.

- **Manner** is expressed by adverbs, adverb phrases or prepositional phrases: (to speak) *(very) confidently, in a confident manner/way, with confidence.* Manner is sometimes combined with comparison: (to play) *like/as an actor/as if one were an actor*

- **Means** is typically expressed by a phrase introduced by the preposition *by*: *by car, by the gate*

- **Instrument** is typically expressed by a phrase introduced by the preposition *with* or *without*: *with a key/without (using) a key.*

Task one **

Identify the adverbials of manner and means in the following texts, classifying them on the basis of grammatical structure.

1. Drive extremely carefully when the roads are icy. Avoid sudden actions as these could cause a skid. You should
   - Drive at a slow speed in as high a gear as possible; accelerate and brake very gently
   - Drive particularly slowly on bends where skids are more likely. Brake progressively on the straight before you reach a bend. Having slowed down, steer smoothly round the bend, avoiding sudden actions
   - Check your grip on the road surface when there is snow or ice by choosing a safe place to brake gently. If the steering feels unresponsive this may indicate ice and your vehicle losing its grip on the road. When travelling on ice, tyres make virtually no noise.

   (from *The Highway Code*, §206)

2. Unlike the man before her she moves like a soldier, at a fast cat-like crouch, weaving and ducking and using the river bed for cover.

   (from Michael Palin, *Full Circle*, p. 293)

Task two **

Complete the following sentences by adding an adverbial of manner, means or instrument on the basis of the noun phrase in brackets. In some cases two or three different forms are acceptable.

1. The trade unions protested against the government's measures. (vigour)
2. The new proposal was received. (enthusiasm).
3. The losing team fought back. (courage)
4. The local tribes were treated. (cruelty and injustice)
5. I was dressing the patient's wounds. (a qualified nurse)
6. Mr Pym was behaving towards the new trainee. (a sixteen-year-old)
7. The front gate was locked, so I tried to get in. (the backdoor)
8. Fortunately, we were able to communicate. (mobile phone)
9. The employers sought to win over the workers. (a pay rise)
10. Why don't we resolve the problem? (a change of tactics)
11. The burglars knocked the night porter unconscious. (a baseball bat)
12. We cannot reduce the flood risk. (proper sea defences)

Task three **

Fill the gaps in the following sentences, adding the most appropriate of the adverbials listed below:

as if it were your last day on earth	*by a perilously slim extending ladder*
by road or by rail	*by sounding your horn*
by the path we always used	*by the use of symbols*
clearly and accurately	*like an Arctic explorer*
so slowly	*using an old-fashioned fountain pen*
with a crowbar	*with a little piece of rope for support*
with fond approval	*with great difficulty*

1. Susan had been writing a letter, _____.

2. I only managed to get leave of absence _____.

3. We got down to the beach _____.

4. Time passes _____ when you are waiting.

5. The burglar forced open the greenhouse _____.

6. Jonathan's bride watched over him _____.

7. You can travel on public transport between cities _____.

8. When morning came, I was dressed _____ and still shivering.

9. Live each day _____.

10. Do not scare animals _____.

11. We boarded the plane _____, _____.

12. This vast amount of detail can only be conveyed _____ _____.

7.15. Prepositions (general)

Sections 657–660

Task one **

Complete the paragraph below by putting in the appropriate preposition.

Sir Ranulph Fiennes is described ....(1).......... the Guinness Book of Records as "the world's greatest living explorer". Born ....(2).......... 1944 and educated ....(3).......... Eton, he served ....(4).......... the SAS ....(5).......... embarking ....(6).......... a series ....(7).......... record-breaking Arctic, Antarctic and desert explorations. ....(8).......... 1979 and 1982 he and fellow explorer Charles Burton became the first men to reach both Poles and circumnavigate the Earth ....(9).......... its polar axis. ....(10).......... 1986 he broke the record ....(11).......... getting ....(12).......... the North Pole unsupported. ....(13).......... 1993 he achieved the first unsupported crossing ....(14).......... the Antarctic, the longest such polar journey ....(15).......... history, 1,345 miles. A year ago he attempted the first unassisted polar trek ....(16).......... the North Pole, abandoned when his sledge slid ....(17)........... the Arctic Ocean. Frostbite cost him a thumb and the tops of four fingers. Sir Ranulph's adventures have raised more than £6 million ....(18)........... charity. After writing several books ....(19)........... them, he has now published his first thriller. ....(20)........... his wife ....(21)........... 31 years, Virginia, he runs a Somerset farm ....(22)........... 100 sheep and 200 Aberdeen Angus cattle. ....(23)........... there, this flamboyant hero told us ....(24)........... his own special hero.

(from *SAGA Magazine*, February 2002, p. 45)

Task two **

In the sentences below state whether the words underlined are *prepositions* (P) or *prepositional adverbs* (PA).

1. These are the books I paid for. Not those.

2. We'll walk down.

3. It was a very steep hill and we had to climb up. There was no other way.

4. Don't stand too near!

5. Should I put more salt in?

6. I looked up and there he was.

7. Which shop did you go into?

8. I don't know what he's looking for.

9. It didn't look a very interesting town. We just drove through.

10. He's not someone I'd work with.

7.16. Two or more adverbials

Section 460

Time adverbials in end-position tend to occur in the order duration + frequency + time–when:

– I used to swim *for an hour or so every day when I was a child.*

When various semantic types of adverbials occur in end-position, the normal order is manner/means/instrument + place + time:

– I was walking *quietly across the lawn that evening.*

When two time or two place adverbials occur together, the more specific one tends to come first.

However, long adverbials of any type often come at the very end of the sentence.

Task **

Arrange the adverbials in brackets in the most appropriate order.

1. Some scientists believe that palm trees will be growing (in fifty years; in Iceland).
2. We moved together (at the front of the building; into the small colonial room).
3. Laura was sitting (in an armchair; with a magazine in her lap).
4. I found this (among the boulders; by the tower).
5. I tapped (at ten past four; on Stella's door).
6. The couple had travelled (on the Transsiberian Express; eastward).
7. The barrel of the gun pointed (in my direction; intimidatingly).
8. Martin Cash arrived (after a career of crimes, arrests and escapes; in 1840; in the penal colony of Port Arthur).
9. Hudson travelled (extensively; for several years; in the North).
10. Mr Lee was (in his office; in Hong Kong; on the fourth floor of a supermarket).
11. Ruth gazed (at the paving stone; fixedly; under her feet).
12. Tallinn became visible (about 1 o'clock; in the afternoon; to starboard).

7.17. Degree

Section 215; 459

Expressions of degree can have a heightening or a lowering effect on some part of the sentence. They are usually adverbs acting as modifiers of adjectives, adverbs, etc. or adverbials typically occurring in mid-position: I'm *very* hungry./We *entirely* agree with you.

Task *

Identify the degree expressions in the following sentences, specifying

(a) whether they have a heightening (H) or a lowering (L) effect
(b) whether they function as modifiers (M) or as adverbials (A).

1. The two pictures looked particularly valuable to me.
2. The word cathedral simply means 'a chair'.
3. Just getting the facts straight is monumentally difficult.
4. There were quite a number of things we didn't know.
5. I had pretty much given up on watching TV.
6. It's almost impossible to get through to New York.

7. Russians care deeply about whether their country is consulted.

8. The government can ill afford to give in to these demands.

9. Observers claimed that the brutal regime had totally collapsed.

10. It's all but certain that the two presidents will reach a deal.

11. Perhaps I should try to be a little more like a stern nanny.

12. We're all terribly grateful to dear Wilfred.

13. It really bothers me that I can't leave right now.

14. Swallowing is piercingly painful, and only partly relieved by a swig from my water bottle.　　　　　(Michael Palin, *Pole to Pole*, p. 125)

15. I let myself into a neat but rather gloomy cabin, barely half the size of Officer B's – the fully furnished life of someone small, slender and dainty in their movements.

(Jonathan Raban, *Hunting Mister Heartbreak*, p. 56)

7.18. Gradable words and degree 1

Sections 216–218

Degree only applies to gradable words: scale words indicate a relative position on a scale (large, small), while limit words indicate the end-point of a scale (black, white).

Degree expressions with adjective scale words can be different from those used with verb scale words, especially when indicating extreme positions (*very* tall vs rain (*very*) *much*) or intensifying the meaning slightly (*pretty* hard vs increase *considerably*).

Downtoners tend to be the same (*slightly* uncomfortable/fall *slightly*).

Degree adverbs with limit words are usually the same whether used with adjectives or with verbs (*completely* black/disagree *completely*).

Task one **

Insert an acceptable degree expression from the set listed below. (A) stands for 'indicating extreme position', (B) for 'intensifying slightly' and (C) for 'toning down'.

a bit	*a great deal*	*a little*	*a lot*	*considerably*	*fairly*
pretty	*quite*	*rather*	*slightly*	*very*	*very much*

1. The situation in the border area is getting desperate. (B)

2. High Street spending has increased over the last two months. (B)

3. Teachers are complaining about class sizes these days. (A)

4. In her early nineties now, Mrs Wilson is beginning to look frail. (A)

5. Ricky's mood swings are making me feel uncomfortable. (C)

6. On the whole, I like these after-dinner speeches. (B)

7. Careful, that wooden chest is heavy! (B)

8. Aren't you getting worried about Mandy's recent behaviour? (C)

9. Teenagers tend to admire pop stars. (A)

10. I think we should reword this letter. (C)

11. We were given an accurate description of the situation. (B)

12. Dear Kenny, I'm looking forward to your visit. (A)

Task two *

Complete the following sentences, using the more (or most) appropriate of the degree expressions in brackets.

1. I felt _____ uneasy at the thought of meeting my rival. (considerably; rather)

2. I remember Aunt Dolly's words _____. (exactly; very much)

3. Henry's work is _____ sentimental for my taste. (a lot; too)

4. Smoking on these premises is _____ forbidden. (rather; strictly)

5. Our victory has proved our enemies _____ wrong. (practically; utterly)

6. Somebody who works _____ is often described as a workaholic. (a great deal; considerably)

7. Jack told me he wasn't _____ bored. (absolutely; in the least)

8. The original edition is still useful as it has only been modified _____. (slightly; virtually)

9. People who drink too much may have to stop working _____. (altogether; quite)

10. Walking on the surface of the sun is _____ impossible. (nearly; quite)

11. I was _____ surprised when I heard these rumours. (a little; a great deal)

12. The idea that _____ any anachronism can be rescued is _____ popular. (almost; completely; extremely)

7.19. Gradable words and degree 2

Sections 219–221

Comparative adjectives and adverbs are modified by degree words used as adverbials: *much* healthier. Superlatives can be intensified by degree adverbs like *altogether* and *very*: *altogether* the best show/the *very* best show.

The adverbial *very much* is often to be preferred to *much*: I liked it *very much*.

The degree adverbs *entirely, fairly* and *quite* tend to suggest a positive meaning, while *completely, rather, utterly* and *a bit/little* often suggest a negative one: *fairly* warm vs *rather* warm.

Task one **

Complete the following sentences, adding degree expressions which indicate 'extreme position on the scale'.

1. A giraffe's legs are _____ longer than an antelope's.
2. Our success _____ depends on your willingness to cooperate.
3. We offer _____ the highest quality in dental care.
4. Some laboratories are using the _____ latest cloning techniques.
5. I like these Beethoven sonatas _____.
6. Dad looks _____ more relaxed these days.
7. Ignoring the problem would be the _____ worst solution.
8. Well, mate, I've done _____ better than you this time, eh?
9. This studio has produced _____ the most enchanting pictures.
10. I know you must be _____ busy but I would _____ welcome a visit from you.

Task two **

Add an appropriate degree adverb to a gradable element in the following sentences. (A) stands for 'indicating extreme position', (B) for 'intensifying slightly' and (C) for 'toning down'.

1. Jimmy looked pathetic standing in the rain outside. (B)
2. Joan seemed at ease in this new environment. (A)
3. It's a pleasant walk now that the heather is in full bloom. (B)
4. The information we received was accurate. (B)
5. The next of kin were devastated by the news. (A)
6. I'm not convinced that this is the ideal approach. (A)
7. For thirty years Mr Lee made an easy living as a fisherman. (B)
8. I've been worried about my health lately. (C)
9. What you were saying is beside the point. (A)
10. It would be foolish to support such a stupid idea. (A)

7.20. Other aspects of degree adverbs

Sections 222–223

Words like *new* and *full* can be used as scale words and as limit words (*very/absolutely* new).

A scale word and a different limit word can deal with the same area of meaning (*very* tired vs *absolutely* exhausted).

A scale word often corresponds to one or more limit words, intensifying its meaning (*very* bad vs *absolutely* terrible).

Words like *barely* and *hardly* are negative degree adverbs, while *at all* occurs in both negative and interrogative sentences. Some degree adverbs tend to intensify specific verbs (need *badly*, enjoy *thoroughly*).

Task one ***

Intensify the meaning of the underlined phrases by replacing them with limit words preceded by matching degree adverbs.

Example: *The late evening programme was <u>quite funny</u>.*

⇒ *The late evening programme was <u>absolutely hilarious</u>.*

1. Some of these 19th century stamps are <u>very rare</u>.
2. After such a long walk we were all <u>really hungry</u>.
3. The health situation in the flooded areas was <u>very bad</u>.
4. All that unfair criticism made me feel <u>quite irritated</u>.
5. Robust economic growth is <u>somewhat unlikely</u>.
6. The latest novel by Tom Wolfe is <u>rather interesting</u>.
7. The results of the investigation are <u>quite unbelievable</u>.
8. At a five-star restaurant the food is bound to be <u>very good</u>.
9. Working yourself to death like this is <u>rather stupid</u>.
10. The preliminary estimates turned out to be <u>quite incorrect</u>.

Task two **

Add to the underlined parts degree adverbs which (a) are inherently negative OR (b) intensify the meaning of the verb.

Examples: *The PM is not a supporter of appeasement.*

⇒ *The PM is not a supporter of appeasement <u>at all</u>.*

We all want to see the surviving sailors.

⇒ *We all want to see the surviving sailors <u>(very) badly</u>.*

An old ruler was complaining that <u>he was not loved</u> by his subjects. <u>However he tried</u> to convince them of HIS love for THEM, it was all to no avail. The old man <u>failed</u> to realize that people <u>disapproved</u> of the way he managed the finances of the realm.

Years of excessive spending had left his country <u>with no money</u>. Endless military campaigns had been draining it of <u>funds needed elsewhere</u>.

<u>Was it possible</u> to make the ruler change his policies? It <u>seemed</u> so. Even though his subjects <u>wanted reform</u>, <u>he disagreed</u> with even the suggestion of change.

7.21. Role, standard and point of view

Section 224

A gradable word can have its meaning qualified in terms of

- **role**: Anna is very good *at swimming./As a swimmer*, she is very good.

- **standard**: Anna is a good swimmer *for a twelve-year-old*.

It is also possible to specify the point of view from which a word or phrase is understood: Anna is a good swimmer *in a technical sense./ Morally*, it was a difficult problem.

Task one *

Identify the expressions indicating **role**, **standard** and **point of view**, determining to which of the three categories each expression belongs.

1. In theory, most of our environmental problems can be solved.
2. Britain is bad at dealing with extreme weather conditions.
3. If you inadvertently wander off the footpath, you are technically trespassing.
4. For a man aged over sixty, running such a distance was quite an achievement.
5. We have become successful by being expert at solving problems.
6. As a football player, David Beckham is unbeatable.
7. In a political sense the uninsured hardly formed a group at all.
8. The coach said we did well for such a young team.
9. On paper, this set of rules looks impressive.
10. Six out of ten is not too bad for a beginner.
11. Ms Carpenter is excellent as a teacher and trainer.
12. Objectively, this war is terrifying. Subjectively, it remains strangely uninvolving.

Task two **

Rephrase each of the above sentences in at least one alternative way.

7.22. Sentence adverbials

Sections 461–463

Sentence adverbials are not integrated in the structure of the sentence but are peripheral to it. They also have a wide variety of possible structures, ranging from simple adverb to finite subclause. Most sentence adverbials occur in front-position and are separated from what follows by a tone unit boundary.

Some sentence adverbials convey speakers' comments on what they are saying:

– *Frankly / If I may be frank*, this isn't good enough.

Other sentence adverbials have a connective role:

– The team didn't like the food. *However*, they have not complained so far.

Task one *

Add a sentence adverbial corresponding in meaning to the expression in brackets.

1. Tracy forgot to lock the front door.

   (this was very odd)

2. What Sam told us is a pack of lies.

   (this is clear)

3. I haven't got the faintest idea why she rebuffed you.

   (I want to be frank about it)

4. Harry will have second thoughts about this.

   (I hope he will)

5. I would say only a trained diver could reach the wreck.

   (I want to speak as an expert)

6. The evidence we've got is not convincing.

   (I have to admit this)

7. Some spectators turned up after the game had started.

   (this was unfortunate)

8. I've never intended to hurt Maggy's feelings.

   (I want to be honest with you)

9. Dennis jilted his girlfriend for a much older woman.

(this really surprised us)

10. Lady Tattle was monopolizing the conversation again.

(this was characteristic)

11. Many more people will be killed in the operations.

(this cannot be doubted)

12. The white powder looks quite harmless.

(on the surface of it)

Task two **

Connect the following pairs of sentences by adding one of the adverbials below to the second sentence of each pair:

after all	*alternatively*	*as a result*	*however*	*in other words*
instead	*moreover*	*on the contrary*	*otherwise*	*similarly*

1. The Prime Minister is suffering from a hernia. He will not be able to attend the European summit.

2. The peace process is in deep trouble. The various parties involved are prepared to continue their efforts.

3. Nursery education has been transferred to community colleges. Teacher training has been shifted to colleges and universities.

4. We could travel by train. We could travel by plane.

5. I did not feel put off by this unexpected confrontation. I was already looking forward to the next challenge.

6. We are not going to buy a sunbed as it is too expensive. Someone told me UV-radiation can cause skin cancer.

7. I think we should show some more understanding for Susan's behaviour. She's been through a lot lately.

8. Is there a cheaper solution? Can you make a cheaper device?

9. Don't forget to tell the boss. You will get into a lot of trouble.

10. The suspect did not answer any of my questions. He kept staring into the distance.

Clause types

8.1. Cause, result, purpose and reason

Sections **198–206**; 323; 365; 613–615

The clauses in this section answer the question "why?"

- **Cause**: This is indicated by an adverbial *because*-clause or by a prepositional phrase beginning *because of, on account of, from, out of*. Also used are *for* with nouns of feeling and *through*. We also use verbs such as *lead to* and *result in*.

- **Result**: **Result** is the opposite of **cause**. This is often expressed by a clause beginning with *so that*, or just *so*.

- **Purpose**: This is an intended result. It can be introduced by an adverbial of purpose, usually a *to-infinitive* clause. We can also use *so that, in order to* or *in case* (for a negative purpose).

- **Reason & consequence**: This can be expressed in a similar way to **cause**, using *because, because of, on account of*. *As* and *since* are also used. Other ways of expressing this are with conjunctions such as *seeing that* and *now that* or the use of *for*-phrases. We can also use the linking adverb *consequently*.

Also important for expressing **cause** or **reason** are linking adverbials such as *therefore, hence, accordingly, so* and *in that case*.

Task one **

In the following examples, underline the phrase or clause in each sentence which expresses **cause/reason** or **result/consequence**. Indicate the meaning of each of these underlined elements as either **cause, reason, result** or **consequence**

1. The trains were badly affected by strikes again last week so I had to go to work by car.

2. Because I set off early, I thought the roads would be clear.

3. However, on account of the strike, everyone had taken the same action as I had.

4. By as early as seven o'clock, the roads were so crowded that there were long queues of traffic.

5. There had been several accidents with the result that nothing was moving.

6. Since I had been stuck for so long, I was over an hour late getting to work.

7. I couldn't face the same problems going home, so I decided to stay in a hotel that night.

8. Because so many people had the same idea, all the hotels were fully booked.

9. As I still didn't want to drive home in all the traffic, I made myself as comfortable as possible and slept in the office.

10. I forgot to put a notice on my office door, so I was woken at five o'clock in the morning when the cleaners came in.

Task two ***

Join the pairs of sentences using one of the conjunctions or constructions below according to the function by each item. In some cases, it will be necessary to rewrite the sentences. e.g.: He wasn't able to afford such an expensive holiday. He decided not to go with his friends. [cause]

Not being able to afford such an expensive holiday, he decided not to go with his friends.

and consequently; as; because; because of; on account of; since; so; so that; to-infinitive clause; with the result that

1. The weather was very stormy. People were advised not to travel. [result]

2. A full survey of the house wasn't done. Many faults were discovered later. [result]

3. The Post Office lost over £2m last year. Some postal deliveries must be curtailed. [reason]

4. A virus was sent through the e-mail. Whole programs were lost on the computer. [result]

5. Public services need more investment. Taxes will have to be raised. [reason]

6. There was a sudden death in the family. His trip to Hungary was cancelled. [reason]

7. He led a busy but sedentary life. Gabor was very overweight. [cause]

8. His doctor told him to do more exercise. He would lose weight. [purpose]

9. The ski resorts lost a lot of money last year. There was very little snow. [cause]

10. The meeting was postponed. The trains were running late. [reason]

Task three ***

Using the conjunctions and phrases listed, make as many sentences as you can by linking the clauses below. Some examples have been done for you.

Examples:

The problem is often psychological so that telling people to diet or take exercise is not the easy answer.

Our parents and grandparents did more manual work in the home because there weren't the labour-saving devices.

Cause: *because, because of, on account of, bound to* and *result in.*
Result: *so that, so.*
Purpose: *to*-infinitive clause, *so that, in order to, in case.*
Reason & consequence: *because, because of, on account of, as, since, seeing that, now that, a participle clause, for*-phrase, *consequently.*

there is so much information about healthy life-styles
people should dedicate time to sit down and eat properly
it is surprising that British people are becoming dangerously overweight
we must look at the real reasons why we eat too much
you can now buy many healthy foods
diets often leave us feeling hungry and miserable
the problem is also psychological
it gets harder to shed weight each time we diet
telling people to diet and take exercise is not the easy answer
people try different diets
many people try diets but then fall back
some experts say there is an epidemic of obesity
our work patterns often give us little time
we take in more calories than we burn off
people get anxious about work
there weren't the labour-saving devices
they eat to cheer themselves up
our parents and grandparents did more manual work in the home
we also need to do more exercise
our eating habits need to change

(adapted from Chris McLaughlin: Losing Weight & Keeping it off, in *World Cancer Research Fund Newsletter*, issue 45, Winter 2001)

Task four **

Complete the following text with conjunctions or phrases indicating **cause, result, purpose, reason & consequence**. The first one has been done for you:
.........(1).............. few people will admit to taking astrology seriously...

As few people will admit to taking astrology seriously, it is surprising how many people read their horoscopes each week. This has ....(2).............. even some serious newspapers and journals publishing horoscopes. It is .... popular

.........(3)............. there has been a huge increase in the number of "professional" astrologers. This is strange ....(4)............. during the 18th & 19th centuries astrology became marginalised. People were becoming more independent and educated ....(5)............. irrational beliefs such as our fate being influenced by the position of the stars on the day we were born seemed absurd. ....(6)............. this, by the beginning of the 20th century, astrologers had almost disappeared from public view. What has brought about the change? In August1930, ...(7)............. boost circulation, the Sunday Express invited an astrologer to draw up a birth chart for the newly born Princess Margaret. ....(8)............. the public was entertained by this press stunt, other newspapers copied the idea. Then, during the second World War, many people turned not only to religion but to the occult ....(9)............. find comfort in difficult times. While many of the stranger activities disappeared when the war was over, horoscopes maintained their hold on the public. Now as life becomes more complicated, people want to know more about their possible fate. ....(10)............. we even have horoscopes on the internet. Many people laugh at themselves ....(11)............. being so foolish. Meanwhile the sales of horoscope year-books continue to rise.

(adapted from Michael Watts: Who says our fate is in the stars, in *Saga Magazine*, January 2002)

Task five **

Read through your own completed text for Task Four and label the conjunctions or constructions you have used, e.g. *reason, result, cause*, etc.

8.2. Concession and contrast

Sections 211–212; 361; 462

The clauses in this section relate to a situation where two circumstances are in contrast. This means that one is surprising or unexpected in view of the other.

Task one **

Connect the pairs of clauses using the conjunction or adverbial phrases indicated. In some cases, it will be necessary to rewrite one of the clauses.

1. It was raining heavily last Sunday. We still went out for a walk after lunch. (although)

2. He lost all his money. He maintained an air of calm reassurance. (in spite of)

3. I admire his paintings. I doubt if he is a major artist. (much as)

4. Film directors in Hollywood have a long training. Young British directors can go straight into making major films. (whereas)

5. He puts in a lot of hard work. He never gets any promotion. (for all)

6. The administration maintains an aggressive stance. There are signs of compromise among some of its members. (nevertheless)

7. These are favourable weather conditions. The rough terrain should persuade them not to make the trip. (notwithstanding)

8. Some critics had written some very bad notices. The play was sold out for all performances. (even so)

9. The evidence points strongly towards a conviction. The defence still believes the woman will be found not guilty. (while)

10. The ruined abbey is in a very beautiful setting. I'm not sure I want to see it. (all the same)

Task two ***

Complete the text with the following conjunctions or adverbial phrases. Each one can only be used once.

although, despite, however, in spite of, nevertheless, so, though, whereas, while, yet

..............(1)............ he walked on the moon in 1969, Edwin Aldrin still has space-travelling ambitions. ....(2)............ his age, he's still interested in space-travel and is involved in developing 'cyclers' as a means of getting to Mars. ....(3)............ he went direct from the earth to the moon in a space-craft, going to Mars is much more complex. ....(4)............ the moon is always the same distance from the earth, the distance between the earth and Mars can vary from 33m miles to 250m miles, and periodically the planets are at opposite sides of the sun. ....(5)............ all the problems this presents, scientists believe it will be possible to go there by 2018. ....(6)............ they are now looking for plants which will provide food and keep the air fresh in the 'cyclers'. ....(7)............ 'cyclers' will be principally shuttles between earth and Mars, they will provide all the comforts of a good hotel. Absurd it may be now, ...(8)..........., two men, one a billionaire and the other a multi-millionaire, have already booked themselves to be among the first to holiday on a space-station. It might seem to be very exciting to be travelling in space, ...(9)............ scientists are concerned about the effects of boredom on long journeys. Mars is a long way away, ...(10)..........., it is no longer a fantasy destination.

Linking

9.1. Linking signals

Sections **351–359**; 238; 470–472

We help people to understand our messages by signalling how one idea leads to another. Most of the words and phrases which have this connecting function in English are sentence adverbials, and they generally come at the beginning of a sentence. Their most important functions are:

- making a new start
- changing the subject
- listing and adding
- reinforcement
- summary and generalisation
- explanation
- reformulation

Task *

Complete the dialogue by adding a suitable linking signal as suggested by the function in brackets.

Andy: Didn't it snow heavily last night. (1. Making a new start), not heavily, but a lot. (2. Reformulation), I've had a bad time getting into work this morning.

Ben: It wasn't easy. (3. Changing the subject), you do realise that that report has to be finished by Friday, don't you?

Andy: Friday? That'll never happen.

Ben: Why not?

Andy: There just isn't the time. We haven't got all the information we need. (4. Explanation), we don't have the figures for the last quarter of the year.

Ben: I can easily get those. (5. Making a new start), what other problems are there?

Andy: (6. Making a new start), (7. Listing): what about staff reductions? How are they to be included?

(8. Listing): what about the "bad debt" write-offs?

(9. Listing): Is the Managing Director's pension enhancement to be included in the whole of last year's figures?

All these things have made a dent in our profits. (10. Generalising), they do not reflect on the increased business, (11. Explanation), the fact that we have opened up new markets, (12. Explanation), in South-east Asia and some of the Russian republics.

Ben: (13. Summary), you want to be able to say that the business is improving, so we have to figure in special items for this year.

Andy: Yes. (14. Adding), I want to stress that things like the bad debts are one-off items, (15. Explanation), of course, they won't be repeated.

Ben: Not even the managing director's pension?

Andy: (16. Summary), no! Not even the Managing Director's pension pro-vision. (17. Reinforcement), I think that was already considered in the mid-year report. (18. Changing the subject), what do you think about the proposed branch closures?

Ben: It's terrible.

Andy: It will be for some people. (19. Explanation) the older staff who won't easily find another job.

Ben: It won't?

Andy: No. Not here at head office. (20. Reinforcement), we may take on more staff.

Ben: Glad to hear it.

9.2. 'General purpose' links

Sections **371–374**; 110–111; 493–494; 686–694

In addition to a positive link between two ideas expressed by 'and', there are other vague or 'general purpose' connections:

- relative clauses
- participle and verbless clauses
- grammatically unlinked clauses

Task one **

Identify the restrictive and non-restrictive clauses by re-writing them to show their connecting function. Insert commas where appropriate.

1. They won't finish the work today and that causes a problem.
2. I don't like mobile phones that have a musical repetitive tone.
3. He was always late and that lost him his job.
4. Be sure to buy a savings bond that gives you a good return on your investment.
5. The books that were badly stacked fell across the floor.
6. They have problems with their neighbours who are very noisy.
7. Many people who found themselves always playing 'Solitaire' on their computer have had the game removed.
8. People shouldn't ski off-piste which is dangerous.
9. The arrangements for the conference which were very bad angered him.
10. He fell madly in love with Barbara who was directing the play.

Task two **

Match the unlinked clauses in columns I and II, and identify the connecting function.

I	II
1. I haven't seen them for some time.	A. I've got to finish this work.
2. Always keep the TV volume down at night.	B. They've been away in Africa.
3. He published the book himself.	C. You'll be late.
4. He drove fast along the road, swerving round the corner.	D. Winter's coming.
5. You must answer truthfully.	E. There was a terrible crash.
6. Get a move on!	F. You can't make a can of peas look sexy.
7. I can't come out to play.	G. It won't disturb the neighbours.
8. The train was delayed.	H. No harm will come to you.
9. The birds are going south.	I. No publisher was interested.
10. Supermarkets put fresh produce in front.	J. There was a cow on the line.

Task three **

Rewrite the following text changing the underlined clauses into participle or verbless clauses.

As he knew it was time to go, Rob finally got his things together. <u>He didn't want to leave</u>, so he had left tidying up to the last minute. <u>Now it was empty of all his books and papers</u>, the office seemed quite large. <u>Just by looking round the room</u>, he recalled the thrill of the first time he had walked in. <u>He had felt proud</u> and determined to succeed in this new position. <u>If he had been seen to be a keen and co-operative worker</u>, he would have had further promotion. <u>But because he didn't understand the corporate culture</u>, he tried to do everything to promote himself above his colleagues. <u>They grew tired of this</u> and made his work difficult. <u>He was soon failing to get things done on time</u>, so he was asked to reconsider his position. <u>He knew there was nothing he could do</u>, so he resigned.

9.3. Cross-reference to noun phrases and substitutes for a noun phrase

Sections 375–382; 510; 529; 597–601; 619–622; 675–680

The personal pronouns *he, she, it, they*, etc. cross-refer to noun phrases, and agree with them in number and/or gender.

Occasionally, 1st and 2nd pronouns substitute for coordinate noun phrases.

Sometimes a plural pronoun cross-refers to quantifier pronouns like *everybody, somebody, no one*, and *anyone*.

Other pronouns such as *one, some, each, none* can act as substitutes for a noun phrase.

The pronouns *that* and *those* can act as substitutes with definite meaning.

Task one **

Replace the phrases underlined with appropriate pronouns.

1. I used to have high blood pressure. <u>The high blood pressure</u> somehow affected my eyes.

2. Thubron's journey takes <u>Thubron</u> through a spectacular area of desert and mountains.

3. The book will deserve, through the beauty of <u>the book's</u> prose, to stand alongside the best of travel writing.

4. Thubron is an extraordinary traveller, but <u>Thubron</u> wears <u>Thubron's</u> knowledge as casually as <u>Thubron's</u> rucksack.

5. Nobody is quite as you remember <u>the person</u>.

6. In <u>the Tajiks'</u> villages of clay and brushwood, the Tajiks walk about in bright colours.

7. People began to laugh. Jacobi turned to glare at <u>the people who began to laugh</u>.

8. Pat and I always went there. It was one of <u>Pat's and my</u> favourite spots.

9. Jacobi found he was bored with the piano and switched over to the violin. The only problem with <u>switching from the piano to the violin</u> was that he had to carry <u>the violin</u> home in a canvas case.

10. My two companions and I were summoned back to the office although <u>my two companions and I</u> still had unfinished business in the town.

Task two **

Complete the sentences with an appropriate pronoun.

1. It was obvious that the two students had cheated though neither of .... would admit it.

2. This early sonata is among his best. .... he wrote later were too formulaic.

3. The daffodils this year have done better than .... last year.

4. They short-listed six of the applicants, but .... of them interviewed well.

5. It's every man for ....

6. I've read all Shakespeare's plays. *Romeo and Juliet* is the .... I know best.

7. He's won many prizes, including several of the most important ....

8. She takes very good photographs. .... have won the top international prizes.

9. He has a house in London, ... in Geneva and .... in the Caribbean.

10. There are too many books here. .... of them belong to you. Take .... back, please.

11. The problem of including sensitive questions in a census is always a delicate ....

12. It was only in 1829 that provision was made for a regular police force in the metropolitan London area. .... was followed by further legislation establishing 43 county and borough forces.

13. Would you like a cup of tea? No thanks. I had .... just half-an-hour ago.

14. I preferred the play they did last year to the .... this year.

15. The herdsmen had all collapsed on the ground, ... here, ... there.

9.4. Substitutes for structures containing a verb

Sections 383–385; 479; 482

The dummy auxiliary *do* can act as a substitute for the whole of a clause apart from the subject.

Other auxiliaries can be used in a similar way. That is, you can omit the whole or part of a sentence following an auxiliary.

Be as a main verb cannot be omitted after an auxiliary.

The main verb *do* acts a substitute for a main verb, normally a verb denoting some action or activity. *Do* requires an object which may be *it*, *that* or *so*.

Task one *

Complete the short answers to the following questions.

1. Who wants to go to the cinema? I (positive)/I (negative)
2. Did you finish the essay last night? Yes, I ....
3. Will you get a ticket for Tom? I already ....
4. Is Joan coming to the party? I don't know. She may ...., she .... not
5. Did Terry get the job? No, he ....
6. Will you be able to meet Fred on Friday? Of course, I ....
7. Have you read Amis's new book? Yes, I ....
8. Do you like our new millennium bridge? No, I ....
9. Who was responsible for all the disturbance last night? She ....
10. Who can deliver this parcel for me? He ....

Task two **

Rewrite the sentences below with an appropriate substitution for the part underlined.

1. John will come with us to the theatre <u>if Susan will come with us to the theatre.</u>
2. He might get the job, <u>but I don't think he will get the job.</u>
3. That is something I can't tell you, <u>but he can tell you.</u>
4. Is Harold Pinter our greatest playwright? <u>Yes, he is our greatest playwright.</u>
5. Why didn't you tell me? I'm sorry. <u>I know I should have told you.</u>
6. Why don't you sit down? <u>Why should I sit down?</u>

7. Is it possible to buy stamps in that shop? <u>It might be possible to buy stamps in that shop</u>.

8. She got the travel brochure for hotels in Australia, <u>but she didn't get the travel brochure for the hotels in Singapore</u>.

9. If you haven't finished the work by now, <u>you should have finished the work by now</u>.

10. Are you going to invite Michael to your party? <u>I could invite Michael to my party, but I don't want to invite Michael to my party</u>. He always quarrels with people.

Task three **

Complete the sentences below with *do that, do it,* or *do so,* etc.

1. A: He told them he didn't like going there. B: Why did he ....?

2. If they invite you to join them at their country house, you should .... It's a wonderful place.

3. He'll ask you to work late, but don't .... You'll simply be seen as an easy touch and you'll get no thanks.

4. A: They say he turned down the job. B: Why should he ....? It's stupid.

5. He's promised to come next week. If he ...., it'll be the first time he's been here in years.

6. Go and see your aunt while you're in London. To .... will cost you nothing and give her a lot of pleasure.

7. It won't help if I do the work for you. In any case, why should I ....? You've never done anything for me.

8. Give up teaching! Why ....? I thought you loved the job, and everyone say you're a wonderful teacher.

9. So you want to spend the next two years just travelling round the world. Well, in order to ...., you'll need to work hard now and save all your money. We can't help you.

10. To continue doing research, you'll need to get a very good degree. To ...., you'll have to work much harder than you do now.

9.5. Substitutes for *wh*-clauses and *to*-infinitive clauses

Sections **387–389**; 94; 99; 376

The whole of a *wh*-clause following the *wh*-word can be omitted.
    With infinitive clauses, you can omit the whole clause following *to*.
    The definite pronouns *it, that* and *this* are widely used as substitutes for noun clauses as well as for noun phrases.

Task ★★

Find simpler substitutes for the clauses underlined.

1. He's gone out, but <u>I don't know where he's gone</u>.

2. A: Let's go and see a film. B: <u>I'd love to go and see a film</u>, but I'm busy tonight.

3. I intend to go to Brazil, but <u>I don't know when I'll go to Brazil</u>.

4. You can go climbing <u>if you want to go climbing</u>. I'm staying here. I'd rather read a book.

5. You should keep exercising. <u>To keep exercising</u> is the best way to stop your knees becoming stiff.

6. The garden is organised into several areas. <u>The organisation of the garden into several areas</u> gives a lot of variety to the garden and makes it seem much bigger than it is.

7. It rained every day while they were in Spain. <u>That it rained every day</u> meant that they couldn't enjoy the beautiful countryside.

8. You need to get a tourist ticket. I can do that for you <u>if you want me to get the tourist ticket</u>.

9. He wants me to go and see that film about a monk's journey to Indonesia, <u>but I don't want to go and see that film about a monk's journey to Indonesia</u>.

10. A: Two hundred jobs are to go in the car factory. B: <u>How do you know two hundred jobs are to go in the car factory</u>?

11. A: Do you ever go back to the restaurant where you and your wife met? B: No, <u>I can't bear to go back there</u> since she left me.

12. Many Internet companies were unable to cope with the slow business build-up. <u>The slow business build-up meant</u> that many went bankrupt.

9.6. Omission with non-finite and verbless clauses

Sections 392–394; 493–494

Non-finite and verbless clauses have no operator (the first auxiliary of a verb phrase) and often no conjunction or subject. They are more economical than finite subclauses and avoid repetition. They are more favoured in formal and written styles of English.

Task one ★★

Rewrite the underlined clauses using non-finite or verbless clauses.

1. This man, <u>who was well-known to me</u>, caused all the problems in the department.

2. I expect <u>that I shall see you while I'm in London</u>.

3. Next month is the time <u>when you should visit Italy</u>.

4. <u>As he was a born leader</u>, James soon attracted the attention of the company management.

5. <u>He had retired from the army</u> and so gave up his title of General.

6. <u>He doubted that she would come</u> and made plans to go with another woman.

7. <u>I know how you have behaved in the past</u>; so I cannot accept you as a member of the group.

8. Ian had thought <u>he would see a film that evening</u>.

9. <u>He was given so much time</u>; he should have completed the work.

10. Please get me a taxi. <u>I've drunk so much</u> I mustn't drive my car tonight.

Task two **

Rewrite the following sentences, using non-finite or verbless clauses but, where possible, keeping the subordinators.

1. While Tom knew Maria had cheated in the exam, he, nonetheless, congratulated her warmly.

2. As he was going to Sweden for his job, he decided to wait until he was there before he bought a new winter coat.

3. Since I've lived here, I've not made any real friends.

4. Whether he was rich or poor, Joe always organised a good party on his birthday.

5. After Mary had read the best-seller about an old woman, she felt she was able to cope with old age.

6. When he met her after several years, he felt very sorry they had not become close friends.

7. After he had retired, he lived in Tasmania.

8. Since I don't know the way, I'd rather you drove.

9. Since he has known the truth about them, he has become very wary of them.

10. Though they were unsuccessful in their last business, they are determined to start again.

Conditions

10.1. Open and hypothetical conditions

Sections 207–210; 275; 366–367

Conditional sentences typically consist of a conditional (sub)clause and a main clause expressing the result which follows if the condition is satisfied. There are three basic patterns:

(i) If Tom wins a fortune in the lottery, he will buy a yellow submarine.
[= open condition: present/future time reference]

(ii) If Tom won a fortune in the lottery, he would buy a yellow submarine.
[= hypothetical condition: present/future time reference]

(iii) If Tom had won a fortune in the lottery, he would have bought a yellow submarine. [= hypothetical condition: past time reference]

The two clauses often appear in reverse order.

Some of the above verb forms are replaceable by other forms, although there are a number of restrictions, especially in terms of tense.

If is by no means the only conjunction introducing a conditional clause.

In some sentences a conditional phrase is used instead of a conditional clause.

Task one *

Study the following sentences, deciding which of the three basic patterns of conditional they can be related to. Also discuss any special features.

Example: *Without an organ transplant, Robert Pennington would survive only hours.*

⇒ *Relatable to type 2: the conditional part 'without an organ transplant' can be replaced by, i.e. be expanded into, 'if he didn't get an organ transplant'.*

1. If low wages were the chief magnet for industry, Haiti would be the manufacturing hub of the world.

2. Our hero will sacrifice the first living being he encounters, provided that he reaches land safely.

3. Supposing the minister concerned had decided to send a fleet of bombers to Tasmania: what would have happened?

4. You will not get an electric shock so long as you don't touch that live wire.

5. Ground coffee loses its flavour within five or six days unless it is specially packaged.

6. If a driver is trying to overtake you, maintain a steady course and speed, slowing down if necessary to let the vehicle pass.

   (*The Highway Code*, §144)

7. This information may be reproduced free of charge provided that it is reproduced accurately.

8. Unless road signs or markings indicate otherwise, you should use the left-hand lane when going left.   (*The Highway Code*, §121)

9. France and Germany might put aside their antagonism if given economic incentives for cooperation.

10. In case of burglary, report any loss of valuables to the local police.

11. In the event of renewed terrorist attacks, civil liberties might have to be curbed.

12. It is inconceivable that any scholar could have attained an important post in 1942 without the official sanction of the Nazi regime.

Task two **

Reword the following sentences, expanding them where necessary and using one of the three basic patterns.

> Example: *Gerry Adams said there would be no peace process but for John Hume's courage and vision.*
>
> ⇒ ... *if John Hume wasn't so courageous and didn't have so much vision.*
>
> (or: ... *if John Hume hadn't been so courageous and hadn't had so much vision* ... = if-clause refers to past time)

1. Given the opportunity, the tax office will take the easy way and grab whatever it can.

2. Without fear, the tax office would have a difficult time maintaining our system of so-called voluntary compliance.

3. In case of anticipated payment, please ignore this invoice.

4. Giving people confidence that information about them on the Internet is safe will boost electronic commerce.

5. The lieutenant governor succeeds the governor in case of the latter's death, removal from office, or disability.

6. Don't drive so fast or you'll smash into a lamppost.

7. Failure to comply with the rules will result in a one point deduction or disqualification.

8. In the event of my not being elected I will be the member of parliament for Holborn and St Pancras.

(British politician Frank Dobson)

9. But for the protesters a passer-by might have mistaken the annual conference of the party for a mass funeral.

10. The Treaty of 1839 guaranteed the neutrality of Belgium in case of a conflict in which Great Britain, France and Germany were involved.

11. What happened to Mr Dias would have been prevented by a proper freedom of information bill.

12. Without reform and better relations with the United States, Iran will face a major drastic upheaval.

13. Cling too long to yesterday's strategy and you could be in trouble, no matter how powerful you are.

14. Intensified violence would make it difficult to reach a negotiated settlement.

Task three **

Complete the following sentences, using forms of the verb in brackets which are compatible with the rest of the sentence.

1. If you (ever visit) _____ this area, (not miss) _____ the Science Centre.

2. Most people (send) _____ their kids to the best schools if they (strike) _____ it rich.

3. Supposing for a moment that sea levels (rise) _____ by several feet, don't you think vast tracts of land (be) _____ flooded.

4. Rodents (cause) _____ severe damage to trees unless proper control measures (be) _____ employed.

5. Modern civilization (probably develop) _____ much more slowly if people (not move) _____ from place to place.

6. If you (be) _____ kind enough to help, we (can) _____ easily move all this stuff to the attic.

7. I (never pay) _____ such a huge sum if you (not lend) _____ me 50,000 dollars that day.

8. If Herbert (not teach) _____ me how to swim, I (almost certainly drown) _____ in the lake that afternoon.

9. I (not have) _____ all these problems with my car now if I (choose) _____ to buy a more sophisticated model.

10. If the Soviet Union (make) _____ honourable use of the idealism it inspired in the West, it _____ still survive and be a happy place today.

11. Our whole strategy (have) _____ to be reviewed in case new problems (arise) _____ over the marketing of our products.

12. If the police (catch) _____ us then, they (send) _____ us back across the border.

Task four **

Complete the following sentences, adding a main clause that is compatible with the conditional subclause or, alternatively, a conditional subclause that is compatible with the main clause.

Example: *If you had listened to me . . .*

⇒ *. . . you wouldn't have run into trouble.* (= continuing past time reference)

⇒ *. . . you wouldn't be in trouble now.* (= present time reference)

1. If you see Arthur ....
2. If you were in my place ....
3. Will you lend me £20 if ....
4. .... would you have paid the bill?
5. I should have had my photograph taken if ....
6. Surely if you .... he would understand.
7. If he had told you everything ....
8. Would you have told him the truth if ....
9. .... unless you come up with better arguments.
10. If you cannot deal with the problem yourself ....
11. If .... he would send me to the principal at once.
12. Wouldn't it have been extraordinary if ....
13. If I were Prime Minister ....
14. The Second World War would have run a very different course if ....
15. If William the Conqueror ....

Task five ***

All of the following sentences are from the 2001 *Britannica Book of the Year: Events of 2000* (pp. 8–55) and use the so-called historic present (see *CGE* §131). It may be argued that these events would not have happened if the underlying causes had not existed. Such sentences could, therefore, be turned into hypothetical statements about the past, as in the following (adapted) example:

> *4 April: Lord Archer is expelled from the Conservative Party for five years for breaches of political ethics and integrity.*
>
> ⇒ *Lord Archer would not have been expelled from the Conservative Party if he had not breached political ethics and integrity.*
>
> ⇒ *. . . if he had acted in accordance with political ethics and kept his integrity.*

Now transform the next twelve sentences in similar ways, making any structural and lexical adjustments that are necessary.

1. 20 January: A leading official in Germany hangs himself as a parliamentary group begins an investigation into illicit payments to his party in the 1990s.

2. 27 February: The Limpopo River in southern Africa overflows its banks after weeks of heavy rains and disastrous flooding.

3. 10 March: A dam in a Romanian mine breaks, causing spillage of toxic metals into nearby rivers.

4. 5 April: A computer glitch closes down the London Stock Exchange for nearly eight hours on the last day of Great Britain's fiscal year.

5. 12 May: UN Secretary-General Kofi Annan criticizes the US for its reluctance to participate fully in peacekeeping operations in Africa.

6. 9 June: Buenos Aires is brought to a virtual standstill as workers stage a one-day strike to protest the Argentine government's austerity plan.

7. 2 July: The former communist rulers in Mongolia are returned to power after a landslide victory in the general election.

8. 12 August: The Russian nuclear submarine *Kursk* sinks in the Barents Sea after the hull is damaged by a series of explosions.

9. 16 September: Public transportation in Los Angeles shuts down as the United Transportation Union goes on strike.

10. 5 October: Responding positively to a challenge from Germany, the European Court of Justice halts a proposed European Union-wide ban on tobacco advertising.

11. 30 November: The city of Bethlehem cancels its traditional Christmas celebration owing to the ongoing violence between Israelis and Palestinians.

12. 7 December: Officials in California declare a stage-three power alert as electricity reserves drop to dangerous levels.

Task six ***

Rewrite the following dialogue, using conditional sentences (eight in all).

Example: *Go home now, otherwise your Dad won't be too pleased.*

⇒ *If you don't go home now, your Dad won't be too pleased.*

Tom: The world will be like paradise twenty years from now. Ever more robots will relieve us of all sorts of boring tasks.

Daisy: I don't agree. Life on earth might be hell. Just imagine these robots becoming more intelligent than humans. Some of them could even develop into monsters. Scientists may decide to fit them with brains.

Tom: What? Scientists behaving like modern Frankensteins? There would be every reason to worry then. No, they will introduce very strict guidelines, so everything will be under control.

Daisy: And what about cloning? Terrible, a few nutty professors reproducing themselves. Let's lock them up, otherwise things will get out of hand.

Tom: You sound like one of those latter-day Luddites. Put a few of them in charge and we're back in the Stone Age.

10.2. Other ways of expressing hypothetical meaning

Sections 277–278

There are three less common ways of expressing hypothetical meaning in subclauses:

(i) the *were*-subjunctive

(ii) *were to* + infinitive

(iii) *should* + infinitive

When the operator occurring in the *if*-clause is subjunctive *were*, *should* or *had*, the conditional clause can alternatively begin with the operator placed before the subject (= inversion).

Task *

Use the alternative, more formal versions of the following sentences, replacing the *if*-clause by a clause characterized by inversion.

1. If we had known the true situation at the Coco Reef, we would not have visited the resort last February.

2. If this were to be true, no one is quite sure what effects it would have.

3. If you should have any health care related questions, please call or visit your physician.

4. If we had realized Brian was cheating on us, we would have distanced ourselves from him.

5. I would be amazed if such an incident were ever to happen again.

6. If this man had been assisted just a little, he might have become a useful citizen.

7. If this should not be satisfactory, a second investigation will be conducted.

8. If they were ever to build another town they would probably profit from past experiences.

9. The proceeds from the book will cover the legal fees, if anything should go wrong.

10. If a solution were to be provided the problem would cease to be philosophic.

11. If the women had been given any real choice, their babies would never have been taken from them.

12. Millions of lives could be saved if someone were to find a cure for cancer.

10.3. Condition and contrast

Sections 213–214; 368

The idea of condition can be combined with that of implied contrast (*even if*) or with that of contrasting alternatives (*whether . . . or, whatever, no matter what*, etc.).

Task ***

Combine the following pairs of sentences, linking them in one or more of the above ways.

> Example: *Almost anything may happen. The few remaining aid workers will stay away.*
>
> ⇒ *Whatever* (or: *No matter what*) *may happen, the few remaining aid workers will stay away.*

1. This pup will win your heart. You don't like dogs, however.

2. Your panoramic view of the lake is breathtaking. It does not matter when you choose to come.

3. Your home is only temporary. Still, you can decorate with style.

4. You may have good credit or a past history of credit problems. Our experts will help you every step of the way.

5. Every child has a legal right to financial support. Children of divorced parents have this right, too.

6. You may be far away. I will always love you, though.

7. We don't know where you are travelling. Still, you'll find a familiar place where you can relax.

8. You may or may not be advanced. Anyway, there's one more trick for you to consider.

9. People are saying so many things. Just do your own thing.

10. I know you are not an art lover. Still, I think this collection is something for you.

11. You are going to have fun. You may or may not like it.

12. The US appeals court has made the right ruling. Admittedly, this ruling may be difficult to enforce.

Comparison

11.1. Comparison 1

Section **227**; 500–504

- Most one-syllable and some two-syllable adjectives and adverbs take the endings -*er* and -*est* for their comparative and their superlative form respectively.
- Some shorter and all longer adjectives and adverbs form comparison with *more* and *most*.
- A small group of short adjectives, adverbs and quantifiers have irregular comparison.

When comparing two things we use comparative forms, when comparing more than two things we use superlative forms. To name these things we add an *of*-phrase, to name the sphere or range of comparison we add an *in*-phrase.

Task one **

Complete the following sentences with the most appropriate comparative OR superlative of the word in brackets, using

- adjective forms in sentences 1 to 5
- adverb forms in sentences 6 to 10
- adjective OR adverb forms in sentences 11 to 15.

1. The (serious) _____ accident I ever got involved in crippled the (old) _____ of my two daughters for the rest of her life.

2. I may be the (able) _____ of all the mechanics in town but as for repairing a 1940s Morris, nothing could be (far) _____ from my mind.

3. The situation is getting (bad) _____ by the day, so even (drastic) _____ measures will have to be considered.

4. Brian had expected old age to be the (unhappy) _____ period in his life but he couldn't have been (wrong) _____.

5. In some ways Hubert is (clever) _____ than most people, but he is also one of the (shallow) _____ minds I've ever come across.

6. Even the (careful) _____ planned campaign can go (disastrous) _____ wrong than anyone would imagine.

7. (hard) _____ hit by the floods is the Mekong delta, one of the (dense) _____ populated areas in Asia.

8. No one is (high) _____ praised by fashion connoisseurs than Ms Heartthrob, who has been dubbed "the (good) _____-dressed woman walking the planet".

9. Political observers are (acute) _____ aware than ever that this is now the (autocratic) _____ ruled country south of the Sahara.

10. (little) _____ talented authors are often (wide) _____ read than their (true) _____ artistic counterparts.

11. The (old) _____ Brian grew, the (close) _____ attached he became to family values.

12. The (heavy) _____ injured of the two victims had to be taken to the (near) _____ hospital.

13. A (thorough) _____ investigation will be needed if we are to find an answer to the (hot) _____ debated issue of the decade.

14. Having an affair with a young intern is one of the (emphatic) _____ denied allegations in US public life. Apparently, speaking the truth is the (little) _____ of some politicians' concerns.

15. The (long) _____-serving chef in London had made the (great) _____ efforts imaginable to make the Christmas pudding taste (delicious) _____ than ever.

Task two **

Use two different superlative forms of 'late' in the following extract. What is the difference in meaning?

The _____ figures show joblessness rising to almost 3.9 million, about 9.3 per cent of the work force. (. . .) Germany currently ranks _____ among the euro zone's 12 in terms of economic growth.

(adapted from *Newsweek*, 27 August 2001, p. 14)

Task three **

Combine the following words and phrases into short sentences, using superlative adjectives and adding connecting words.

Examples: *Joan/professional/these five photographers.*

⇒ *Joan is the most professional of these five photographers.*

Joan/professional/photographer/town.

⇒ *Joan is the most professional photographer in town.*

1. the Red Bull/good/pub/the northern hemisphere
2. Winnie/attractive/the three girls
3. religious fundamentalism/bad/our enemies
4. the Ibans/fierce/tribe/Borneo
5. the moon landing/exciting/event/the 1960s
6. Gregory/tough/Sam's opponents
7. Shirley/competent/secretary/the department
8. the Thirty Years' War/bloody/conflict/17th century Europe
9. David/bright/my overseas students
10. malaria/common/present-day tropical diseases
11. Bologna/old/university/the world
12. Nero/ruthless/the Roman emperors

11.2. Comparison 2

Sections 225–226; 505–507

To compare two unequal things various structures can be used:

● We are *taller than* most Sherpas (are).

● Most Sherpas are *shorter than* we are/ ... *than we* (= formal)/ ... *than us* (= informal).

● Most Sherpas are *less tall than* we are/ ... *than we* (= formal)/ ... *than us* (= informal).

● We are *less short than* most Sherpas (are).

For stating or negating an equal comparison the following structures are used:

● Some Sherpas are *as tall as* we are/ ... *as we* (= formal)/ ... *as us* (= informal).

● Most Sherpas are *not as/so tall as* we are/ ... *as we* (= formal)/ ... *as us* (= informal).

Task one **

Rephrase the following sentences without changing their basic meaning, giving at least two alternatives to each. Add any stylistic variants as well.

1. My skin is darker than Angela's.
2. Our politicians are more optimistic than most voters.
3. Cynthia was feeling better than I was.
4. Boris looks healthier than I do.
5. There were not as many casualties in the train as in the coach.
6. I arrived later than Adrian.
7. The hooligans were dealt with more leniently than the anti-globalists.
8. Shy children speak more quietly than assertive ones.
9. My home is not decorated as lavishly as Madonna's.
10. The British athletes were not running as fast as their Ethiopian counterparts.

Task two ***

Study each row of statistical data below, then write four sentences similar to those that have already been done for you with reference to 'area'.

	Country ⇒	United Kingdom	Ireland	Canada	Australia	South Africa
Ex	Area (sq km)	244,101	70,285	9,970,610	7,682,300	1,219,090
1	Population	59,210,300	3,622,000	30,770,000	19,165,000	43,421,000
2	Density (per sq km)	244.6	52.1	3.3	2.5	35.6
3	Birth rate (per 1,000)	11.9	14.4	11.4	13.0	22.2
4	Under 15s (%)	19.3	23.7	19.8	21.6	33.9
5	Life expectancy (yrs)	77	76.7	78	78.5	53
6	Life expect. males (yrs) Life expect. females (yrs)	74.4 79.7	73.9 79.5	74.9 81.2	76.0 81.0	51.9 54.2
7	GNP (per capita) ($ US)	21,410	18,710	19,170	20,640	14,100
8	Annual rainfall (mm)	593	929	946	1,181	709
9	Annual temperature (°C)	11	10	6	17	16
10	Distance from London (km)	–	500	5,500	17,000	9,000

Example: *Australia is a large country.*

> ⇒ *(a) Australia is larger than the UK, Ireland and South Africa.*
>
> *(b) Australia is smaller than Canada.*
>
> *(c) Canada is the largest of the five countries.*
>
> *(d) Ireland is the smallest of the five countries.*

1. South Africa is a populous country.
2. Canada is a sparsely populated country.
3. The UK has a low birth rate.
4. Ireland has a young population.
5. Canadians live long.
6. Ireland has a wide gender gap as regards life expectancy.
7. Australia is a rich country.
8. Canada has a wet climate.
9. South Africa has a warm climate.
10. South Africa is far away from the UK.

Task three **

Convert the following sentences by replacing an adjective-and-noun pattern with one structured around an adverb. In some cases antonyms can be used in a number of alternative ways too.

Example: *I am as avid a reader of Punch as my granny.*

> ⇒ *I read Punch as avidly as my granny (does).*
>
> ⇒ *My granny reads Punch as avidly as I do.*
>
> *(or: . . . as I <formal> . . . as me <informal>)*
>
> ⇒ *My granny and I are equally avid readers of Punch.*

1. Simpson is a more elegant writer than Williams.
2. Chuck is not as good a baseball player as Pete.
3. Lady Carcrash is a more reckless driver than Lord Slowlane.
4. Americans are less ardent supporters of euthanasia than Europeans.
5. Sarah is as firm a believer in life after death as Monica.
6. Keith Michell was not such a brilliant actor as John Gielgud.
7. Barbara was not as peaceful a protester as Sandra.
8. Conchita is a more fluent speaker of English than Andrikos.
9. Arthur is a much harder worker than Hyacinth.
10. Dorothy is a less energetic swimmer than Sybil.

11.3. Comparison 3

Sections 228–229 & 233

Comparative forms are often repeated with *and* to express continuing change. In some cases there is an accompanying adverbial clause of proportion introduced by *as*: Things got *better and better* (*as* time went on).

Another construction expressing proportion consists of two clauses beginning with *the* + a comparative word: *The earlier* (we start), *the better* (it will be).

Task ***

Rewrite the following text, replacing the underlined parts with one of the above structures. In some sentences a change of word order is necessary within the underlined strings.

As the food situation in Malnutritia was deteriorating, the authorities were becoming increasingly worried.

Waiting too long before taking action would add to the risk of violent outbursts among the native population.

These people had felt mounting anger at the growing scarcity of food.

They knew that, if their complaints were loud enough, their plight would soon come to an end.

Fortunately, as the international community has become increasingly aware of such crises, it has been responding to them with ever greater speed.

11.4. Comparison 4

Sections 230–232

Comparison is implicit in structures with *enough* and *too* followed by a *to*-infinitive:
– You are *old enough/too young to travel on your own.*
Degree or amount constructions with *so . . . (that)* and *such . . . (that)* express a similar meaning. The *that*-clause adds a meaning of result:
– Mr Simpson is *so old/such an old man that he can't travel on his own any more.*
The various types of comparison can also be applied to gradable count-able nouns:
– I'm *as much of a pessimist* now as I've always been.
– I'm *more/less of a pessimist* now than before.

Task one *

Complete the following sentences, adding a subclause that is compatible with the main clause.

Example: *David is so poor . . .*

> ⇒ *David is so poor that he can't even afford to eat three decent meals a day.*

1. Ann is not earning enough . . .
2. The trainees were too inexperienced . . .
3. The fog is so dense . . .
4. Tony is such a fool . . .
5. The witness was too afraid . . .
6. The suitcase is so heavy . . .
7. The patient was too weak . . .
8. Professor Puniverse is such a bore . . .
9. We had been practising long enough . . .
10. It had been snowing so heavily . . .
11. Some of the interviewees were too nervous . . .
12. Ms Lovelace is such a hard worker . . .
13. The president is too much of a realist . . .
14. Ted's sudden departure was as much of a surprise . . .
15. Tracy's poor marks at school are less of a worry . . .

Task two *

Rephrase the completed versions of the above sentences without changing their meaning in a significant way. In some cases there may be more than one acceptable alternative.

Example: *David is even too poor to afford three decent meals a day.*

> or: *David is very poor so (that) he can't even afford three decent meals a day.*

Addition, exception and restriction

12.1. Addition

Sections 234–235

Addition can be expressed by

- **prepositions**: *in addition to, as well as, besides*
- **words typically used in coordinate constructions**: *and, not only . . . but (also)*
- **adverbials**: *in addition* (front-position), *also* (mid-position), *as well* and *too* (end-position)
- **the adverbs** *so* and ***neither/nor***, which have a positive and a negative meaning respectively. All three adverbs cause subject-operator inversion.

Task one ***

Rewrite the following (pairs of) sentences, replacing the underlined part by the word or phrase in brackets. Pay attention to both structure and word order.

> Example: *This food is not only delicious but also safe. (besides)*
> ⇒ *Besides being delicious this food is (also) safe.*

1. In addition to being far too long, the play was badly acted. (also)
2. At the party, Bianca not only sang but also danced. (too)
3. Besides offering a BA in political science the department also serves the community in various ways. (in addition)
4. Jane spoke English and Russian, and fluent Arabic as well. (besides)

5. Slaves <u>not only</u> built the South, <u>but also</u> created the wealth of the North. (in addition to)

6. Ms Moore was a frequent guest on NBC's *Weekend Today*. <u>In addition,</u> she has done more than 200 television interviews. (as well as)

7. Arkansas has hundreds of hotels and motels, and more than 170 bed and breakfast inns, <u>too</u>. (in addition to)

8. Getting a good guide in that area is an absolute necessity. It is <u>also</u> very affordable. (as well as)

9. <u>Besides</u> the Amazon rain forest, another Brazilian jewel faces peril. (too)

10. We have a tradition of sparkling wine and have just begun brewing beer <u>as well</u>. (not only . . . but also).

11. Prisoners of war received the same rations and supplies. <u>In addition,</u> they received comparable medical care. (as well)

12. Healthy aging depends on social <u>as well as</u> physical activity. (not only . . . but also)

Task two **

Complete the following dialogue, using *so* or *neither/nor* in combination with the subject mentioned in brackets.

> Examples: *A1: Uncle Joe is a social worker.*
>
> *B1: (Aunt Betty) _____.* ⇒ *So is Aunt Betty.*
>
> *A2: Uncle Joe is not a social worker.*
>
> *B2: (Aunt Betty) _____.* ⇒ *Neither/Nor is Aunt Betty.*

Ron: My train was delayed again this morning.
Tess: (mine) _____.
Ron: I didn't get to work on time.
Tess: (I) _____.
Ron: I've decided to look for a job closer to home.
Tess: (lots of other people) _____.
Ron: You may not believe it, Tess, but I can't drive a car.
Tess: (I) _____. Actually, I would have preferred to live in an earlier age, when there were no cars at all.
Ron: (I) _____.
Tess: People like my grandparents managed quite well without a car.
Ron: (most of their generation) _____. The trouble these days is so many people behind the wheel don't behave like humans.
Tess: (some people sitting behind desks) _____.
Ron: Still, motorists shouldn't be blamed for all the problems on our roads.

Tess: (lorry drivers) _____. They are all too often made scapegoats.

Ron: (cyclists and pedestrians ... and even animals crossing roads.) _____.

Tess: Well, I think we should all try to be more understanding towards each other.

Ron: (I) _____.

12.2. Exception

Section 236

Exception is the opposite of addition and can be expressed by

- **prepositions**: *except (for), apart from, bar, but*
- **the conjunction** *except (that)*
- **adverbs of exception**: *otherwise, else; even* (= negative adverb of exception)

Task **

Complete the following sentences, using each of the connecting words or phrases below at least once:

apart from	bar	but	else	even
except	except for	except that	otherwise	

1. I have a bit of a headache, but _____ I'm fine.
2. Our turnover is expected to increase considerably this year _____ any unforeseen events.
3. The weather was mild last winter _____ one cold spell in January.
4. Mumbai proves to be India's capital in everything _____ name.
5. _____ English, what language will be most important in the global market place?
6. There were no further details _____ the 15-year-old was released on bail.
7. We spent the next few days playing games and partying and not much _____.
8. Do not call the fire department _____ in case of an emergency.
9. I didn't keep any of my books, not _____ my dictionaries.

10. _____ diaries or personal journals, most writing is intended for one or more readers.

11. Some of the paint has gone but _____ the woodwork is in good condition.

12. _____ vets, who _____ can treat an animal?

12.3. Restriction

Sections 237–238

Restriction can be expressed by words like *only*, *just*, *merely* and *simply*, which combine negative meaning with the idea of exception. The word *only* can often be paraphrased as *nothing but, no one except, no more than*, etc.

Adverbs of addition, exception and restriction often focus their meaning on a particular part of the sentence. A sentence can be ambiguous, depending on the element that is focused, but contrastive intonation can help to clarify the meaning.

Task ***

Complete the following sentences in two different ways to bring out the ambiguity of the introductory clause. Underline the parts which are 'focused' in the two versions of each sentence.

Example: *The tourist merely wanted to touch the statuettes,..........*

⇒ (1) *The tourist merely wanted to touch the statuettes, she didn't want to steal them.*

⇒ (2) *The tourist merely wanted to touch the statuettes, she didn't want to touch the jewels.*

or: (2) *The tourist merely wanted to touch the statuettes, not the jewels.*

1. The reporters only interviewed the Prime Minister,..........

2. Sarah isn't just a keen tennis player,..........

3. The politician merely suggested changing priorities,..........

4. The police didn't even try to deal with the worst types of crime,..........

5. We also had to underline the adjectives,..........

6. Thelma isn't merely against modern music,...........

7. The young man not only envied his cousin,..........

8. Chris couldn't even understand simple questions,..........

9. We didn't just go to Arizona to meet Native Americans,..........

10. Tom was also fined for not wearing his safety belt,..........

Information, reality and belief

13.1. Questions and answers 1

Sections **240–242**; 536–541; 609–612; 681–683

Questions are sentences by which someone asks the hearer to give information. The most natural response to a question is an answer, giving the information needed. The commonest types of questions are:

- *yes-no* **questions:**
  - limited to only one of two answers (*'yes'* or *'no'*)
  - subject-operator inversion and usually rising intonation
- *wh*-**questions:**
  - unlimited number of answers
  - initial *wh*-word, subject-operator inversion (except when the *wh*-word is subject) and usually falling intonation
- **alternative questions:**
  - limited to one of two or more alternatives
  - similar in form to *yes-no* or *wh*-questions.

Wh-questions are introduced by
  - interrogative determiners/pronouns (personal only): *who(m)* and *whose*
  - interrogative determiners/pronouns (personal and non-personal): *what* (indefinite reference) and *which* (definite reference)
  - interrogative adverbs: *where, when, why, how.*

Task one *

Turn the following statements into corresponding *yes-no* questions.

1. They are going to build a new bridge across the river.
2. Motorists can park in the town square on Sundays.
3. Arthur has lived in South Africa all his life.
4. Two gunmen were killed by the security forces yesterday.

5. Inflation will start rising again in the next few months.
6. Charlotte caught pneumonia last winter.
7. Skin-diving is Uncle Toby's favourite pastime.
8. Patients had been waiting for hours before seeing a doctor.
9. These measures should have been taken years ago.
10. The postman always rings twice.
11. Susan was disappointed after the job interview.
12. The principal has a fourteen-year-old daughter.

Task two **

Complete the following questions, adding the most appropriate *wh*-word.

1. _____ was the first man to walk on the moon?
2. _____ form of English do you like best: British, American or Australian?
3. _____ criminals should serve life sentences?
4. _____ did the CIA suspect of terrorism?
5. _____ is your cousin, a fashion model?
6. _____ of you are going to take early retirement?
7. _____ caused the hurricane to change course all of a sudden?
8. _____ motorbike did you borrow, your dad's?
9. _____ were you talking to in that dark corner of the library?
10. _____ leg hurts most, Mr Sillitoe?
11. _____ on earth are people prepared to risk their lives climbing Mount Everest?
12. _____ can you possibly expect me to forgive you?
13. _____ is the most wanted man in the world hiding?
14. _____ will humans visit the planet Mars?
15. _____ often have you been abroad?

Task three **

Respond to the following questions in an appropriate way. Where possible, give both a complete and a shortened answer.

Examples: Q: *"Are you going on holiday this summer?"*
⇒ A1: *"Yes, we're going to the Maldives." / "No, we're staying at home."*
⇒ A2: *"Yes, we are." / "No, we're not."*
Q: *"Where did you buy those magazines?"*
⇒ A: *"(I bought them) at the newsagent's."*

1. Will Mr Walker try to get in touch with one of our senior staff?

2. What time do you think the first election result will be declared?

3. Shall we buy a new car or a mobile home?

4. Which of the four candidates is most suitable for the job?

5. Did the police catch one of those burglars?

6. What are we going to do now? Sell the house, get rid of the jewellery, or cancel the cruise?

7. How many of these novels do we have to read in fact?

8. Have all the necessary precautions been taken to prevent this from happening again?

9. Did they teach you how to pronounce the word "thoroughly"?

10. Why do so many people eat junk food?

11. Which would you prefer: a flat in a tower block or a house in the country?

12. Who wrote *Moby Dick*?

Task four ***

Turn the statements in the following text into questions, replacing the underlined parts by corresponding *wh*-words.

Example: *The burglar got into the warehouse by smashing a window.*

⇒ wh-Q1: *Who got into the warehouse (by smashing a window)?*

⇒ wh-Q2: *How did the burglar get into the warehouse? / How did he get in?*

CONGO VOLCANO: THE FACTS

Mount Nyiragongo in the Democratic Republic of Congo is one of Africa's most active volcanoes. In all, there are eight volcanoes along the borders of Rwanda, Congo and Uganda. Nyiragongo was last active in 1994, when a lava lake reappeared in its summit crater.

The latest eruption is more serious. Lava from Nyiragongo can travel at 60 kilometres per hour and some of it might reach a nearby lake and do further damage.

Bill Evans of the US Geological Survey said lava could react with gas in the lake, with catastrophic consequences. The gas is composed of carbon dioxide and methane and could suffocate local people living around the lake.

Both Nyiragongo and another active volcano are located in the Virunga mountain range, which straddles the Rwandan border. The pair are responsible for nearly two-fifths of Africa's historical eruptions.

(adapted from *www.news.bbc.co.uk*, 18 January 2002)

Task five ***

Add the missing questions (neutral *yes-no* or *wh-*) addressed to Pat by the recruitment officer in the following job interview.

R.O.:
Pat: Patricia Lonsdale.
R.O.:
Pat: In Cape Town, South Africa, on the 23rd of March 1980.
R.O.:
Pat: No, we moved to Durban when I was three.
R.O.:
Pat: Yes, I went to local schools until the age of 18.
R.O.:
Pat: No, my parents sent me to Britain.
R.O.:
Pat: Because they thought the tuition system at British universities would suit me better.
R.O.:
Pat: Manchester. I got a BA in accounting and finance there.
R.O.
Pat: Oh, yes, I also studied two foreign languages, Spanish and Russian. After my BA, that is.
R.O.:
Pat: Well, by taking odd jobs, serving food in restaurants, teaching English to foreigners, etc.
R.O.:
Pat: Yes, I would really like to be employed full-time.
R.O.:
Pat: Something in the range of 1,500 to 2,000 pounds a month.
R.O.
Pat: Yes, I've got two references here, but these were both part-time jobs.
R.O.: Thank you. Well, that will do for the time being. You will be hearing from us soon.

13.2. Questions and answers 2

Sections 243–244

Yes-no questions containing words like *any*, *ever*, *yet* are neutral, while words like *some*, *sometimes*, *already* suggest a positive bias.

Questions in statement form with rising intonation have a positive or a negative bias depending on the absence or presence of a negative element.

Task ***

Form acceptable and fully explicit questions suggesting a neutral attitude (NEU), or a positive (POS) or negative (NEG) bias to match the following answers.

> Example: *A: Yes, they've all been locked already. (NEU)*
>
> ⇒ *Q: Have all the gates/doors been locked yet?*

1. Yes, some of them are unsuitable for such a job. (POS)
2. No, we didn't see any of them at all. (NEU)
3. No, it won't make much difference. (NEG)
4. Yes, they have been successful sometimes. (NEU)
5. No, none of them are being taken care of. (NEU)
6. No, not many people knew about it. (NEG)
7. Yes, we had already met all of them. (POS)
8. Yes, I've written to some of them. (NEU)
9. Yes, they definitely do protest sometimes. (POS)
10. No, there is no one on earth who can. (NEG)
11. No, it's going to get a lot worse. (NEG)
12. Yes, it could make a big difference for some of them. (POS)

13.3. Questions and answers 3

Sections **245–248**; **612**; **684**

Special types of question:

- Tag questions are shortened *yes-no* questions consisting of an operator and a subject pronoun. They are added to the end of statements to ask for confirmation. If the statement is positive, the tag question is negative, and vice versa.

- *Yes-no* questions with a negative form have a mixture of positive and negative bias and express surprise.

- If there are two *wh*-elements in a sentence, one of them is moved to the front or the two are coordinated.

- Questions can be made more polite by adding *please* or by using an introductory formula.

Task one *

Add question tags to the following statements, using contracted forms.

1. Kenny is being very naughty again.

2. Several dozen men didn't turn up for work.

3. You can't drive a lorry at all.

4. In some countries people eat horse meat.

5. It will take a long time before the situation is back to normal.

6. English spelling isn't going to be changed.

7. There have been more reports of incidents near the border.

8. Speed limits should be reduced still further in some areas.

9. Deborah loves one of our local celebrities.

10. Some prisoners have never committed a crime.

11. These bigots are extremely hard to convince.

12. The police wouldn't intimidate such young offenders.

Task two ***

Form question sentences with two *wh*-elements to match the following answers.

> Examples: A: *It happened in an underground car park shortly after midnight.*
>
> ⇒ Q: <u>*Where and when*</u> *did the shooting happen?*
>
> A: *Larry was accusing Fred and Jim was accusing Tony.*
>
> ⇒ Q: <u>*Who*</u> *was accusing* <u>*who(m)*</u>*?*

1. Carol wants to visit an exhibition, and Joyce wants to visit an arts and crafts centre.

2. We gave it away to the neighbours, because they hadn't got one yet.

3. Tim is flying to Honolulu, Ted is sailing to Madeira and Tony is hitchhiking to Turkey.

4. I killed it with a spade, early this morning.

5. She ordered six of them for tomorrow and ten for next Sunday.

6. This is Mr Cheng, over there is Mrs Udolpho, and the third person is Tracy, our secretary.

7. I've put the letters on your desk and the photos on the dresser.

8. Paul was driving 80 and Ralph 90 miles per hour.

9. It is going to take place in Singapore next summer.

10. The football fans stayed on to watch the game while the hooligans stayed on to pick a fight.

13.4. Responses

Sections **249–252**; 22–23

Responses to statements:

- In conversation we often make a response to a statement to express interest, surprise, pleasure, etc. Many of these responses are 'backchannels' like *Yes, Yeah, Mm, Really?, That's right.*

- In informal English, shortened *wh-*questions can be used as responses to statements (a) when the hearer wants more information or (b) when it is not clear, in some respect, what the speaker says.

- *Yes-no* echo questions are used as requests for repetition when the information given by the speaker was surprising or not fully audible. Either all or part of the statement can be echoed. In *wh-*echo questions one specific element of the statement is singled out for further clarification.

- General requests for repetition include expressions like *Pardon?, Excuse me?,* etc. and more complete sentences asking the speaker to repeat the original statement.

Task one **

Complete the following conversation by adding a variety of 'backchannels', using each one of them only once.

Dad: Tom, I'm not too pleased with the way you've been behaving lately.
Tom:
Dad: Professor Crawford tells me you're not turning up for some of his lectures . . .
Tom:
Dad: . . . especially those taught in the morning.
Tom:
Dad: Look, son, there's nothing wrong with going to bars and discos from time to time.
Tom:
Dad: I did that too when I was your age . . .
Tom:
Dad: . . . but I knew when to stop.
Tom:
Dad: I belonged to a different generation, of course.
Tom:
Dad: Some of us would even go to lectures with a bad hangover.
Tom:

Dad: Look, you've got enough talent to get a good degree...

Tom:

Dad: ...and you would probably want to keep your monthly allowance, I suppose.

Tom:

Task two **

Add to each of the following statements a shortened *wh*-question asking for more information (relating to the point in brackets) followed by an appropriate answer.

> Example: A: *Would you give me that book, please. (specification)*
>
> ⇒ B: *What/Which book?/Which one?*
>
> A: *That novel by V.S Naipaul over there / on your desk.*

1. Ian is studying chemistry and physics. (place)
2. Charles insisted on having a word with me. (topic)
3. I've received angry letters from our main customer. (number)
4. We don't want to emigrate to New Zealand any more. (reason)
5. One of the missing children was spotted near a cliff edge. (time)
6. Two flights have been cancelled. (specification)
7. I went to the movies in those days. (frequency)
8. The circus artist had been in a coma. (duration)
9. I'll try to make it up with Caroline. (manner)
10. Put the stuff into our garage, will you? (specification)
11. The victim had been knocked down. (instrument)
12. I've bought a pearl necklace. (recipient)

Task three **

Respond to each of the following statements with

(a) a *wh*-echo question focusing on the underlined part, using two types of word order where possible.

(b) a *yes-no* echo question in all other cases, using both a complete and a shortened version.

> Examples: *I lost one of my contact lenses this morning.*
>
> ⇒ *What did you lose? / You lost what?*
>
> *Would you give me a screwdriver, please.*
>
> ⇒ *Give you a screwdriver? / A screwdriver?*

1. I lost a finger when I was a child.
2. Johnny Reckless considers himself an excellent driver.
3. Martin should have his head examined.
4. A sister of mine became a pavement artist.
5. I spent two months in Kuala Lumpur.
6. We're going to buy a speedboat next summer.
7. Mr Clay earned half a million dollars last year.
8. I admire body builders for their big muscles.
9. Aunt Rachel was born in 1910.
10. The government wants to privatize the prison system.
11. Brother Francis is a specialist in medieval manuscripts.
12. The two youngsters killed the hamsters for fun.

13.5. Omission of information

Sections 253–255

Information which is already obvious from the preceding context is often omitted, so that many responses lack the structure of a complete sentence.

The situation outside language may also make certain information unnecessary, giving rise to brief incomplete or formulaic utterances (short commands, questions, public notices, headings, etc.).

In casual speech, sentence-initial elements like pronoun subjects and/or auxiliaries are often omitted.

Task one ***

Respond to the following statements in an appropriate way by using sentences in which some of the information is omitted, taking into account the general feeling indicated in brackets. Do not use the same response twice.

Examples: Rita: *"Most young kids need to be re-educated, I think."*

Steve: (surprise) ⇒ *"What a strange thing to say!"*

Rita: *"And computers should be banned from primary schools."*

Steve: (strong disagreement) ⇒ *"Rubbish."*

Andy: There's too much crime on our streets these days.
Bill: (complete agreement)

Andy: So many burglars and robbers that aren't caught any more, let alone big criminals.

Bill: (partial agreement)

Andy: Well, if I had my way, I'd even put petty thieves behind bars . . . for years.

Bill: (disagreement)

Andy: I think the worst offenders should have their hands chopped off.

Bill: (indignation)

Andy: Sorry, I got carried away a bit . . . There's this new thing, of course, electronic tagging.

Bill: (enthusiasm)

Andy: But the problem is that some of these convicts are experts in electronics.

Bill: (surprise)

Andy: The cleverest of the bad boys – and girls – could start tampering with the devices.

Bill: (reluctant agreement)

Andy: So I'm all for prisons and, as for overcrowding, there's the alternative of using convict ships.

Bill: (scepticism)

Andy: And as soon as we've run out of ships, we can send our excess of prisoners to Australia . . .

Bill: (disbelief)

Andy: . . . or, better still, to the Antarctic.

Bill: (scorn)

Task two **

Use an incomplete sentence or formula to respond appropriately to the situation described by the sentence in brackets.

1. (you are sitting next to someone who is driving much too fast:)

2. (your guest might like another helping of pudding:)

3. (someone has just played a very dirty trick on you:)

4. (you want your colleague to join you for a drink in a nearby bar:)

5. (your partner has said something that doesn't make sense at all:)

6. (your canoe has overturned and you cannot swim:)

7. (your best friend has won the first prize in a contest:)

8. (blood is suddenly trickling down the wall:)

9. (you want the Democrats to win the election:)

10. (you've just trodden on someone's toes:)

11. (you didn't quite catch what your interlocutor was saying:)

12. (you're pushing people out of the way while heading for the exit:)

13.6. Reported statements

Sections 256–258

Speech can be reported directly or indirectly. When the reporting verb is in the past tense the following changes are normally made in converting direct into indirect speech:

- present tense forms become past tense forms
- 1st and 2nd person pronouns and determiners become 3rd person pronouns
- pointer words like *this, now, here*, etc. are replaced by *that, then, there*, etc.

Past perfect verbs and some modal auxiliaries do not change. The present tense can be left unchanged if the reported clause refers to something still applying to the time of reporting.

Task one **

Convert the following reported statements from direct into indirect speech.

Example: *"I'm seeing my boss next week and will ask him for a pay rise,"*
Alice said.

⇒ *Alice said that she was seeing her boss the next week and would ask him for a pay rise.*

1. Edith said: "I'm leaving for Thailand this evening."
2. A spokesman declared: "Two suspects were caught by the police yesterday."
3. Helen confided to her friends: "I don't want to stay here for the rest of my life."
4. "There will also be widespread frost tomorrow", the weatherman added.
5. "I haven't touched a drop of alcohol since last weekend", claimed the drunken driver.
6. "You can't imagine what the situation was like two years ago", the chairman told his audience.
7. "I refuse to reveal the truth now because I'm being blackmailed", Tom replied to the detective.
8. "If you lend me your sportscar for a day or two, I'll invite you to my party", Susan promised Mark.
9. "We hadn't realized you were taking care of these problems", the old couple explained to the social worker.

10. "The United Nations must become more active", the Secretary-General emphasized, "if the organization is to keep its credibility."

11. "You may be in pain for a few days", the doctor warned his patient, "but you will definitely feel better by the end of this week."

12. "It's regrettable", the principal told the parents, "that children watch so many violent programmes on TV these days."

Task two ***

(a) Underline any reporting clauses and equivalent expressions in the following text.

(b) Rewrite the text by giving all the reporting clauses front position or adding such a clause to sentences that do not have one. While doing so, shift all of the text into the past.

Example: *According to reliable sources new measures may be introduced to deal with these problems.*

⇒ *Reliable sources said / told us / pointed out that new measures might be introduced to deal with these/those problems.*

CARE CUTS PUT OAPS' 'LIVES AT RISK'
The government is putting the lives of elderly people at risk and is jeopardizing its own plans to reform the health service, according to a report published on Thursday, 31 January 2002.

It says residential care and support in people's own homes is being rationed and more than a million old people are suffering as a result.

A spokesperson stresses that the report was compiled by 21 organizations, including Help the Aged, Age Concern and the Alzheimer's Society.

It suggests that, while the National Health Service might grab the headlines and the lion share of resources, social care is in crisis.

There are more old people than ever, yet the number receiving support in their own homes is actually falling with only the most needy qualifying for help, the document says.

Some 35,000 residential care beds have been lost in the past three years, it adds.

The organizations claim that many elderly people do not receive the help they need with washing, dressing and other forms of personal care.

Others have to wait, sometimes in NHS hospital beds, because they cannot be discharged anywhere else.

Ministers acknowledge that funding for social care has not kept up with the health service.

The report suggests that, without substantial investment, the problems in this area could jeopardize attempts to modernize the NHS.

(slightly adapted from *www.bbc.co.uk*, 31 January 2002)

13.7. Indirect questions

Sections 259–260; 681

Indirect *yes-no* questions are introduced by *if* or *whether*, the *yes-no* type of alternative questions by *whether . . . or*, indirect *wh*-questions by a *wh*-word.

The rules for changing direct into indirect questions are similar to those for statements. The reported interrogative clause can also be a *to*-infinitive clause beginning with a *wh*-word.

Task **

Convert the following reported questions from direct into indirect speech, reversing the clause order in 5–12. Give two versions for 11–12, using a finite and a non-finite reported clause each time.

> Example: *"When did all the trouble start and when will it end?" I asked her.*
>
> ⇒ *I asked her when all the trouble had started and when it would end.*

1. Margaret suddenly asked her roommate: "Are you right-handed or left-handed?"

2. The consultant asked the personnel manager: "Which of these candidates do you prefer?"

3. Mr Patten kept wondering: "Why can't the council put off the meeting until tomorrow?"

4. The talk show host asked the superstar: "Have you ever suffered from stage fright?"

5. "What caused the car crash on the railway bridge two days ago?", the insurance man asked.

6. "May I give the patient two pills instead of one?", the nurse wanted to know.

7. "Where exactly do you store the yoghurt?", the inquisitive woman asked the shop assistant.

8. "Did parents teach their children good manners in the 1970s?", the 10-year-old wondered.

9. "Which platform does the number 17 bus leave from?", I wanted to know.

10. "Will the foreign delegations start arriving this afternoon?", the PR woman inquired.

11. The learner driver asked the instructor: "How should I reverse the car?"

12. "Shall I send a card or a bunch of flowers?", I wondered.

13.8. Denial and affirmation 1

Sections **261–262**; 581–585; 610–611; 697–699

The truth of something can be denied by using a negative sentence containing one of the negative items *not, no, nowhere, nothing*, etc. The element *not*, or its contracted form *n't*, is put immediately after the operator. When there is no operator the auxiliary *do* is introduced as operator.

The part of a sentence which follows the negative word is the scope of the negation, i.e. the part which is negated. A final adverbial may or may not be in the scope of negation. Inside the scope of negation are words like *any, yet, ever*. Outside of it are words like *some, already, sometimes*.

Negative determiners and pronouns are often replaceable by *not/n't* . . . *any*. Other negative words can often be replaced in similar ways.

Task one *

Deny the truth of the following sentences in a formal and at least one informal way.

> Example: *We are going to the theatre tonight.*
>
> ⇒ *We are not going to the theatre tonight.*
>
> *We aren't going to the theatre tonight. / We're not going to the theatre tonight.*

1. I have been here before.
2. We will be running out of money shortly.
3. Charles teaches English to Asian immigrants.
4. We had received an invitation from the local council.
5. Some people like watching soap operas.
6. I would buy a holiday cottage if I were you.
7. Jessica is being stalked by her ex-boyfriend.
8. Bill has been listening to the concert.
9. David struck me as a very dedicated young man.
10. They built a new tunnel to link the two islands.
11. I shall see the leading actress after the performance.
12. Our gardener cut down the big chestnut trees.

Task two **

Paraphrase the following pairs of sentences to bring out the difference in meaning.

Example: a. *Peter definitely hasn't taken the job.*

b. *Peter hasn't definitely taken the job.*

⇒ a. *It's definite that he hasn't taken the job.*

b. *It's not definite that he has taken the job.*

1 a. I truly can't believe what happened last night.

b. I can't truly believe what happened last night.

2 a. Jim particularly doesn't like his mother-in-law's fruitcakes.

b. Jim doesn't particularly like his mother-in-law's fruitcakes.

3 a. Smoking clearly isn't forbidden in this canteen.

b. Smoking isn't clearly forbidden in this canteen.

4 a. Frank really doesn't know why Paula is so upset.

b. Frank doesn't really know why Paula is so upset.

5 a. We possibly couldn't come tomorrow.

b. We couldn't possibly come tomorrow.

Task three ***

Explain the ambiguity in each of the following sentences by paraphrasing the two meanings and referring to the scope of 'not'.

Example: *The suspect wasn't seen near the scene of the crime.*

⇒ (a) *The suspect was (probably) not seen anywhere else either.*

(scope of 'not': 'seen')

(b) *The suspect was seen somewhere else.*

(scope of 'not': 'seen near the scene of the crime')

1. The applicants were not interviewed by the human resources officer.

2. I haven't discussed the children's future with my wife.

3. The opposition is not going to stage a demonstration next week.

4. I didn't offend Patricia by telling her she looked a bit under the weather.

5. I don't vote for the New Democrats to please my dad.

6. The patient didn't suffer any pain while she was in hospital.

7. The local party leader was not re-elected as a result of a smear campaign.

8. Monica didn't get injured when she collided with the van.

9. I haven't been able to contact Jack on my mobile phone.

10. I didn't want to see Sylvia because I felt depressed.

Task four ***

(a) Decide whether the underlined word is inside OR outside the scope of
not / n't.

(b) Paraphrase the sentences without changing their meaning.

1. I haven't seen <u>some</u> of the famous Walt Disney films.

2. Alice hasn't visited the Taj Mahal <u>yet</u>.

3. We hadn't <u>ever</u> been notified of the health risks involved.

4. Young Mr Plimsoll doesn't <u>sometimes</u> attend Professor Barnaby's lectures.

5. There wasn't <u>anybody</u> around to show me the way to the boardroom.

6. Look, it's not as if we didn't <u>already</u> have enough problems.

7. The problem with Terry is that he will not <u>sometimes</u> listen to what I'm saying.

8. The suspect said he hadn't got <u>anything</u> to do with the recent spate of burglaries.

9. There isn't <u>yet</u> a sign that relations between the two countries are improving.

10. This untalented and boorish 'artist' shouldn't <u>ever</u> be allowed in here again.

11. We haven't seen <u>some</u> of the applicants <u>yet</u>.

12. The relief bus can't <u>already</u> have arrived to pick up <u>any</u> of the stranded passengers.

Task five **

Complete the following text by adding one of the following negative words:

few	*little*	*neither*	*never*	*no*	*nobody*
none	*nor*	*nothing*	*nowhere*	*rarely*	*scarcely*

As I was looking for the fruit juice this morning, I found there was
_____ any left in the refrigerator. I wondered why there was so
_____ of it so early in the week, but _____ Pam _____ Ruth
could give a reasonable explanation. "Well," I sighed, "I suppose there's
_____ to be done about it."

   Going back to the refrigerator, I also found that there were very _____
oranges left. And as for grapefruits, there were _____ whatsoever.
This was something that had _____ happened before. I was about to
ask Pam and Ruth again, but they were _____ to be seen any more. As
I had _____ to turn to now, I saw _____ option but to hurry to
the shop around the corner. _____ had I felt so let down by my two
roommates, sending me off to the grocer's on an empty stomach like this.

Task six **

When you have completed the above text, try to express negation in an alternative way by using synonymous phrases where possible.

> Example: *I have <u>nowhere</u> to go these days.*
>
> ⇒ *I <u>don't</u> have <u>anywhere</u> to go these days.*

13.9. Denial and affirmation 2

Section 263; 586–587

- Occasionally a negative word only applies its meaning to a phrase or part of a phrase elsewhere in the sentence.
- Non-finite clauses are made negative by placing not before the verb phrase.
- With main clause verbs like believe, suppose and think the element not can be transferred from the subclause to the main clause.

Task one ***

Replace the underlined phrases with alternative expressions requiring the use of *no* or *not*, keeping the meaning (more or less) intact.

> Example: *Donald is <u>only moderately</u> gifted.*
>
> ⇒ *Donald is <u>not particularly / not especially</u> gifted.*

1. <u>Lack of</u> news is good news.
2. Hubert gave me a <u>rather unconvincing</u> reply.
3. <u>Only some</u> of the students disliked their history teacher.
4. It is <u>quite usual</u> for tribespeople to behave in this extraordinary way.
5. A <u>rather important</u> detail was overlooked by all those present.
6. Beatrice did sell her caravan, but <u>with</u> some regret.
7. Most observers agreed that the workers' demands were <u>quite reasonable</u>.
8. <u>The absence of</u> electricity means that people have to live in primitive circumstances.
9. In spite of everything, <u>some</u> of these deprived children are <u>happy</u>.
10. The President will visit South Korea in the <u>relatively near</u> future.
11. Dyslexia in children <u>quite frequently</u> goes unrecognized for years.
12. We can put off the scheme for some time, but <u>there is a limit</u>.

Task two **

Replace the underlined part with an infinitive OR an *-ing* clause, keeping the meaning intact.

1. I tiptoed through the room <u>so that I wouldn't wake up the sleeping toddler</u>.
2. <u>As I couldn't tell the difference between the twins</u>, I asked them both to wear name tags.
3. The ideal solution would be <u>if drivers didn't think of their vehicles as race cars</u>.
4. <u>The fact that you aren't rich</u> doesn't necessarily mean that you are unhappy.
5. Mr Templar was the only person <u>who didn't drink a single drop of alcohol</u>.
6. Laura was livid with rage as <u>she hadn't been invited to the wedding party</u>.
7. The instructor began by telling us <u>how we should not respond in an emergency situation</u>.
8. One student objected to <u>the fact that he didn't have access to the Internet</u>.
9. Most observers expect <u>there won't be too many problems</u>.
10. As <u>I didn't know</u> where to go, I simply decided to stay at home.

Task three **

Transfer the negative element to the main clause in the sentences making up the following dialogue.

Amy: Boris, I think I won't be coming to your party after all.
Boris: No problem. I suppose nobody will miss you.
Amy: What a rude thing to say! I believe you don't realize how badly some of your guests behaved last month.
Boris: Well, I expect that bunch of lager louts won't show up this time. They haven't been invited.
Amy: Oh, good. You see, I thought I would have no chance at all of enjoying myself with them around.
Boris: Look, I'm sorry about what I said. I suppose you wouldn't be willing to change your mind?
Amy: Hmm. I feel I shouldn't give in too easily. I can be very stubborn, you know.
Boris: Yes, I do know that. Still, I would expect you not to be too stubborn, just for my sake.
Amy: Turning on the old charm again? OK, you win. I think I shouldn't make you feel miserable for the rest of your life.
Boris: Great! I believed I could never win you over. Thanks for proving me wrong.

13.10. Denial and affirmation 3

Sections **264–269**; 611–612

To emphasize the positive meaning of a sentence or to deny what someone has suggested or supposed, the intonation nucleus is put on the
operator. When the negative is not contracted, the nucleus falls on *not*.

Shortened forms can be used to affirm a question or statement or to
deny a statement.

The construction *not/n't . . . but* is used to deny one idea and to affirm
another, contrasting, idea.

Task one **

Respond to the following sentences by denying them. Use complete sentences, indicating the intonation-nucleus.

> Example: *The postal workers have decided to go on strike, I hear.*
>
> ⇒ *They haven't decided to go on strike (they still have to vote on it).*

1. There won't be an inquiry into the railway disaster then?
2. So the new stadium isn't going to be built after all?
3. Where did you buy that garden swing?
4. What a shame your visitors arrived so late!
5. You can't lend a hand with these heavy cases, I suppose.
6. Surely this organization has secret funds somewhere?
7. Why do you keep refusing to learn a foreign language?
8. Teachers shouldn't get upset when children skip classes, I would think.
9. This great innovator deserves special praise, surely?
10. I wonder when Jane and Dick are coming over for their annual holiday.
11. Clearly, your sister doesn't want to see me any more now.
12. Tell me, why hasn't anyone called an ambulance?

Task two **

Complete the following dialogue by adding short affirmations (A) or short
denials (D).

Lynn: Mark, are YOU interested in history?
Mark: (D) ...., I think it's extremely boring.
Lynn: You are not being serious.
Mark: (D) .... People should be interested in the future,
not in the past.

Lynn: I hope you understand that SOME people take an interest in the past.

Mark: (A) ...., it's just that I've always disliked the subject.

Lynn: You probably had teachers who insisted on students remembering lots of dates.

Mark: (D) .... as a matter of fact. One of them even got the dates wrong himself.

Lynn: Well, he can't have been fully qualified for the job.

Mark: (A) .... He told us one day that Napoleon had died in 1812.

Lynn: Oh, he should have said 1821, of course.

Mark: (A) .... And he claimed that the Battle of Waterloo had taken place in 1805.

Lynn: That was an even more stupid thing to say.

Mark: (A) .... So I became convinced that history was a subject for nerds.

Lynn: And you didn't want to become a nerd yourself.

Mark: (A) .... That's why I started reading science fiction novels instead. They are very interesting books indeed.

Lynn: (D) .... Nothing's more boring than sci-fi. Anyway, librarians will take such unscientific books off the shelves in the years to come.

Mark: (D) .... Some of those books are works of literature. You've never read Wells, Huxley ... Orwell, I suppose.

Lynn: (D) ....

Mark: Well, there you are! We seem to agree at last.

Task three **

Complete each of the following sentences by adding another, contrasting idea.

1. Geoffrey isn't particularly gifted, but ...

2. I don't earn a fortune, but ...

3. This country may not be a model democracy, but ...

4. The tropics don't really appeal to me, but ...

5. Melissa shouldn't be suspended from school, but ...

6. We couldn't find the ticket office, but ...

7. I didn't sell my film script to the national broadcasting company, but ...

8. This article deals not with the collapse of communism, but ...

9. Our secretary DOESN'T speak foreign languages, but ...

10. The suspect DIDN'T plant the bomb, but ...

Modifying

14.1. Restrictive and non-restrictive meaning

Sections 110–112

Modifiers before or after the noun help to specify the meaning exactly.

There is also a non-restrictive type of modifier, such as a non-defining relative clause.

Sometimes a modifying adjective before a proper noun can be non-restrictive.

Task one **

Modify and make more restrictive the items below by adding one of the phrases here. Each phrase may only be used once.

delayed; from Latvia; heavy; Hungarian; local; marketing; on the hill; that went bankrupt; who reported the crime; for sale

1. the house
2. the business
3. the history society
4. a visitor
5. a fall of snow
6. the manager
7. the President
8. the 6.45 train
9. the woman
10. the school

Task two **

The noun phrases below could have restrictive (R) or non-restrictive (N-R) modifiers. Show how the meaning would differ in each case.

1. The large animal parks are now closed.

2. The old houses in the main square were razed to the ground.

3. The unreliable train services have upset the travelling public.

4. The Finnish students enjoyed the course.

5. The hard-working students were given a week's break.

6. The democratically sophisticated voters wanted equality and transparency.

7. The under-staffed hospitals may get more money.

8. The French teachers had good exam results.

9. The poor students had to work during the vacation.

10. The famous portraits by Reubens attracted a lot of attention.

Task three **

Show how the pairs of phrases may differ in meaning.

1. Naïve French paintings	French naïve paintings ......
2. The first sunny day	The sunny first day ......
3. Their second disastrous game ...	Their disastrous second game ...
4. Classical Greek music	Greek Classical music ......
5. Her last romantic novel	Her romantic last novel ......

14.2. Post-modifiers

Sections **641–649**; 70; 106; 110; 128; 132; 151; 170; 194; 198; 392; 443; 470; 531; 589; 593; 596; 654; 686–687; 728; 740

Modifiers after the noun head are called post-modifiers. There are several types of post-modifiers:

● relative clauses

● prepositional phrases

● non-finite clauses equivalent to relative clauses

● appositive clauses

● clauses of time, place, manner and reason

● adverbs

● adjectives.

In addition two or more modifiers can modify the same noun.

Task one ***

Join the pairs of sentences and define the type of post-modifier.

1. I'll always remember that moment. The lawyer realised he'd lost the case.
2. What you wrote in that article about the new laws offended people. The people had fought hard for changes in the law.
3. You don't have to go there. There's no reason.
4. We have to do it this way. There is no other way.
5. It's next to the old building. They're going to pull down the old building.
6. The doctor will have time. He can see you.
7. I'll do it some time next week. I'll be free then.
8. There is just one reason. He should not be allowed to go.
9. That's the best play. If you want to see something good.
10. That was not the right time. You should not have done it then.

Task two **

Rewrite the relative clauses and rewrite them as other types of post-modifiers.

1. I shall be detailing the plans in a paper which I'll distribute next week.
2. Everyone who worked in that department was angered by the proposal.
3. The couple who live next door both work in the Social Studies department.
4. All those who are wary of walking too close to the edge of the cliff should stay near the leader.
5. Hillary and Tensing were the first men who got to the top of Everest.
6. I have nothing which I have to do this afternoon.
7. People in the train that was delayed for three hours were given a full refund for the ticket.
8. There is no more which anyone can do.
9. I have nothing which I want to say.
10. The train which goes to London will leave from platform 4.

14.3. Pre-modifiers

Sections **650–653**; **440**; **459**; **522**

Modifiers after a determiner but before the noun head are called pre-modifiers.

There are several types of pre-modifiers:

- adjectives
- adjective phrases
- *–ing* participles
- *–ed* participles
- nouns.

In addition two or more modifiers can modify the same noun.

Task one **

Underline and identify the type of pre-modifier.

1. Is that a new car?
2. It's better than being an anorexic model.
3. They were sworn enemies.
4. It's in the published text.
5. There's still a very long way to go.
6. That's an interesting question.
7. The train company is in great trouble.
8. It's a government organisation.
9. That's a very exciting idea.
10. There's the punishment room.

Task two **

Modify the noun underlined with pre-modifiers based on the information in the sentence. Put hyphens where necessary.

1. That house is Victorian and part of a terrace.
2. He was wearing a jersey that was red and made of lambswool.
3. He was a man who had made himself successful.
4. The table was designed artistically and made of oak.
5. The institute financed itself.
6. The television was very old and only showed films in black and white.
7. The car was an estate with three doors.
8. The student worked hard.
9. That rose flowers early.
10. The date on the credit card shows when it will expire.

Task three ***

Complete the sentences below by putting the modifiers in the correct order before the noun.

1. We've had some .... weather this year. (very wet, English, Spring)

2. He bought a .... rug in Switzerland. (oriental, beautiful)

3. They loved the .... beer. (German, strong, wheat)

4. He had the accident during the .... vacation. (university, summer, long)

5. She admired all the .... surfers. (Australian, strong, blond)

6. The business was a sold to a .... company. (textile, very small, French, unknown)

7. He loved the .... hills. (south-facing, Welsh, craggy)

8. The sheep were lost on the .... mountains. (snow-covered, cold)

9. He's a .... man. (patient, very kind, old)

10. It tasted like that .... wine. (dessert, Hungarian, classic)

Task four **

Underline the pre-modifiers in the text, and classify them as i) adjective; ii) noun; iii) genitive; iv) -*ing* participle; v) -*ed* participle; vi) compound; vii) numeral.

> The famous Manchester flat cap, designed to keep off the rain and act as a shield against bailiffs, foremen and wives, is to enjoy a new lease of life as a symbol of the Commonwealth Games.
>
> At the risk of splitting northern opinion between the modernisers who abhor "flat cap syndrome", and the nostalgics who wallow in it, the headgear will top off the official uniform of thousands of games staff and volunteers.
>
> Made of cotton cloth, dyed a no-nonsense northern black, the squashy symbol defeated the all-conquering baseball cap in a play-off for the games contract. Melding the tested shapes of the Yorkshire pudding beret and Soviet worker's cap as worn by Lenin, it was launched yesterday in the homely setting of a Manchester Asda supermarket.
>
> "We're particularly pleased with it as a concept," said Beth Watson, chief designer for the supermarket chain, which is running-up over 125,000 pieces of uniform as part of its sponsorship for the 11-day event in July and August.
>
> The cap is the nearest thing to a traditional item in the kit for Crew 2002, as the helpers, enablers and greeters will be known. It comes with a snazzy bag, water bottle, poncho and umbrella.
>
> (from *The Guardian*, 6 March 2002)

14.4. Relative clauses

Sections **685–694**; 110–111; 371–372; 461; 595; 659; 747

The main function of a relative clause is to modify a noun or phrase. There are several relative pronouns to choose from. The choice depends on:

● whether the clause is restrictive or non-restrictive

● whether the head noun-phrase is personal or non-personal

● what role the pronoun has in the relative clause.

The uses of relative pronouns are shown in this table:

	Restrictive & non-restrictive		Restrictive only
	Personal	Non-personal	Personal & non-personal
Subjective	who	which	that
Objective	who(m)	which	that, ZERO
Genitive	whose	of which, whose	

Task one *

Match the clauses in column A with those in column B.

A	B
1. I didn't get the job	a. that gave me no spare time.
2. That's the room	b. which I will not put up with.
3. There was a time	c. I applied for.
4. I couldn't do a job	d. in which there were often huge rats.
5. I don't know the woman	e. when people helped each other.
6. Australia is a country	f. you mustn't go into.
7. That's something	g. at the top of which was an old stone monument.
8. They got to the moon in the year	h. who you were talking to.
9. They climbed the hill	i. which is very arid in the centre.
10. During the war they hid in cellars	j. in which I was born.

Task two **

Link the clauses below with a relative pronoun, omitting the part of the second sentence corresponding to the relative pronoun.

1. It is something. I'm expected to do it.

2. She was a clever woman. The company exploited her.

3. He was an actor. No-one had ever heard of him.

4. I like being married to a chef. His sister owns the restaurant.

5. I enjoyed the production of 'No Man's Land'. Ian Holm starred in it.

6. I've finished the book. You got as a prize.

7. How do you like living in the town? You work there.

8. It was a lovely day. We went to Brighton then.

9. He's got a new computer. He can't use it.

10. He told me about it in the letter. The letter came this morning.

Task three **

Complete the following text by using a relative pronoun. On some occasions the pronoun will be governed by a preposition.

The wide range of skills and trades ......(1).......... was needed to maintain a big Victorian country estate is shown by the large number of workers ......(2)...... were on the staff of any large manor house. At Wallington, Northumberland ......(3).......... was the home of Sir Charles Edward Trevelyan (1809–86), ...(4).......... was the second baronet, there were over 30 male staff most ......(5).......... would have lived on the estate. There would also have been a large female staff most ......(6).......... work would have been within the house. Photographs from the late 19th century ......(7).......... male and female staff are always shown separately reflect a bygone way of life ......(8).......... we find little has survived in the great houses of today. On the Wallington estate, there is still a saw-mill ......(9).......... three foresters are based, but such posts as footman and rabbit-catcher have long disappeared. These have been replaced by employees ......(10).......... are known as education and events staff.

(adapted from the *National Trust Magazine*, no. 95, Spring 2002)

Task four **

Rewrite the phrases below with a reduced relative.

1. The bike which was tethered to a tree ....

2. The house which was in need of repair ....

3. The man who was driving too fast ....

4. Any company which hides its accounts ....

5. The article which discussed the use of nuclear power ....

Task five *

Rewrite the following sentences with a sentence relative.

1. He's working very hard now and this is a good thing.

2. Jane's finished her thesis and that's amazing.

3. Jack's working in Tokyo for two years. Then he's hoping to go to Hong Kong.

4. The old lady died on her husband's birthday. That's sad!

5. The train was an hour late. This was not unusual.

14.5. Apposition

Sections 470–472; 397; 589; 593; 646

Two or more noun phrases which occur next to each other and refer to the same person or thing are said to be in apposition.

Just like **relative clauses**, appositions can be restrictive and non-restrictive.

Task one **

Rewrite the sentences so that the relative clause is replaced by a noun phrase in apposition to the person or thing referred to.

1. David Brown, who owns the garage across the road, has a good reputation.

2. Mrs Davies who is a teacher at the local school is loved by all the children.

3. Anne and Peter Austin, who are the executors of my aunt's will, have retired and gone to live in New Zealand.

4. I once knew James Kane who was the star in last year's Oscar-winning movie.

5. John Williams, who writes poetry, has won several prizes.

6. That building over there was designed by James Stirling who was a celebrated architect in the 1970s and 80s.

7. The production is by Richard Jones who directs both opera and theatre.

8. I always book my holidays at Compston's which is the travel agency opposite the bank.

9. Impact 92 which is a language consultancy does a lot of work in Scandinavia.

10. Nokia which is now a mobile phone company started as a company selling rubber goods such as tyres.

Task two **

Look at the uses of apposition in the items below and decide whether they are restrictive (R) or non-restrictive (N-R) and make the appropriate changes to the punctuation.

1. A: David James has bought the house next door to mine.

   B: Which David James? David James our old school friend or David James the dentist?

2. (on the phone) Hello! Is that Robert Hunt the builder?

3. I was at university with the actor James Marlow.

4. Barbara Castle the British socialist politician died on 2 May 2002.

5. One of my oldest friends is Keith Godard the New York-based graphic designer.

6. Your doctor John Beasley is retiring next year. Did you know?

Task three ***

Complete the text below with an appropriate expression to show explicit apposition. *chiefly; especially; for example; for instance; in particular; mainly; namely; notably; particularly; such as*

In the late 1940s, after the Second World War, there was a flowering of the film industry in many countries, ...(1)............ India, Italy and Japan. There were many good, young film directors, ...(2)............ in Italy, ...(3)............ De Sica, Rosselini and Visconti. Working as assistants for them were several young people who would later become directors of world-importance, ...(4)............ Antonioni and Fellini. These directors established a clear identity for the Italian film, ...(5)............ the neo-realist cinema. In the same way, Asian film directors, ...(6)............ Kurosawa in Japan and Ray in India, established an identity for the Japanese and Indian cinema.

Modality

15.1. Agreement and disagreement

Sections **270–273**

It is often a good idea to be polite when agreeing or disagreeing with another person's opinion.

- When agreeing with an unfavourable opinion, we can qualify the agreement with an expression of regret.
- When we deny or contradict what has been said, we can disagree tactfully by softening the denial or contradiction in some way.
- Sometimes we may only partially agree with what has been said. Then we can qualify our agreement with a statement that suggests another view.
- We can also strengthen our agreement by adding comments which give further support to what has been said.

Task one *

Make a qualified agreement or tactful disagreement with the following unfavourable opinions.

1. I didn't like that movie at all. It was a very silly story.
2. The management made a big mistake employing that woman.
3. The food in that restaurant is always undercooked.
4. He comes up with some stupid ideas. And the latest is the worst.
5. Fancy painting a door that colour!
6. You really can't believe everything he says.
7. United played a poor game on Tuesday. They shouldn't have won.
8. He's not the man for the job. That's the problem.
9. The book had some good ideas, but in the end it amounted to nothing.
10. The exam results were very poor this year.

Task two **

Make enthusiastic or emphatic responses to the utterances below.

1. United should have won last Tuesday.
2. The exam results won't please everybody.
3. I loved that film. I could see it again.
4. What a beautiful picture that is!
5. You can always rely on him to give a good presentation.
6. The trouble is there aren't any real leaders in politics any more.
7. It was a very good course.
8. I've given up the car. On long journeys, the roads get so crowded.
9. I'm not sure John's going to be very happy working under Alan.
10. Didn't you enjoy that play!

Task three **

The underlined responses to the utterances below may be thought somewhat "impolite". Soften them in some way to make the disagreement more tactful.

1. A: I really didn't like that film. B: It was very good.
2. A: The government must do what the people want. B: Nonsense. The people want so many different things.
3. A: Well done, the Danes. No to the Euro! B: That's not a very sensible attitude.
4. A: She's the most stupid person I've ever met. B: That's very unfair.
5. A: They shouldn't have let him become a member. B: He works very hard for the club.
6. A: He's not a very good teacher, is he? B: I like him.
7. A: I don't like any of these paintings. B: Why not? Some are good.
8. A: I didn't understand anything he was talking about in that lecture. B: It was very clear to me.
9. A: There's never been a better time to invest in securities. B: Whatever gave you that idea? I wouldn't do it.
10. A: He must be the richest man in the country. B: There are a lot of people richer than him.

15.2. Fact, hypothesis and neutrality

Sections **274–282**; **416**; **493**; **589**; **609**; **706–708**

There are many statements where truth or falsehood is assumed rather than directly stated.

Fact is usually expressed by a finite verb or by an *-ing* clause.

Hypothesis is usually expressed in the past tense in dependent clauses. Here the past tense has nothing to do with past time, but refers to the present or future time. Often this is done with a conditional clause, but there are other expressions that can be used.

Neutrality is often expressed by infinitive clauses or a *wh*-clause in reported speech.

This can also be expressed with the use of *should* or the *subjunctive*.

Should is also used to express **factual** and **hypothetical** meaning.

Task one **

Mark each of the underlined dependent clauses in the following sentences as **fact** (F), **hypothesis** (H) or **neutral** (N)

1. I'm glad you decided to come.
2. It's time you came to visit me.
3. I'm surprised they let you out.
4. The best thing for him is to resign.
5. I wish you had decided to come.
6. If we'd been in Hungary in 1999, we'd have seen the total eclipse.
7. Did you know James was going to marry Emma?
8. If I were you, I'd refuse to do it.
9. If he should postpone the meeting again, we won't have time to submit the application.
10. I doubt if the application will succeed anyway.

Task two **

Add one of the following initial phrases to the utterances below to make each one **fact**, **hypothesis** or **neutral** as stated.

Did you know that

Do you know whether

Had you known

I'd be surprised if

I doubt whether

I'm glad

It's time

Should you get the job,

Suppose

They were surprised

1. would you be willing to move home so that you are not so far from the office? (H)
2. Colin was hurt during the raid? (N)
3. Anna got the job. (H)
4. we had a change of government. (H)
5. NATO had ignored the situation. (H)
6. most of the charity money from the Lottery goes to projects in the capital? (F)
7. Jane's settled in Barcelona at last. (F)
8. about Ian and Judith, would you still have come on this holiday? (H)
9. when they got the letter confirming the loan. (F)
10. we'll ever know the whole truth. (N)

Task three **

Compare the pairs of sentences below and give reasons for the use of *should*.

1. If he comes, give him my apologies for not being here to greet him.
   If he should come, give him my apologies for not being here to greet him.
2. It angers me that people are given honours just for doing their job.
   It angers me that people should be given honours just for doing their job.
3. He says the race will take place next year.
   He says the race should take place next year.
4. I'm surprised he's invited.
   I'm surprised he should be invited.
5. The government has decided to incorporate Human Rights legislation into British law.
   The government has decided that Human Rights legislation should be incorporated into British law.

15.3. Degrees of likelihood

Sections **283–292**; 461–463; 483; 501; 542

We need not always think in terms of truth or falsehood. There is also a scale of likelihood.

Certainty (or Logical necessity) expressed with *must* or *have to*

Ability expressed with *can, be able to, be capable of*

Predictability expressed with *will* or *must*

Probability expressed with *should* or *ought to*

Possibility expressed with *can, may, could, might*

Tentative possibility expressed with *could* or *might*

Improbability expressed with *shouldn't, oughtn't to, it is improbable/unlikely that*

Impossibility expressed with *can't, may not, mustn't*

Task one ***

Describe the degrees of likelihood shown in the sentences according to the list below.

Possibility of the fact

Possibility of the idea

Impossibility

Hypothetical possibility

Tentative possibility

Ability

Hypothetical ability

Certainty or logical necessity

Hypothetical necessity

Prediction and predictability

Probability

1. If the people were persuaded that the Chancellor was lying, the government could lose the next election.
2. He might have been lying.
3. You don't have to be good-looking to be a star, but it helps.
4. Don't worry. Gerry's probably on his way by now.
5. You shouldn't have any trouble with this.
6. I'm sorry. There must have been a fault in the connector.
7. My grandmother must have been having children over a period of almost thirty years.
8. The politician couldn't give his view on the matter because of forthcoming legal proceedings.
9. There will be fighting in the streets if he claims to have won the election.
10. Do I have to put down every single detail of what I've done during the day?

Task two **

Complete the sentences below with a modal verb or phrase showing the degree of likelihood shown in brackets at the end of the sentence.

1. Surely they .... have chosen him. He's such a difficult person. (Impossibility)

2. There .... be someone in this room who saw the accident. (Logical necessity)

3. There ......(a)........ be at least forty people at tonight's meeting, and there ......(b)........ be fifty or even sixty. (a) Probability; (b) Possibility of fact

4. It's not your fault. Someone .... have told him. (Certainty)

5. He's not up to the job. He .... make decisions. (Negative ability)

6. Anything .... happen if you drive when you're tired. (Possibility of the idea)

7. .... that the northern ice cap will have melted by the end of the century. (Possibility of fact)

8. If I .... do that, I'd just walk out of the job. (Hypothetical possibility)

9. .... she still be the head after all the trouble there's been? (Possibility of fact)

10. The train didn't stop in time. There .... be something wrong with the braking system. (Logical necessity)

Task three ***

Rewrite the following sentences replacing the modal verb with a suitable expression reflecting the degree of likelihood shown by the modal verb.

1. Well, she may get the grades she needs for university entrance.

2. Jobs have got to go. The company has to restructure itself.

3. Don't worry. They will give in in the end.

4. The play should have started by now.

5. John could make that business work if he wanted to.

6. There might have been an accident. You don't know.

7. After all these years, she can't still be living in Brook Street.

8. There should be a bus home after the concert. After all, the concert finishes at 9.30.

9. She may not be the best 400-metre runner in the world, but she deserves a place in the team.

10. I must be dreaming. It can't be you after all these years.

Task four **

Rewrite the sentences below, replacing the phrase underlined with a modal verb where possible.

1. It was <u>necessary</u> for someone to tell him to stop; otherwise we'd have had a lot of trouble from the management.
2. Right from the beginning, <u>it was very unlikely</u> that they would have selected her for the team.
3. It is <u>possible</u> that by mid-century people will be taking holidays on the moon.
4. It is <u>almost certain</u> that the financial director was in deep trouble and has chosen to disappear.
5. It's <u>not necessary</u> to finish the project by the end of the week. The boss told you he doesn't want the results until the end of the month.
6. It's a pity for the old people, but, <u>unavoidably</u>, the bus service will be cancelled. Hardly anybody uses it.
7. <u>Do you know how to</u> increase the fonts available on this computer?
8. <u>It's possible</u> for them to order a review of the way the money was spent.
9. <u>They are bound</u> to have questioned her about the missing documents.
10. <u>If it were necessary</u> to choose, would you want to do research or to teach?

15.4. Attitudes to truth

Sections **293–297**; 508; 587; 733

To express attitudes to the truth, we often use: a *that*-clause; a *wh*-clause; an adverbial or a comment clause.

We express such attitudes as **certainty**; **doubt** or **uncertainty**; **belief** or **opinion**; **assumption**; **appearance**

Task one **

Look at the examples below and then describe ways of showing attitudes to the truth and what each one of the examples expresses.

1. I just know that he won't be here on time.
2. There's no doubt that, by expressing her disapproval of the plan in such a manner, she upset all her colleagues and lost the argument.
3. You did take down all his details, I presume.
4. Obviously he was going to tell us.
5. It's unlikely that she will be willing to take on that job.

Task two **

Complete the statements below with a suitable word or phrase which reflects the attitude shown in brackets after the statement. Avoid using a word similar to the one in brackets – e.g. for item 1, avoid using the verb 'assume'.

1. I .... you've made all your travel arrangements. (assumption)

2. .... nobody bothered to check if the customer had been properly informed. (appearance)

3. ...... my ...., the case should never have gone to court. (opinion)

4. It's my .... she actually arranged for books to arrive too late. Then she could have the test delayed. (belief)

5. Everyone has .... been told that they will have to come in to work on Sunday. (assumption)

6. It .... to me that we're all to blame for the accident. (appearance)

7. David really .... he could persuade the company to give him special leave. (belief)

8. Pete was rather naïve to believe that story, ...? (opinion)

9. The chairman .... that everyone will make special arrangements to be able to attend the meeting. (assumption)

10. I ...... (not) .... we should ever have gone to war over such a minor issue and one that didn't concern us. (opinion)

Task three **

Rewrite the statements below replacing the phrase underlined and state whether your rewritten phrase shows a) a belief or opinion; b) an assumption; c) an appearance; d) certainty; e) doubt or uncertainty.

1. I think the newspaper report suggested she had committed suicide.

2. He really believes the world revolves around him.

3. It appears that she never had the ring in the first place.

4. I assumed you knew exactly what the results of such an action would be.

5. In my opinion, we should give in now and take what we have.

6. It looks as if he's not coming.

7. It is my belief that during this century overhead cables will disappear and all telecommunication and electricity supplies will come via satellite.

8. You do know, I presume, that this work must be completed within two weeks.

9. You did behave rather stupidly, didn't you? Telling him he'd made a fatal error of judgement.

10. I suppose he's got there by now.

15.5. Volition

Sections 319–324

We distinguish four types of volition. These are listed in order of increasing strength.

(i) **Willingness**: this is expressed by the auxiliary *will* (or *'ll* informal). For past or hypothetical willingness, use *would*.

(ii) **Wish**: for neutral volition *want* is less formal than *wish*. For hypothetical circumstance, use only *wish* or the exclamatory *if only* . . . When expressing your own wishes or inviting the wishes of others, you can make the wish more tactful by using *would like*, *would prefer*, *would rather*. *Should* can replace *would* for the first person. *Shall I/we* is another way to consult another person's wishes.

(iii) **Intention**: This is expressed by the verbs *intend*, *plan* and *aim*. It can also be expressed by *be going to*, or, in the first person by *will* or *shall*.

(iv) **Insistence**: This can be expressed by *insist* or *be determined* and also by *will/shall* with a strong stress.

Task one ***

Rewrite these examples avoiding *will/would* or *shall* and using another verb construction to convey nearly the same meaning. If there are any noticeable differences of meaning, say what they are.

1. The government will press ahead with the new security bill in spite of strong opposition.

2. Shall we work together on this new project?

3. She wouldn't spend time watching programmes like *Coronation Street*. She considers them to be trivial and no more than a fantasy world.

4. The chairman won't postpone the shareholders' meeting just because the venue is considered to be too small.

5. They will help you in the garden. They enjoy doing that.

6. I would put money into it if they could guarantee a minimum return for the investment.

7. Would you like to be rich and famous like Cliff Richard?

8. I'd like her to succeed. She's worked very hard.

9. The minister won't admit he was wrong about the Sports stadium.

10. Ivan would like Tim to teach with him in Hungary.

Task two **

Complete the sentences with an appropriate verb or phrase.

1. I .... help you with your luggage, sir.

2. He's very rich and he loves the old art gallery. He .... leave a lot of his money to look after the building.

3. I .... this work finished by the week-end.

4. I .... to thank all of you for the contribution you have all made to our success this year.

5. They .... they'd bought the house now, instead of renting.

6. .... you'd told me about the problem.

7. The room's too small and too noisy. I .... another one. There must be somewhere in this hotel where I can rest comfortably.

8. .... I get the tickets?

9. They .... stay until the end of the performance, although it doesn't finish until after midnight.

10. He's like that. He ......(always)........ do everything himself. He never asks for help.

15.6. Permission and obligation

Sections 325–329; 483

The tasks below examine ways of expressing:

Permission

Obligation

Exemption

Prohibition

Task one **

Identify the meanings expressed in the following sentences by completing the chart below.

1. If you were a member, you could get in free.

2. Could I take my holiday at the end of August?

3. You must return those books by the end of the week.

4. Children under fourteen should have parental permission to see this film.

5. If he's the leader, he should know the way.

6. You mustn't walk on the grass.

7. You can't park there.

8. Can I stay overnight? It's too late to drive back now and I've drunk too much.

9. If you have a season ticket, you don't need to book a seat in advance.

10. But you can't go that day. It's Joan's 60th birthday party.

Permission:	
Hypothetical permission:	
Obligation or compulsion:	
Hypothetical obligation:	
Prohibition:	
Exemption:	

Task two **

Below are the rules for a Karate Club. Show what meaning is expressed in each rule with the appropriate letter.

A Permission, B Hypothetical permission, C Obligation, D Hypothetical obligation, E Exemption, F Prohibition

This club is dedicated to the high performance of karate

1. All members must regularly satisfy the committee that they have maintained the standard they achieved at the previous supervision.

2. Any member failing to do so will not be allowed to continue without further training.

3. Members who agree to a prolonged period of supervision will not need to undergo further training, unless there is sign of improvement.

4. Members may decide what they prefer to do.

5. The annual two supervisions must be completed within twelve months of the second supervision in the previous year.

6. If the member of the committee is deemed to be unsympathetic, members do not have to submit themselves for supervision at that time.

7. Such a refusal must be submitted in writing one week before the supervision.

8. Members can appeal against the result of supervision.

9. Members don't have to undergo periods of supervision, if they are seeking advice from a personal trainer.

10. Members must not challenge other members who have not reached the same standard.

11. Each member will carry at all times the card showing the standard he/she has achieved.

12. This card must be seen by an opponent before a challenge is accepted.

Task three **

You are writing to a friend who is looking for a job as an assistant teacher in Britain. Tell him/her how to do it and how to get the best out of his/her time here. Use the sentence topics in the function boxes below and find an appropriate modal verb to express the function required. Pay attention to the construction of the whole sentence.

Example: *in my opinion – spend some time in Britain – improve your English (obligation)*

Answer: *In my opinion, you must spend some time if Britain if you want to improve your English.*

1. write to head teacher of a school at once. (obligation)

2. pay your travelling costs to Britain. (obligation)

3. register with the police. (exemption)

4. take no disciplinary action yourself – unruly pupils. (prohibition)

5. take your car to Britain if you want. (permission)

6. contact anyone you know who has done this before. (permission)

7. arrive in Britain at least three weeks before the beginning of the term. (obligation)

8. live more than four miles from the school. (prohibition)

9. attend any special induction courses. (exemption)

10. take pupils out of school without special permission. (prohibition)

15.7. Influencing People 1

Sections 330–335 & 339; 417

The tasks below examine ways of expressing:

Commands

Requests

Advice

Suggestions

Warnings

Promises

Threats

Task one **

1. Choose what kind of communication the following utterances are.
   a) command; b) request; c) advice; d) suggestion; e) warning; f) promise;
   g) threat; h) invitation
2. Indicate where the important stress is.

1. I wonder if I could join you for lunch.

2. Please stop doing that.

3. Won't you sit down?

4. You stay at home and do your homework.

5. You ought to get out more.

6. How about going to see the new exhibition at the Royal Academy?

7. Careful!

8. I'll be sure to put it in the post for you tomorrow morning.

9. You come here again and you'll regret it.

10. Hands up or I shoot!

Task two **

Complete the utterances below by adding a word sequence to make each
the form of communication shown at the end of the item.

1. .... It's a very slippery surface. (warning)

2. I want the money by Thursday .... (threat)

3. .... let me have a small advance until the end of the
   month. (polite request)

4. .... be back here by eight o'clock. (command)

5. .... possibly postpone the meeting until early in the
   New Year. (request)

6. .... It's a very popular play. (advice)

7. I'll be there. .... (promise)

8. .... on Monday instead of tonight? (suggestion)

9. .... a good holiday. (advice)

10. .... me for a good night out. (invitation)

Task three **

Complete the dialogues in the situations below with the various forms of communication stated.

SITUATION ONE

A: This is a very good room.
B: Yes. It's good for my work here.
A: Work a lot do you?
B: At home, yes. I'm quite busy now.
A: That must be nice. Working at home.
B: Yes.
A: But you're busy. I mustn't bother you.
B: No.
A: There is just one thing.
B: I am very busy. ....

B wants A to leave. Write

a) a request

b) a command (be careful not to be rude)

c) a suggestion

SITUATION TWO

A: The government isn't going to allow you to testify.
B: I have important things to say.
A: You mustn't say them.
B: Why not? In a democracy, you're free to say anything.
A: The government isn't happy.
B: Is that important?
A: ....

A doesn't want B to testify. Write

a) a request

b) a prohibition (be careful not to be rude)

c) a suggestion

d) some advice

e) a threat

f) a warning

SITUATION THREE

Mother: The river's very deep here.
Child: Please can I go for a swim. I won't go far.
Mother: All right. But remember ....

The mother tells the child to be careful. Write

a) a warning

b) a weakened command

c) some advice

SITUATION FOUR

A is discussing plans to build a double garage with his next-door neighbour.

A: Those bricks for us to build a garage are coming today.
B: How many will there be?
A: I don't know. I just gave them the measurements for my part and your part.
B: I don't want them in my garden.
A: Does anybody? But some are for you. We don't want to upset the other neighbours.
B: No. But –
A: ....

A insists B accepts some of the bricks. Write

a) a warning

b) a suggestion

c) some advice

d) a request.

15.8. Influencing People 2

Sections 336–338 & 340; 608; 730

The tasks below examine ways of expressing:

Commands

Requests

Advice

Suggestions

Prohibitions

Refusals

Warnings

Promises

Threats

. . . in reported statements.

Task one *

Match the direct statements in A with the indirect statements in B.

A

1. Pauline, let David tell us himself.
2. You can be sure I'll be at the station to meet you.
3. Why don't we spend the day walking in the hills?
4. No parking.
5. You come home late and you won't be allowed out again for a month.
6. Be careful if you go walking in the hills alone.
7. Could you help me with this work, please?
8. No, I'm sorry. I haven't the time.
9. Could I go to see that film with you?
10. Sit down!

B

A. It is forbidden to park here.
B. She asked if she could go to see the film with him.
C. He refused to help as he didn't have the time.
D. He told him to sit down.
E. They told Pauline to let David tell them himself.
F. He asked her to help him with the work.
G. She suggested they spent the day in the country.
H. His father threatened to keep him home for a month if he came home late.
I. She was warned about walking in the hills alone.
J. She promised to be at the station to meet him.

Task two **

Write the original statements. There could be several possibilities for each item.

1. John suggested that he and Mary invested in the new company.
2. Mrs McNorton warned her son not to go near the station after dark.
3. They asked her to stand for President of the society.
4. The doctor told her to do more exercise.
5. The politician refused to support his government on the matter of lowering taxes.

6. They threatened to sue the newspaper if it didn't publish an apology.

7. He promised to give back all the money he'd borrowed by March.

8. He was prohibited from going into the club until he had paid his debts.

9. It was recommended that they should spend at least four weeks travelling round Australia.

10. Customers were told flights would be delayed because of a strike in France.

Task three ***

Write the reported statements for the statements below, using an appropriate verb according to the description in brackets at the end.

1. Management: There will have to be some redundancies. (warning)

2. Boss: You're definitely being considered for promotion. (promise)

3. Rob to Don: Let's finish the work tonight, so we can have a free day tomorrow. (suggestion)

4. Shirley to Mary: You couldn't lend me £50, could you? (request)

5. I wouldn't invest in a dot com company, if I were you. (advice)

6. You must finish this by nine o'clock. (command)

7. You finish this quickly or we stay here all night. (threat)

8. Club rules: No member can introduce a person under eighteen years old into the club. (prohibition)

9. Secretary to Manager: The report will be on your desk tomorrow morning. (promise)

10. Will you get the tickets for me. (request)

Addressing

16.1. Vocatives

Sections 349–350

Vocatives such as *Alice, Mr Pym, Dr Hyde* are often used to get someone's attention.

Other vocatives mark the speaker's relation to the hearer. They can range from formal (*Sir, My Lord, Your Excellency*) to informal (*daddy, my dear*).

Some occupational vocatives (*waiter, driver*) may sound impolite. A good alternative in such cases is the expression *Excuse me!*

Task **

Add suitable vocatives to the sentences below, taking into account the addressee(s) mentioned in brackets.

1. I'm sorry it took me so long to answer your letter. (your pen friend Sarah)

2. Your European allies are fully behind you. (the elected leader of the United States)

3. Come over here! (your brother Eric)

4. Could you put me through to Mrs Alice Hawkins, please. (telephone operator)

5. I wish you a very happy birthday. (your grandmother)

6. May I have your attention, please. (a mixed audience of adults)

7. The witness has been traumatized by the events. (an American judge)

8. Shall I prepare you a candle-lit dinner tonight? (your sweetheart)

9. Report back in ten minutes! (private Harry Slocombe)

10. Can I use your car tomorrow? (your father)

11. Do you think I'll make a complete recovery? (your GP)

12. Please accept our sincere apologies. (the ambassador of Australia)

16.2. Commands

Sections 497–498

2nd person commands involve the use of the imperative verb, often accompanied by the downtoner *please*: *Shut* the door (*please*).

The only auxiliary used in commands is *do*, also in combination with *be*: *Stay* here./*Do be* quiet.

The implied subject *you* is sometimes expressed overtly, although this can sound impolite: *You stay* here!

1st and 3rd person commands often involve the use of the verb *let*:

– *Let me* answer your question first./*Let's* go now.

– *Let each nation* decide its own fate./*Someone* help me, please.

Task one **

Complete the following extracts using one of the imperative forms below:

be	bear	beware	climb	cross
keep	leave	make	take	turn

Teign-e-ver Bridge leads onto an island formed where the river divides. _____ the island by the other bridge and _____ for Scorhill Circle to the north. _____ the meandering track that passes to the right of the stone circle. (. . .)

_____ careful not to miss the deflection from the main track at the first clearing. _____ half-right here along a lovely path that threads through bluebells and begins to descend steeply. When it reaches the river, _____ right along a shady riverside path until you reach the footbridge. _____ here and _____ a steep path to reach a broad drive at the top. (. . .)

At the top the gate through which the footpath passes bears a sign saying, '_____ of the Bull'. _____ the hedge on the left to a gate at the top of the field (the bull, one hopes, being busy elsewhere).

(adapted from *Dartmoor Walks*, p. 47)

Task two **

Rephrase the sentences below, using a 1st or 3rd person command.

1. I would just like to give you another example.
2. I would like the two of us to go for a drink.
3. I would like somebody to move all that stuff out of the way.
4. I think they'd better eat cake.
5. It would be better not to pretend that we support the idea.

6. I would like to warn you just one more time.

7. We had better settle the problem once and for all.

8. There should be no doubt at all about our resolve.

9. I would like us to move as fast as we can.

10. I don't really want to detain you any longer.

Focusing

17.1. Focusing information

Sections 396–401; 744

Tone units represent the way we structure information when speaking.

A general rule is that a tone unit is the way we separate each piece of information.

Each tone unit has a nucleus which marks the focus of information in the unit.

Often, the nucleus is at the end of the tone unit, or rather on the last major class word. This is known as **end-focus**.

Sometimes, however, it is shifted to an earlier part of the tone unit when the speaker wishes to draw attention to something which is in contrast to something already mentioned or understood in the context. This is known as **contrastive focus**.

Task one **

In the following statements, mark the places where you would expect the boundaries of tone units. Some positions for a tone unit are more certain than others. Where you think the boundary is certain, mark it II. Where it is less certain, mark it I.

1. I like Kent, but I prefer Sussex.

2. I find that with so many of these problems – marriage, sex education – as soon as you try to make it a sort of formal lesson, the whole thing falls flat.

3. The fact that Burti feels only bruised and battered after the accident with Schumacher is a measure of the progress we have made on the safety measures over the past two seasons.

4. We had our breakfast in the kitchen and then we sort of did what we liked.

5. We took some children to the environmental study centre the other day, and they have various animals around there.

6. And the thing is that the journalists – I mean I've met some of these people – they know nothing about the country at all.

7. Spectator sports are dying out. I think people are getting choosy. There's more to do, of course. More choice.

8. Sundays in London. If we're all working or cooking or things like that, it can get fearfully dull.

9. Dave rang me about this business of changing the groups.

10. Of course the children have their own inhibitions about talking about sex. They're just not frank about it.

> (from D. Crystal & D. Davy (1975) *Advanced Conversational English*, Longman)

Task two ***

For each item in Task One, explain which of the following general rules informed your decision.

a. clause or adverbial phrase at the beginning of the sentence

b. non-restrictive modifier in the sentence

c. medial phrase or clause

d. vocative or linking adverb

e. a clause or long noun phrase acting as a subject

f. two or more clauses are co-ordinated

g. (overriding rule) each piece of information deserves a separate tone unit.

Task three ***

Mark the nucleus in each of the tone units in the following items. (Some items need more than one nucleus.) Show whether the tone is falling, rising or fall-rise. There may be more than one solution.

1. She's been painting that door for three days now.

2. Sue teaches at the school in Queen Street.

3. No. Sue teaches at the school. She's not the social secretary.

4. A: That's a fine penguin. Are you taking it to the zoo?

    B: No, I took it to the zoo yesterday. I'm taking it to the cinema today.

5. I saw that film at the Duke's.

6. It was the film version of Orlando that I saw at the Duke's.

7. The phone's ringing.

8. Ivan lives in London in King Street.

    He lives in London, but he also has an apartment in Cambridge.

9. Can you understand all that? If you can't, just phone again.

10. I want more time, more money and more coffee.

11. The editor was John Wrigley.

12. Studio production was by Paul Moore; the editor was John Wrigley.

Task four **

Mark the nuclear tone in the underlined clauses below. (Where necessary divide a single sentence into more than one tone unit.)

1. Weren't you working in Berlin last summer?
   No. It was the summer before last.

2. You haven't visited our new art gallery.
   Yes, I have. I've been several times.

3. All the voting papers were sent out early, but only forty-six per cent of the voters replied on time.

4. He gets a lot of work on television, but he's not a very good actor.

5. They say he was very good in that job. I say he's just an opportunist who arrived at the right time.

6. Have you still got that old car? Yes. And it still drives well.

7. Why have you changed your e-mail address? I haven't. The one I gave you was incorrect.

8. It looks as if it will take ages to get there, but the time will fly past.

9. I can't learn things just by reading the instructions. I have to be hands-on.

10. Give him another chance. He's had four already.

Task five **

Below is an interview given by a TV star. The answers have been changed. Rewrite the answers, so that the important information becomes its end-focus.

1. What is your idea of perfect happiness?
   A good meal with good friends is perfect happiness for me.

2. What is your greatest fear?
   It is drowning that I fear most.

3. With which historical figure do you most identify?
   Queen Victoria, a small lady, is the most obvious one.

4. What is the trait you most deplore in others?
   An inability to laugh at yourself is something I hate.

5. What vehicles do you own?
   A car is the only one I have.

6. What is your greatest extravagance?
   Shopping is something I love to spend money on.

7. What is your greatest regret?
   Life is too short and that I regret.

8. How would you like to die?
   Suddenly and painlessly is what I hope it will be.

9. How do you relax?
   Crossword puzzles are a great form of relaxation.

10. What is the most important lesson life has taught you?
    To take each day as it comes is the most important thing I've learned.

17.2. Organising information – Given and new information

Sections 402–407

Given information is something which the speaker assumes the hearer knows already

New information is something which the speaker does not assume the speaker knows about already.

Sometimes **given information** is not spoken but is suggested by the situation.

For the main information, we use a falling tone for emphasis.

For subsidiary or less important information, we use a rising tone.

In writing, the most important new information is saved until the end of the sentence.

Task one **

Indicate where the nuclear stresses should be in the following items.

1. "Did they enjoy Singapore?" "No, it was raining all the time."

2. "That's a lovely vase Anne gave you." "Joan gave it to me, not Anne."

3. The driver wasn't going very fast when he crashed through the barrier.

4. I know you find the noise from the trains disturbing, but here the planes are worse.

5. I took my holiday in Hungary.

6. There's someone at the door.

7. Can I speak to Alison, please?

8. Tell her it's Mike.

9. I went to Berlin in February because the U-Bahn was a hundred years old.

10. It's true. He won the lottery.

Task two **

(In 2001, Foot and Mouth Disease was widespread throughout Britain. Other countries in Europe were concerned about the disease spreading to their animals. Below is part of a document issued to travellers between Finland and Great Britain.)

Reorganise the sentences in the paragraphs in the following text where necessary to give proper emphasis to the main information in each case.

How to prevent the spread of foot and mouth disease to Finland

1. on 20 February
   in England
   the outbreak of foot and mouth disease was detected

2. since then
   in an explosive manner
   it has spread in the UK

3. the disease was found in England, Wales, Scotland and Northern Ireland by 2 March

4. the virus causes foot and mouth disease only in hoofed animals
   in horses and people
   but may cause a transient infection

5. hoofed animal species include
   cattle, pigs, sheep, goats, deer, reindeer and elks

6. no risk for humans
   the disease causes

7. you may use diluted citric acid available from pharmacies
   as a disinfectant

8. as pets may transport the virus
   wash them thoroughly with shampoo after arrival
   if you bring animals to Finland from the risk areas

9. it is the duty of travellers to be cautious
   as the situation in the UK is critical

10. for at least 48 hours
    where animals are kept
    do not visit premises

17.3. Organising information – Order and emphasis

Sections 411–414

Instead of the subject, you can make another element the topic, by moving it to the front of the sentence. This shift gives the element a kind of psychological prominence, and has three different effects:

(i) Emphatic topic

(ii) Contrastive topic

(iii) Semi-given topic.

Task one **

Indicate which type of topic is fronted in the following sentences –
Underline the fronted element E–emphatic topic; C–contrastive topic;
S–semi-given topic.

1. Some awful films they have recommended.

2. Poor they may be, but they are generous to a fault.

3. Most of this work an assistant should do.

4. Some days he works very late, but others he's home by lunch-time.

5. Hard work you say it is!

6. Not many people want to live in an old property; but new houses in a traditional style, buyers are willing to pay a lot for.

7. Stupid he isn't, but he's often careless.

8. Romantic novels you can buy cheaply; serious works you must pay a lot for.

9. You're diving straight into the pool. This I must see.

10. I'm good at remembering people's names. Street names I always forget, though.

Task two **

Rewrite the following sentences so that the part underlined is the topic of the sentence. State what kind of topic it is.

1. They just don't look after that cat properly.

2. The company has already put into practice these new working conditions.

3. They show some foreign films, but they don't show the really important ones.

4. He may be very clever, but he isn't practical.

5. She behaved in a very strange way at the meeting.

6. They painted the house an awful colour, didn't they?.

7. His speech at the funeral offended a lot of people.

8. I don't understand the reason for this celebration.

9. They gave the money to her; but they gave the painting to him.

10. The management looked into the problems you're speaking about last week.

Task three ***

Rewrite the following letter freely, making the following elements of the story into topics: i.e. subject or fronted topics:

story structure

shifts between characters

name of main character

movement of characters in the story

descriptions

the philosophy

opportunity for others

Dear Edward,

Many thanks for giving me a chance to read your story. I think it is of importance to all people like us and most will find it reflects their own experience. I was very impressed by the structure of the story. I liked the way the story shifted back and forth between the two protagonists and, because of this, shifted between the seasons to show the development of the main character. I was a bit frightened by the introductory monologue. I think this was because I am shy of exposing myself and you had written this in the first person. I was relieved when I discovered you had called the character Tim. I liked the way the characters moved in and out of the story reflecting the parallels of experience.

I also liked the way you described the town, the sea and the vineyard. I could imagine myself there, especially by the sea and in the vineyard. I found the philosophy underpinning the story interesting. There is never a beginning. Where we think there is a beginning, it is really a development of ideas and events that have gone before. You conveyed this brilliantly.

Well done, Edward. Many thanks again for letting me read this. I hope others will have this opportunity. Your story has a lot to say.

Yours,

Ivan

17.4. Organising information – Inversion

Sections 415–417; 584–585; 590–594; 681–684

There are two types of inversion:

(i) Subject-verb inversion

(ii) Subject-operator inversion

Subject-verb inversion is normally limited as follows:

- The verb phrase consists of a single verb word in the past or present tense
- The verb is an intransitive verb of position
- The topic element is an adverbial of place or direction

Subject-operator inversion occurs when a negative element is fronted for emphasis.

Task one **

Give end-focus or end-weight to the parts of the sentences underlined below.

1. John's there by the fence.
2. The house for sale is over there.
3. Look, the person you want is there.
4. Rick is on the left; Nick is on the right.
5. Janet and Paul came down the road laughing and shouting.
6. The kite flew up into the sky.
7. John Nehemiah lies here – looking up at his friends.
8. The car of his dreams stood outside the house.
9. A city stood on the hill, proud surveyor of the valley below.
10. An enormous tree crashed down as the storm raged.

Task two **

Rewrite the sentences below to give greater emphasis to the negative element.

1. The government would only agree to bail out the company if the managing director quit.
2. England has never played better than with its new manager.
3. Your proposal doesn't touch on the real problem in any way.
4. The Prime Minister didn't make even the smallest concession to the opposition.
5. Their son not only failed his exam; he also refused the chance to repeat it.
6. They were not left a penny in their mother's will. All the money went to charity.
7. She had hardly had time to take in the new rules for welfare payments when she was put in charge of the office.

8. The head of department could do little to stop the erosion of confidence in any future developments.

9. He gave little away about his own future plans.

10. I've rarely seen such a poor display of sportsmanship.

Task three ***

Rewrite the passage using an appropriate form of inversion wherever possible, and where necessary a change of vocabulary, to achieve greater emphasis. The first one has been done for you. There are ten others.

<u>Eccles is not far from Manchester.</u> It is not only famous for its special cake; it also has the world's only swinging aqueduct, carrying water from the Manchester Ship Canal. Now the people of Eccles are afraid that no-one will come to experience these jewels. Why?

A town called Eccles is nowhere on the new ordnance survey map.

"We're very sorry about this. We rarely make such mistakes," confessed a spokesman for the ordnance survey team.

"They understand little about how we feel," said a town councillor. "I had hardly sat down at my desk this morning before the phone started ringing with complaints. I shall only be satisfied when we are back on the map."

Unfortunately, that can't happen in any way until the next edition of the map.

Another mistake is the map shows Ladywell and Salford Royal Hospitals. These hospitals no longer exist.

Residents of Eccles have seldom felt so confused and angry. "There's no way strangers to the region can find us now," sighed one resident.

Not far from Manchester is Eccles.

17.5. Organising information – Fronting with 'so/neither'

Section 418

So is placed first:

- as a substitute form with subject-operator inversion for end-focus
- as a substitute form without inversion to express emphatic affirmation
- for emphasis with subject-operator inversion when it introduces a clause of degree or amount.

In the case of a negative comparison, we use *neither*.

Task one *

Read through the information about the people below, then write sentences that show additional information using *so* as a substitute form with subject operator inversion.

	DAVID	MARC	MILES	SARA	ROWAN	HELEN
Born	12.5.64	29.3.78	16.6.69	9.3.69	4.5.53	29.6.64
Married	15.10.93	not yet	16.7.93	31.8.91	10.7.75	15.10.93
Children	2 boys, 1 girl	none	2 girls	2 girls	4 boys, 1 girl	2 boys, 1 girl
Education	university physics	until 16	university physics	until 18	until 16	university history
Work	pilot	clothes shop manager	teacher	secretary	housewife	journalist
Sport	most, esp. swimming	tennis only	none	most, esp. tennis	climbing	all sport, esp. swimming and climbing
Plans	go to USA next year	get married next year in USA	work in USA next year	France next year	buy a house in France next year	spend next year in USA
Wants	start own business	own his own shop	be a writer	be a teacher	be a writer	sail round the world

1. David read physics at university.
2. Marc hasn't been to university.
3. Sara is a keen tennis player.
4. Helen is fond of climbing.
5. Sara got married before 1993.
6. Rowan wants to be a writer.
7. Miles doesn't have any sons.
8. David got married in October.
9. Marc will go to America next year.
10. David wants to have his own business.

Task two **

Rewrite the following text so that, where possible,

1. *So* as a substitute form without inversion is fronted to express emphatic affirmation
2. *So* introducing a clause of degree or amount is fronted for emphasis.

The event was so catastrophic that most people couldn't take in the enormity of the disaster. In reality, the area covered was so small that the majority of the world could only look on in disbelief. However, the building was so enormous that, as it crumbled, it brought others down in its wake.

"We have seen the end of an era," claimed one commentator.
"We have indeed," replied the politician.
"I had friends in there."
"In fact, we all did."
"The world will never be the same again."

The messages that flashed round the world were so extraordinary that only pictures could help people understand what had happened. Commentators described the scene as if it were from a Hollywood movie so often that the comparison became devoid of meaning.

"I saw that film '*Independence Day*' ".
"We all did."
"It had scenes like this"
"It did indeed."

And the people were so shocked and frightened that they went home and left an eerie silence on the streets.

17.6. Organising information – Cleft sentences

Sections **419–423**; **496**; **592**

Cleft sentences

"*It*"-type:

- This construction is useful for fronting an element as topic and also for putting focus on the topic element.
- It cannot focus on the complement of a clause.
- It cannot focus on the verb, by using the substitute verb "*do*".

"*Wh*"-type:

- It can focus on the complement of a clause.
- It can focus on the verb, by using the substitute verb "*do*".
- It can be linked by the verb "*be*" to a demonstrative pronoun.
- It is more common at the beginning of a sentence.

Task one **

Rewrite the following sentences so that the focus (the underlined word) is a cleft with the introductory *It*.

1. I spent last week in Sweden not Switzerland.

2. No, Shakespeare wrote '*Much Ado about Nothing*' not Marlowe.

3. At the meeting of the fiscal committee, she supported the lower interest rate.

4. The prince was filmed by our camera crew.

5. Nobody will ever forget the 1960s.

6. My sister got married in 1969 not 1970.

7. I didn't tell them and I don't know who did.

8. We now face a global recession.

9. They bought the house as an investment, not to live in it.

10. Michael Apted directed the movie I liked.

Task two **

Rewrite the sentences below so that the part underlined is the focus using a "wh" cleft.

1. We now face a global recession.

2. I was working with the army, not the navy.

3. It isn't known when he will get here.

4. Emily Dickinson wrote poetry not plays.

5. Cybereconomics attracts the over fifties.

6. E-crime is on the increase.

7. The head of department needs the annual turnover figures tomorrow morning.

8. A last minute error delayed him.

9. The streets of London are paved with concrete, not gold.

10. Mick Jagger has become a film producer.

17.7. Organising information – Postponement

Sections 424–429

Postponement with introductory "it"
  This is used to postpone a subject clause for purposes of end-weight or end-focus:

● when the subject is a 'that' clause

● impersonal passive introduction

Occasionally it can be used to displace a clause in object position. This must occur when the object clause is a 'that' clause or an infinitive clause.
  It is also possible to postpone sentence elements to give more emphasis and to avoid awkwardness.

Task one **

Complete the sentences by starting each one with the introductory 'It' and adding one of the words or phrases here.

amazing, a problem, disappointing, expected, hard, lovely, not clear, stupid, very gratifying, very important

Example: .... *to see so much waste paper in the countryside. (annoy)*

It annoys me to see so much waste paper in the countryside.

1. .... to be here.
2. .... they will soon attack.
3. .... why the government was being so cautious.
4. .... that he failed his exams so badly.
5. .... how long elephants live.
6. .... to be proved right in this case.
7. .... to walk all the way to the university.
8. .... if you always refuse.
9. .... to predict what will finally happen.
10. .... for him to win the prize.

Task two **

Rewrite these sentences postponing certain elements to give them more emphasis or to avoid awkwardness.

1. A place for him to stay has been found.
2. The train coming from Berlin was late.
3. What a problem finding this address has been!
4. How serious about resigning are you?
5. The commander himself gave the order to shoot.
6. The manager himself paid for the breakages.
7. Footballers have more status than they used to as celebrities.
8. All the bills except the one for the new computer system have been paid.
9. He's earned more money in a year than his father earned in his whole life writing that one novel.
10. What a story about her adventures in Thailand she had to tell.

Task three **

Rewrite the report to make it sound more impersonal and authoritative, using introductory 'It' with passive verb forms to replace the underlined expressions.

People think that the British National Health Service is badly run, when generally many know that it is underfunded. You hear tales of vastly overcrowded hospitals, and frequently there are reports that people have had to wait months if not years for minor surgery. Set against this, however, is the fact that the British people value the principle of the National Health Service, and most people acknowledge that no government would dare try to dismantle it. When politicians suggest that there could be some kind of private investment, there is strong opposition; but, on the other hand, there is equally strong opposition, when they say that there will have to be tax increases to fund the service properly. Most analysts acknowledge that, in many ways, the service is the most efficient in Europe and that with more investment, it could be one of the best. There are many people who assume it will always be there, but there are also many who fear it will disappear because of lack of financial support. They don't appreciate how determined the government is to see it survive.

17.8. Organising information – Other choices

Sections **430–432**; 488; 608; 613–618; 730; 740

Choices of position
The passive can be used to give a sentence end-focus or end-weight.
The position of the direct and indirect objects can be postponed for the same purpose.

Task one **

Rewrite the sentences below to give end-focus or end-weight to the underlined sections.

1. How could he afford such a large house?
   His parents gave him the money.
2. They have proved the reasons he gave for meeting that woman false.
3. How did such a successful company collapse like that?
   The Chief Executive made some poor decisions.
4. In 2001, they gave Peter Carey the prize for the second time.
5. The writer checked the samples he'd been sent carefully.

6. Don't leave <u>work for the exam</u> to the last minute!

7. <u>That he'd done so well in his career</u> finally pleased his father.

8. <u>That Marc insisted on spelling his name with a 'c' instead of a 'k'</u> irritated his girl friend.

9. Ivan often failed <u>to contact his friends</u> for months.

10. Cathie asked <u>if she could leave early</u> for a second time.

Task two **

Give end-focus or end-weight to the sections underlined in the article below.

More than fifty years after the event, it is instructive to look at how honestly <u>Second World War leaders</u> treated the civilian population. Were we regarded as delicate flowers? Did they give <u>all the truth and nothing but the truth compatible with security</u> to us?

"There may always be another reality. To make fiction of the truth we think we've arrived at," said the playwright, Christopher Fry. Goodness knows he saw enough reality in the pioneer corps.

<u>Beady-eyed people who have second thoughts about mighty events</u> are revisionist historians. They can really make a veteran's moustache bristle and steam gush from his ears. <u>Burrowers and snufflers through the once-secret archives</u> sometimes force us to face freshly revealed unpalatable truths: in the war, there was the usual tarnished brass – <u>cowards, deserters, psychopaths and black marketeers</u> supported the military geniuses, heroes, yeomen who were worthy of their country.

17.9. Organising information – Avoiding intransitive verbs

Sections 433–434

We tend to avoid predicates consisting of just a single verb as there is a feeling that the predicate of a clause should be longer or grammatically more complex than the subject. This is connected with the principle of end-weight.

Task **

In the following comment, Lionel is talking about himself to Miriam. Rewrite the text by using a more complex predicate: replacing *drank* by *had a drink*.

"You must excuse my chatting away like this, my dear. It's so long since anyone called round, especially an old friend like you. The children have all gone away now. I know I could visit, but I don't like to travel much now. Christine is living in the south of Portugal. I visited her. I suppose it's a lovely spot. Nice beach. Every day at ten o'clock, Christine swims. Then in the afternoon from two to four, she rests. I got bored being there. It's like that really, I suppose. We older folk always had to work hard. They work very little. They've got the money. I don't know how. Don't like to ask. And they're so organised. Everything has to be in its place. You won't believe this, but one day, Tom . . . He's her husband, partner . . . I don't know what they call them now. Well, Tom was showering. Suddenly he shouted. We rushed upstairs. Couldn't get in. The door was locked. I kicked the door hard. It didn't give. Christine called out, asking what was wrong. You really won't believe this. They have a lot of plants in the bathroom. He'd noticed two were out of place. I couldn't live there. They have different standards from us. But then we knew hard times. We did, didn't we? Will you dine with me tonight? Please do. It's been such a long time. We'll have my best wine."

Answer key

Spoken and written English

1.1. Informal spoken English

Sections **17–19**

Task one **

Non-grammatical features: *er(m)* (×7) / *you know* (×2) / repeated elements (suggesting stammer), especially in line 4 / *WHOOSH!*

Grammatical features: *me* (instead of 'my') / half a dozen sentences beginning with '*and*' / free direct speech: *She said fill it up . . .* / subject dropped in two sentences beginning with '*Was . .*' / omission of other sentence elements: *Just take it back . . .* (= answers '*what*' in preceding sentence) – *Straight across the counter. – Dust coal everywhere.*

Task two **

We lived in Cambridge when I was young. One day, my mother got very angry because the coal had some rocks and bits of scale in it. She told me to get a strong bag and fill it up with the coal and stuff. Then we took it by bus to the coal office at the bottom of Hills Road Bridge. Inside the office, there was an old oak table, about as long as this room. I thought she was just going to take it back and tell them coal wasn't very good. But she went in, bent down, picked up the bag and threw it straight across the counter. There was coal dust everywhere. "Take it back," she said. "And come and get the rest of it." They couldn't believe it. I can see their faces today.

Task three ***

1. At the polling station tell the clerk your name and address. It's on the front of the card. After that the Presiding Officer will give you a ballot paper. Make sure that he or she stamps it before they give it to you.

2. Then you go to one of the booths. You'll see some instructions, telling you how to vote. The main thing is that you can only put one cross in the box next to the name of your favourite candidate. Some people put two or three crosses, but these votes are not counted.

3. Now suppose you've made a mistake. That would mean you've spoilt your ballot paper. No problem, though. You just show it to the Presiding Officer and they'll be happy to give you another one.

4. Then fold the ballot paper into two. Show the official mark to the Presiding Officer, but be careful; no one should see who you voted for. The last thing you do is, of course, put the ballot paper in the ballot box and then simply leave the place.

5. There are also two alternative ways of voting. You can, for example, appoint somebody else to vote for you. Such a person is called a proxy. However, some people change their mind at the last minute and want to vote themselves. No problem again, as long as the proxy hasn't voted before you.

6. The other alternative is postal voting. That's a different thing. Once you've been allowed to vote through the post, you can't change your mind anymore.

Task four ***

1. – *(your name and address) as shown on the ballot paper*: as + past participle clause sounds very official

   – *(s)he*: conventional gender neutral way of referring to any male/female (person), only used in writing

2. – *(Mark only one cross) as stated in* . . . : as + past participle clause (cf above)

   – *alongside*: (slightly) more formal preposition than 'next to'

   – *place*: more formal than 'put' (= lexical feature)

3. – *if by mistake you* . . . : rather formal word order

4. –

5. – *you may*: rather formal way of granting permission

   – complex sentence: *if*-clause + infinitive clause, followed by main clause, followed in turn by *if*-clause and time clause

6 – fairly complex sentence

   – *to be entitled to* . . . : expression which is typical of official documents, regulations, etc.

General comment: None of the imperatives in the original text is preceded by the covert subject 'you', while this is quite common in spoken English.

1.2. Cooperation in conversation

Sections **21–23**

Task one ★★★

1. Comment on features of turn-taking:

   – At first turn-taking is restricted to brief contributions by S2 (*laughs/ yes/yeah*).

   – When S3 joins in, he makes a truly interactive comment, followed by a question addressed by S2 to S1. This is followed in turn by a counter-question by S1 addressed to S2.

   – Next we get a succession of discourse markers by all three speakers. The third speaker (S3) goes on to add an interactive comment, is briefly interrupted by S2, then completes his comment and also gets a minimal response from S1.

   – S3 elaborates on his comment, which contains an indirect question. S1 abruptly answers his question and gets '*laughs*' from both S2 and S3.

   – S1 'takes the initiative' again, contributing several sentences. S2 asks for further information, which S1 hesitates to answer straight away. S2 helps to get S1 'going again'.

   – S1 resumes where she left off and continues her story. At first she gets a minimal response from S3 and a somewhat more meaningful one from S2. Towards the end of the conversation the balance between S2 and S3 shifts, with S2 only producing minimal responses to what S1 is saying and S3 participating in a more meaningful way.

2. Discourse markers:
   (i) purely interactive: (*laugh*) – *oh* – *yes* – *er* – *yeah* – *yeah* – *yeah* – *yeah* – (*laugh*) – (*laugh*) – *yeah* – *er* – *er* – *oh* – *mmm* – *oh* – *yeah* – *oh* – *mmm* – *mmm*
   (ii) mainly interactive: *you see* – *well* – *you see* – *now* – *you know* – *that's right* – *well* – *you know* – *you know* – *er* – *well* – *no*
   (iii) also interactive: *maybe* – *maybe* – *anyway* – *of course*

1.3. Tag questions and ellipsis

Sections **24–25**; 684

Task one ★

1. didn't you; 2. didn't it; 3. aren't they; 4. will we; 5. didn't it; 6. has he; 7. do you; 8. would it; 9. aren't I; 10. won't we

Task two *

1. He is . . . ; 2. I . . . ; 3. It's . . . ; 4. It was . . . ; 5. You're . . . ; 6. You . . . ;
7. I . . . ; 8. He will . . . ; 9. You will . . . ; 10. We've . . .

Task three *

1. I . . . ; 2. Would (or: do) you . . . ; 3. I . . . ; 4. I('ve) . . . ; 5. I . . . ; 6. Could
you . . . ; 7. It . . . ; 8. I . . . 9. Do you . . . ; 10. We've . . .

Task four **

1. Hope you don't mind me asking, but you really threatened to resign?
2. Can't believe a word he says.
3. Saw them out together last night. Getting on very well, aren't they?
4. Didn't help you were half an hour late.
5. Gotta get this in the post by tonight.
6. Doesn't matter if you don't get the best grades.
7. Don't know why he thought we weren't coming.
8. No problem about leaving so early.
9. Didn't bother to let him know, did you?
10. Can't help thinking we should have done more to help her.

1.4. Coordination

Section 26

Task one **

1. Be late again and you'll be fired.
2. He's been to Italy, and now he wants to live there.
3. John can't answer the question and neither can Mary (or: and Mary can't either).
4. Go to the new coffee bar and you'll meet Sally there.
5. You've been paid, be happy now.
6. Irene can't understand this new tax form and neither can I (or: and I can't either), and we're both accountants.

   Or: Irene and I are both accountants and yet neither of us can understand this new tax form.

7. That tree will grow higher and damage the telephone lines.

8. Stop eating so late and you'll sleep better.

9. The Wilsons went to Egypt for their holiday and so did the Brooks.

10. He upset the old lady, so I don't want to meet him.

Task two **

1. If you finish that work tonight, you can take the rest of the week off.

2. Now (that) he's got the manager's job, he won't speak to his old friends.

3. Now they've got a new car, they will be telling everyone how much it cost.

4. I don't like that house because it's too dark and miserable.

5. Now that / Because he's been all over the world, he thinks he knows everything.

6. Now that we've changed our money from Francs to Euros, everything costs more.

7. As the fire spread quickly, the whole factory was destoyed.

8. The crowds were waiting patiently at the sides of the road, when suddenly it began to rain.

9. If you get there late, they won't let you in.

10. If you get the early train, you'll have a good day in the city.

1.5. Finite clauses in spoken English

Section 27; 360–374

Task one **

1. He won the race and enjoyed the prize money.

2. The boy had been in trouble in school before and was afraid to tell his mother why he was home so late.

3. He had missed the last train and stayed at his sister's overnight.

4. He felt ill and decided not to go work that day.

5. The theatre had been built in 1903 and was too big for small, contemporary plays.

6. A number of mothers were interviewed who were not in paid work, and the majority of them intended to return to work when their children were older.

7. The stairs were very steep, so it was an accident waiting to happen.

8. He took the dog for a walk across the fields and realized that the new road they were going to build would go very near his own house.

9. She read the biography of Sophia Loren, and determined to become an actress.

10. He got home late and found everyone had gone to bed.

Task two ***

1. Peter reminded Anne about the visit, hoping she would come.

2. Having reorganized the shop, they still didn't get a lot of customers.

3. (On) seeing her in the street, I told her the good news.

4. Having bought an old house and modernized it, they made a lot of money when reselling it.

5. On getting to the top of the hill, you get a good view over the plain.

6. Not liking that stuff they gave us to eat last night, I left most of it.

7. Having gone to a lot of trouble to get the picture, he expected they would pay him a good price.

8. They felt very depressed, their team having lost for the third time.

9. Not having been to Mexico before, I don't know what to expect.

10. Although we yelled at the top of our voices, nobody took any notice.

1.6. Stress

Sections 33–35; 633; 743–745

Task one *

1. The 'rain in 'Spain 'stays 'mainly in the 'plain.

2. The 'tourist for'got to 'buy a 'ticket at the 'counter.

3. 'Janet is 'throwing a 'party for her 'twentieth 'birthday.

4. We 'met in 'Rome, 'visited the 'sights and 'then 'flew 'home.

5. 'John is 'fond of 'chocolate but 'Mary 'thoroughly dis'likes it.

6. I was ad'miring the 'landscape that un'folded in 'front of my 'eyes.

7. This unex'pected en'counter with my 'worst 'enemy 'really up'set me.

8. Do you re'member the dra'matic e'vents of Sep'tember the e'leventh?

9. The U'nited 'Nations de'cided to 'lift the em'bargo im'posed on 'military e'quipment.

10. As a 'true 'democrat, I sin'cerely 'hope that de'mocracy will 'always pre'vail 'over 'tyranny.

11. 'Slow 'progress has been 'made in per'suading the 'warring 'factions to ac'cept a 'compromise.

12. The pho'tographer had 'taken a 'dozen 'pictures, 'all of which ap'peared in 'glossy maga'zines.

Task two **

Stressed: *off; in; up; by; out; on; by; un(der); down; out; off; on; on; out; down; (a)way; by; down; up; in; down; up; off*

Unstressed: *of; on; in; to; for; to; for; through; in; of; on; for; of*

Task three **

(a) prepositional adverbs: *off; in; up; by; out; on; by; down; out; off; on; on; out; down; (a)way; by; down; up; in; down; up; off*

prepositions: *of; on; in; to; for; to; for; un(der); through; in; of; on; for; of*

(b) prepositional adverbs are stressed, whereas prepositions remain unstressed unless they consist of more than one syllable, cf 'under'

1.7. Nucleus and tone units

Sections 36–37

Task **

1. | My only sister is married to an accountant. |

2. | Would you give me the bottle opener, please. |

3. | Shirley was watching a film by Alfred Hitchcock, | the master of suspense. |

4. | Hurricane Freddy swept across Indonesia last night | and is now heading for Japan. |

5. | Although the war has been over for years, | there are still occasional clashes along the border. |

6. | The new car model comes in four colours: | red, | dark blue, | grey | and white. |

7. | Driving on the left-hand side | is something most people get used to in no time at all. |

8. | I haven't got the faintest idea | if the evidence given by Karen | will prove her innocence. |

9. | Either your informant is completely ignorant of the <u>facts</u> | or he is deliberately dec<u>ei</u>ving us, | which is even w<u>or</u>se. |

10. | In contrast with conventional w<u>i</u>sdom, | forests in northern countries are exp<u>a</u>nding | rather than shr<u>i</u>nking. |

11. | The politician said he wasn't involved in the c<u>o</u>ver-up | but he w<u>as</u>, | as appeared from an incriminating d<u>o</u>cument | found in the flat of his former m<u>i</u>stress. |

12. | For Christ's s<u>ake</u>, | why couldn't you behave pr<u>o</u>perly | in the company of such distinguished g<u>ue</u>sts, | whose only f<u>au</u>lt was | that their English sounded slightly p<u>o</u>mpous? |

1.8. Tones

Sections 38–42

Task one **

1. rise: | Are any of these titles still av<u>ai</u>lable? |

2. fall: | Don't lean too far out of the w<u>i</u>ndow. |

3. fall-rise: | I don't want to spend <u>ALL</u> my dollars. |

4. fall: | How many passengers survived the pl<u>a</u>ne crash? |

5. rise: | You've seen some of these films bef<u>o</u>re? |

6. fall: | George Stephenson was the inventor of the st<u>ea</u>m engine. |

7. fall-rise: | In terms of profitab<u>i</u>lity |
   fall: | the current year has been quite exc<u>e</u>ptional. |

8. fall: | Why didn't you turn up at the m<u>ee</u>ting |
   rise: | because you had oversl<u>e</u>pt again? |

9. fall-rise: | Technically sp<u>ea</u>king |
   fall: | these devices are extremely soph<u>i</u>sticated. |

10. (fall-)rise: | If you haven't got enough time n<u>ow</u> |
    fall: | you can write those letters tom<u>o</u>rrow. |

11. fall-rise: | Edith may not be a very good c<u>oo</u>k |
    fall: | she knows at least how to appreciate good f<u>oo</u>d. |

12. fall: | There's a wide choice of ch<u>ee</u>se here |
    rise: | Ch<u>e</u>ddar |
    rise: | St<u>i</u>lton |
    rise: | Cam<u>e</u>mbert |
    rise: | Gorg<u>o</u>nzola |
    fall: | and Danish bl<u>ue</u>. |

Task two (suggested answers) ***

1. fall: | Members of the jury |
   fall: | I thank you for your attention during this trial. |
   rise: | Please pay attention |
   fall: | to the instructions I am about to give you. |
   (fall-)rise: | Henry Johnson |
   rise: | the defendant in this case |
   rise: | has been accused of the crimes of First Degree Murder with a
         Firearm |
   fall: | and Aggravated Assault with a Firearm. |
   rise: | In this case |
   fall: | Henry Johnson is accused of First Degree Murder with a Firearm. |
   rise: | Murder in the First Degree |
   rise: | includes the lesser crimes of Murder in the Second Degree |
   rise: | Murder in the Third Degree |
   fall: | and Manslaughter, |
   fall: | all of which are unlawful. |
   rise: | If you find Mr. Peter Smith was killed by Henry Johnson |
   rise: | you will then consider the circumstances surrounding the killing |
   rise: | in deciding if the killing was First Degree Murder |
   rise: | Second Degree Murder |
   rise: | Third Degree Murder |
   fall: | or Manslaughter. |

2. R: (fall-)rise: | Steve |
     fall: | where's my handbag? |
   S: fall: | Over there, |
     fall: | on the windowsill. |
     fall: | You're not going out shopping |
     rise: | are you? |
   R: fall: | Of course I am. |
     fall: | How else am I to prepare dinner tonight? |
   S: rise: | Oh |
     fall | I thought we were going to a restaurant. |
   R: fall-rise: | The last time we went to a restaurant |
     fall: | you kept complaining about the food. |
   S: fall-rise: | It was one of those very exotic places. |
     fall(-rise): | You know I don't like them. |
   R: fall: | What would you suggest then? |
     fall-rise: | As long as it isn't fish and chips, of course. |
   S: rise: | Well, shall we go to an Italian restaurant? |
     fall-rise: | That's not too exotic as far as I am concerned. |
   R: fall(-rise): | All right. |
     rise: | You still remember the terms of the agreement we made last
     time? |

S: fall-rise: | I <u>don't</u>, quite frankly. |
R: fall-rise: | In <u>that</u> case |
    fall: | let me <u>just</u> refresh your <u>memory</u>. |
    fall-rise: | Whoever chooses the <u>restaurant</u> |
    fall: | pays the bill for the <u>two</u> of us. |
S: fall: | You <u>will</u> have your <u>revenge</u> |
    fall: | <u>won't</u> you. |

Emotion

2.1. Emotive emphasis in speech 1

Sections **298–301**; 528

Task one *

Interjections: 1. *well*; *why*
2. *Christ*; *oh*
Exclamations: 1. *How brave . . . at home!*
Emphatic so/such: 1. *such*
Other emotive elements: 2. *goddamned*; *the hell*
Repetition: 1. *Down, down, down.*
2. *fought* (= echo);
We were . . . we were . . . and we . . . (= structural parallelism for rhetorical effect);
wider and wider;
a fight, an actual fight;
You were great. You were fantastic. You really were .... You were great!
Nuclear stress on certain words: 1. *nothing* (?); *anything* (?); *never*
2. *really*; *she*
(Note exclamation marks)

Task two (suggested answers) *

1. John Thaw was SUCH a brilliant actor.

2. WHAT A beautiful tie you're wearing!

3. That was an awful thing to say...... AN AWFUL THING ...... REALLY AWFUL.

4. HOW stupid of you to insult the ambassador like that!

5. I'm really disappointed .... DISAPPOINTED .... REALLY DIS-APPOINTED now.

6. The lounge is SO elegantly decorated.

7. It would be far better .... FAR, FAR BETTER to ignore that man altogether .... IGNORE HIM.

8. When I came back, I felt SO exhausted.

9. HOW SUDDENLY Joan's mood changed again!

10. The Wilsons are SUCH nice people.

11. WHAT a charming hostess Olive can be!

12. A bedbug .... A BEDBUG .... is a tiny .... TINY .... TINY creature.

Task three **

Helen: George, what <u>are</u> you doing so early in the morning?
George: I'm <u>awfully</u> sorry, but I <u>had</u> (or <u>DID</u> have) to get out of bed.
Helen: <u>DO</u> tell me what's the matter with you, then.
George: <u>Well</u>, I had the most <u>horrifying</u> nightmare.
Helen: You <u>will</u> have to calm down, you know. This <u>isn't</u> an isolated thing. Something <u>must</u> be bothering you.
George: I <u>can't</u> deny that. I've been <u>terribly</u> worked up lately.
Helen: I <u>DO</u> wish you'd tell me more. I <u>DO</u> have a right to know.
George: If <u>I</u> told (better: <u>DID</u> tell) you, you'd be <u>incredibly</u> angry.
Helen: You <u>DO</u> owe me an explanation. I <u>am</u> your wife, after all.
George: I decided to buy a <u>hugely</u> expensive car and it <u>could</u> ruin us.

Task four **

1. utterly; 2. tremendous/great; 3. absolute; 4. definitely; 5. gorgeous; 6. literally; 7. horrendous; 8. raving; 9. terribly; 10. really; 11. great/tremendous; 12. indeed

2.2. Emotive emphasis in speech 2

Sections 302–305; 417

Task one **

1. at all; 2. on earth/in heaven's name; 3. a bit; 4. a wink; 5. ever; 6. in heaven's name/on earth; 7. whatever; 8. a thing; 9. by any means; 10. a fig

Task two *

1. NEVER HAD I met the Sultan of Brunei before.

2. BY NO MEANS IS IT clear that the United States will sign the agreement.

3. NOWHERE ELSE ARE these magnificent flowers to be found.

4. NOT A SINGLE INSURGENT'S LIFE WILL the harsh ruler spare.

5. IN NO WAY SHOULD WE lend credibility to the witness's account of the facts.

6. UNDER NO CIRCUMSTANCES WHATSOEVER WILL I support Mr Barlow.

7. NOT UNTIL AFTER THE FIRST WORLD WAR DID British women get the vote.

8. NOT ONLY DID this evil man murder his wife, he also mutilated her body.

Task three ***

Dick: Oh boy, AM I tired!
Emma: You've NOT been overdoing it again, have you?
Dick: WHAT ALTERNATIVE have I got?
Emma: COULDN'T YOU ask me to lend you a hand from time to time?
Dick: ISN'T THAT a most generous offer!
Emma: DO I detect some irony in your voice?
Dick: HOW MANY TIMES HAVE I asked you in the past?
Emma: WASN'T I suffering from a depression then?
Dick: ISN'T hard work the best antidote to depression?
Emma: Oh, but DID I FEEL sleepy all the time, taking those pills!
Dick: WOULDN'T I have been a far better doctor for you, then?
Emma: Oh Dick, YOU ARE hopeless!

2.3. Describing emotions 1

Sections 306–308; 499

Task one *

1–e; 2–i; 3–g; 4–a; 5–l; 6–b; 7–c; 8–k; 9–d; 10–f; 11–h; 12–j

Task two **

1. AMAZINGLY most passengers of the crashed airliner escaped unhurt.

2. I would like to buy a flat, and PREFERABLY (to have) one with a good view.

3. TRAGICALLY, five skiers died in the avalanche.

4. Barbara FOOLISHLY carried thousands of dollars in her handbag.

5. UNFORTUNATELY too little is being done to protect the environment.

6. REGRETTABLY some people failed to appreciate my point of view.

7. LUCKILY I was not at home when the gas explosion occurred.

8. The government SENSIBLY launched a new campaign against drink-driving.

9. HOPEFULLY the economy will pick up again later this year.

10. The minister UNEXPECTEDLY handed in his resignation.

Task three **

Max: ....I'm afraid. Putting it more bluntly ....
Nora: .... to be honest.
Max: ....you see. What's more ....
Nora: ...., I believe, ...
Max: You bet ....
Nora: ...., so to speak, ..., I'm sure.
Max: ....., I see. ....

2.4. Describing emotions 2

Sections **309–318; 722–723**

Task one **

1. sitting; 2. to drive; 3. walking – cycling; 4. cooking; 5. to be;
6. performing/to perform; 7. sack(ing) – to introduce; 8. to say; 9. going;
10. to work; 11. being; 12. travelling – staying / to travel – to stay

Task two **

Basic emotion: 1. E; 2. G; 3. F; 4. B; 5. A; 6. C; 7. D; 8. E; 9. G; 10. C
Stronger emotion: 1. a; 2. b; 3. a; 4. b; 5. b; 6. a; 7. b; 8. b; 9. a; 10. a

Task three ***

Walt: Viv, I'm LOOKING FORWARD to indulging in a five-course dinner this evening.
Viv, I'm EAGER to indulge in a five-course dinner this evening.
Viv: UNFORTUNATELY you'll be stuffing yourself with fattening food again.
It's unfortunate that you'll be stuffing yourself with fattening food again.
Walt: I THINK IT'S STRANGE THE WAY you envy people who like a hearty meal from time to time.
IT'S SURPRISING THE WAY you envy people who like a hearty meal from time to time.

Viv: THE WAY more and more of those people are becoming overweight these days IS DISTURBING.

I'M CONCERNED THAT more and more of those people are becoming overweight these days.

Walt: HOPEFULLY, that's not going to happen to me.

That's not going to happen to me, I HOPE.

Viv: I'M SORRY you don't seem to realize that too much food is bad for your health.

IT'S A PITY you don't seem to realize that too much food is bad for your health.

Walt: I'M SURPRISED you don't realize that I'm taking a lot of exercise now.

SURPRISINGLY you don't realize that I'm taking a lot of exercise now.

Viv: I'M GLAD you've at least changed that part of your lifestyle.

IT'S GOOD you've at least changed that part of your lifestyle.

Walt: IT'S A PITY some of the physical activities make me feel exhausted.

WHAT A PITY some of the physical activities make me feel exhausted.

Viv: HOPEFULLY, as you lose weight, the activities will seem lighter too.

I HOPE THAT, as you lose weight, the activities will seem lighter too.

Structure

3.1. Clauses

Sections **486–495**; 151; 170; 198; 202–204; 211; 499; 573–577; 588; 613; 686; 718; 724; 727; 737; 739

Task one **

1. SVO[A]; 2. SV; 3. SVO; 4. SVOO; 5. SVOO[AA]; 6. SVC[A]; 7. SVC; 8. [A]SVA; 9. SVO; 10. SVC

Task two *

1. *when you've finished*: finite; 2. *ignoring the accident*: non-finite; 3. *babies among them*: verbless; 4. *to work for the charity*: non-finite; 5. *covered in mud*: non-finite; 6. *angered by the manager's attitude*: non-finite – *to resign her job*: non-finite; 7. *happy with the result*: verbless; 8. *sending lots of Christmas cards*: non-finite; 9. *him to leave*: non-finite; 10. *opening an art gallery in such a small town*: non-finite – *to do*: non-finite

Task three **

1. comparative: conjSV; 2. comment: VC; 3. nominal: conjSVO; 4. adverbial: [A]SV; 5. relative: SVC; 6. comparative: conj SVA; 7. comment: VC; 8. relative: SVC; 9. adverbial: conjSVO; 10. nominal: conjSV[AA]

3.2. Combinations of verbs

Section **739**; 735–737

Task one *

1. can do; 2. could have been; 3. are never going; 4. must have been built; 5. is being completed; 6. has been working; 7. has already seen; 8. can't be going; 9. might have gone; 10. hasn't made

Task two **

1. must have got up; 2. hadn't arrived; 3. was only just getting; 4. had been intending; 5. couldn't believe it; 6. were still locked; 7. should have remembered; 8. had been locked away; 9. would only be opened; 10. had been made; 11. had been losing; 12. hadn't done; 13. had lost; 14. couldn't

Determiners

4.1. Count and non-count nouns

Sections **57–69**; 510; 597–601

Task one **

set of keys; clump of trees; herd of cows; crowd of people; pack of wolves; swarm of bees; flock of sheep; stack of chairs; bundle of clothes; shoal of fish

Task two **

Note: some items may be interchangeable (e.g. 'load' and 'pile')

blade of grass; lump of sugar; cup of tea; block of ice; slice of bread; load of hay; pile of dust; sheet of paper; length of string; bottle of wine; piece of cake

Task three **

count nouns: *bank; book; carrot; engineer; group; joke; quarrel; year*
non-count nouns: *advice; behaviour; butter; clothing; conduct; education; furniture; homework; information; money; news; progress; scenery; shopping*
count & non-count nouns: *ceramic; cheese; fruit; industry; language; night; variety; work*

Task four **

1. pile; 2. bottles (or: glasses); 3. scraps; 4. flock; 5. clump; 6. haze; 7. cup; 8. piece; 9. herds; 10. flocks

Task five **

1. information; 2. is; 3. work; 4. needs; 5. variety; 6. skills; 7. need; 8. engineers; 9. have; 10. language; 11. experience; 12. management;

13. advice; 14. has ; 15. help; 16. situations; 17. seem; 18. weather; 19. is; 20. transportation; 21. is; 22. education; 23. is; 24. methods

Task six **

Vienna; Beijing; (South) Africa; Mayerling: U; past: U; diet: C; cake: U; beef: U; potato: C; dish: C; wine: C; wood: C; sensation: C; apartheid: U; city: C; conversation: C; greatness: U; reference: C; way: C; question: C; rank: U; status: U; influence: U; romantic: C; story: C; prince: C; mistress: C; baroness: C; pact: C; house: C; tale: C; predilection: C; city: C; Sunday: C; grave: C; churchyard: C; command: C; time: U; lady: C; – age: C; affair: C; guest: C; case: C; trace: C; irony: U; daughter: C; bourgeois: C; tram: C; familiar: C; suit: C; middle: shopping: U; bag: C; umbrella: C; toaster: C; electrician: C; stare: C; ketchup: U; charm: C; absurdity: U; cosiness: U; anarchist: C; flesh: U; people: (irregular) plural only; child: C; father: C; majesty: C; day: C; attitude: C; glue: C; flavour: C; adhesive: C; envelope: C

Both C and U: cake; wine; wood; conversation; reference; rank; status; influence; predilection; age; irony; charm; absurdity; majesty; attitude; glue; adhesive

Both C and plural only: people

4.2. Amount and quantity

Sections 70–81; 675–680; 697–699

Task one **

2. (D); 3a. (P); 3b. (P); 4. (P); 7. (D); 10a. (P); 9. (P); 8. (P); 1. (D); 10b. (P); 6. (D); 5. (P)

Task two **

1a. the staff considered collectively; 1b. the members of staff considered individually ⇒ same basic meaning

2a. a number of students (= not all of them); 2b. theoretically, all of them ⇒ different meaning

3a. whichever date is chosen (= positive); 2b. neither one date nor the other (= negative) ⇒ different meaning

4a. whichever date is chosen (= only one date needs to be chosen); 4b. the two dates suggested (= two dates need to be chosen) ⇒ different meaning (this may depend on context, though)

5a. there were some names he couldn't remember; 5b. there were no names (at all) he could remember ⇒ different meaning

6a. a very small number number indeed (= negative); 6b. a relatively small number (= more positive) ⇒ (somewhat) different meaning

7a. speak to both my father and my mother (separately); 7b. speak either to my father or to my mother (one of them will do) ⇒ different meaning

8a. all the things he said; 8b. some of the things he said ⇒ different meaning

9a. neither the speaker nor a second person; 9b. neither the speaker nor a second, third, etc. person ⇒ different (implied) meaning

10a. whichever Sunday you choose; 10b. each Sunday without exception ⇒ same basic meaning

Task three **

1. all; 2. few; 3. many; 4. a few; 5. many; 6. majority of; 7. most; 8. half; 9. majority of; 10. few

Task four ***

1. little (or: not much); 2. a lot of; 3. a majority of; 4. a great deal of; 5. a small number; 6. lot; 7. much; 8. more; 9. a lot; 10. a little

4.3. The use of the article

Sections **82–90**; 448; 475; 579; 597; 641; 747

Task one ***

Definite article:
- general rule: definite meaning of any type of noun (singular and plural count nouns; mass nouns):
- identity established by postmodifier (*of*-phrases and complete or reduced relative clauses: *the owner of a pet shop; the life of a lizard; the loss suffered up to . . .* , etc.)
- identity established by premodifier (*the guaranteed time*)
- unique in the context (*the beat; the virus*, etc.)
- institution shared by the community (*the internet; the UK*)
- second, third, etc. mention (*the disease*)

Indefinite article:
– general rule: indefinite meaning of singular count nouns
– first mention (*a pet shop*; *a lizard*; *a locust*; *a transient infection*, etc.)

Zero article:
– general rule: indefinite meaning of plural count nouns, plural-only nouns and mass nouns
– plural count nouns, both specific and generic (*bobbies*; *hoofed animals*; *humans*; *lost or damaged items*, etc.)
– plural-only nouns (*police*)
– concrete mass nouns, including those preceded by a premodifier, both specific and generic (*stolen property*; *money*)
– abstract mass nouns, including those preceded by a premodifier, both specific and generic (*mouth-to-mouth resuscitation*; *foot-and-mouth disease*; *compensation*, etc.)

Task two ***

Other uses:
Definite article: generic use with singular count nouns
Indefinite article: generic use with singular count nouns

Task three **

1. C; 2. A; 3a. C; 3b. D; 4a. D; 4b. D; 4c. D; 4d. C; 5. C; 6a. F; 6b. B; 6c. B

Task four **

a *morose, tubby man*; *by* the *name of*; a *story*; (the) *scum*; a *sympathetic but slightly bored way*; the *gun*; a *car salesman*; a *sale*; the *technical virtues and drawbacks*; the *various models*; an *odd feeling*

Task five **

1. *a morose, tubby man*: specific, indefinite, first mention – *by the name of*: identity established by postmodifier (*of*-phrase) – *a story*: specific, indefinite, first mention – *(the) scum*: identity established by postmodifier (relative clause) – *a sympathetic but slightly bored way*: specific, indefinite, first mention – *the gun*: second or third mention – *a car salesman*: generic use (any member of the species) – *a sale*: specific, indefinite, first mention – *the technical virtues and drawbacks*: postmodifier (*of*-phrase) – *the various models*: postmodifer (relative clause) – *an odd feeling*: specific, indefinite, first mention
2. *on impulse*: used in a generic sense (abstract mass noun) – *drawbacks*: indefinite article shared with '*technical virtues*' – *on sale*: generic use (abstract mass noun)

Task six ***

1. Generic uses of the article:
– Definite article before singular noun: *the tiger; the lion, cheetah and leopard; the pride; the large male lion; the pride('s); the lion; the female*
– Indefinite article before singular noun: *a fully-grown tiger; a fully-grown lion; an area*
– Zero article before plural noun: *lions, tigers, cheetahs and leopards; strong, razor-sharp teeth and claws, muscular bodies and excellent senses; unwary zebras, giraffes and other prey; big cats; snow leopards; jaguars; lakes; trees; lions; groups; prides; other males; lions, tigers, and other big cats; carnivores; flesh eaters; lions; large prey; antelopes and zebras*
– Zero article before mass noun: *such awe*

2. Few creatures are held in such awe as <u>the lion, the tiger, the cheetah</u> and <u>the leopard</u>, which we often call the big cats. These agile predators have strong, razor-sharp teeth and claws, muscular bodies and excellent senses. Their beautiful striped and dappled fur camouflages among the trees, allowing them to leap from the shadows to ambush <u>the unwary</u> <u>zebra, giraffe and other prey</u>. There are seven kinds of big cats. <u>Tigers are</u> <u>the largest. Fully-grown tigers</u> may measure more than three meters from nose to tail; <u>fully-grown lions are</u> almost as big.

The first cats lived 45 million years ago. Many, including the lion, cheetah and leopard, still inhabit parts of Africa. <u>The snow leopard dwells</u> in the mountains of Asia. <u>The jaguar is</u> the largest of the big cats in North and South America. <u>It is</u> equally at home swimming in <u>a lake</u> or climbing in <u>a tree.</u>

<u>The lion is</u> the only big cat that <u>lives</u> in <u>a group</u>, called <u>a pride</u>, which may be up to thirty strong. <u>Prides roam</u> over <u>areas</u> of 100 sq km or more, depending on the abundance of prey in <u>those areas. Large male lions</u> protect a pride's territory against other prides. <u>Lions</u> also <u>defend females</u> against other males.

<u>The lion, the tiger</u> and other big cats are true carnivores (flesh eaters). <u>A lion</u> usually <u>eats</u> large prey such as <u>the antelope</u> and <u>the zebra.</u> One giraffe is often enough to feed a whole pride of lions.

4.4. Other words of definite meaning

Sections 91–101; 521; 619; 667

Task one *

1. the – the; 2. the – the; 3. Ø; 4. the – the; 5. Ø; 6. Ø – the – the; 7. the; 8. Ø; 9. – ; 10. a; 11. – ; 12. the

Task two **

1. She; 2. Doctors in the emergency departments of hospitals sometimes have to deal with violent patients so they need police support.;

3. they – him; 4. These days teachers aren't paid enough money and they often leave . . . ; 5. It – it (or: she) – It (or: She); 6. she; 7. he; 8. They – it – it; 9. He – they; 10. it

Task three *

1. E; 2. I; 3. I; 4. E; 5. I; 6. I

Task four *

You shouldn't take it for granted that you'll be admitted to a top university simply because you've been to the right school. People say that, on occasion, you can be rather disadvantaged if you've been to certain schools. They say that colleges like to have a balance of scholars from different backgrounds. So if your background group is full, nothing can be done.

Task five **

1. F; 2. B; 3. B; 4. F; 5. B; 6. F – S; 7. F – S; 8. S; 9. B – F; 10. F

4.5. Expressions using 'of' and the genitive

Sections **102–107; 530–535**

Task one *

Genitive phrases: *the art gallery's; the Shearers'; David Shearer's; the local school's; the Cambridge college's; Mason's; the region's; Mason's*
Of-phrases: *of the early drawings; of Keith Mason; of the region; of David Shearer's; of a very individual talent; of the Cambridge college's regular visiting lecturers; of several galleries in the region; of his paintings*

Task two **

1. a teacher's work; 2. the writers circle; 3. the over-fifties' club; 4. Shakespeare's plays; 5. Bruce Willis's/Willis' early films; 6. the United States' economic policies; 7. the government's performance; 8. the Managing Director's car; 9. yesterday's news; 10. an old boys network

Task three **

1. people who live in Africa; 2. the main entrance; 3. the workers have concern (or: are concerned); 4. some journalists are dishonest; 5. there are no ideas; 6. ordinary people are courageous; 7. a bottle which contains wine; 8. a number of things (have) caused the economic crash; 9. his complaint resulted in; 10. the meeting has been (or: was) postponed

Task four **

1. subject-verb (his mother despairs) – the despair of his mother
2. 'have' relation (the sovereign has certain rights) – the rights of the sovereign
3. subject-complement (the actor is charming) – the charm of the actor
4. 'have' relation (the town has traffic problems) – the traffic problems of the town
5. subject-verb relation (the government has fallen): the downfall of the government
6. verb-object (someone (has) arrested the killer) – the arrest of the killer
7. verb-object (someone (has) murdered the child) – the murder of the child
8. 'have' relation (the moon has an effect on the tides) – the effect of the moon on the tides
9. subject-complement relation (the father is angry) – the anger of the father
10. subject-verb (the orchestra (has) performed) – the perfomance of the orchestra

Task five ***

1. the girl told a story – the story told about the girl
2. Scott made a discovery – somebody discovered Scott
3. somebody examines a doctor – a doctor examines somebody
4. the dream he has had for many years – the dream he has of what (his) life should be like
5. an award given in recognition of a long career – the most important award one is not likely to get
6. a portrait by Manet – Manet is the subject of the portrait
7. Peter may have just one friend – one of Peter's friends
8. The story written/told by Mary – the story about Mary
9. a particular part of that period – (about) 30 days
10. a part in a play – the job of an actor

Task six *

1. today's meeting; 2. the world's most successful airline; 3. an hour's wait; 4. Britain's oldest married couple; 5. Scotland's highest mountain; 6. a month's delay; 7. a minute's pause; 8. Liverpool's favourite son; 9. London's worst kept secret; 10. last year's bush fires

Time, tense and aspect

5.1. Auxiliary verbs

Sections **477–478**; 582; 735

Task one *

primary auxiliaries: *was (biting); had (cut); had (never heard); had (met); be (telling); did (laugh); have (appreciated); don't (mock); wasn't (mocking); didn't (like); (to) be (laughed at)*

modal auxiliaries: *can (count); might (not be telling); would (have appreciated); must (know)*

Task two *

1a. It's going; 1b. I'll do; 2a. I'd made; 2b. didn't notice; 3a. needn't worry; 3b. haven't come back; 4a. Jim's been; 4b. he'd better; 5a. We're getting; 5b. who've been; 6. everybody's listening; 7a. We mustn't; 7b. we're not setting; 8a. I don't approve; 8b. you've done; 8c. I won't tell; 9a. I'd be; 9b. I'm afraid; 9c. I can't; 10a. Shouldn't the Robinsons have told us; 10b. they weren't going

5.2. The auxiliary verbs *do, have* and *be*

Sections **479–482**; 736

Task one *

1a. main; 1b. auxiliary; 2a. auxiliary; 2b. main; 3a. main; 3b. auxiliary; 4a. main; 4b. main; 5a. auxiliary; 5b. main; 6a. auxiliary; 6b. main; 7a. main; 7b. auxiliary; 8a. auxiliary; 8b. main; 9a. main; 9b. auxiliary; 10a. main; 10b. auxiliary

Task two *

1. It isn't true that we weren't trying to help people in need.
2. Karen doesn't realize that I didn't do her a favour by also inviting her boyfriend.
3. Those who didn't have dinner with Mr Partridge haven't been told about his latest project.
4. Brian isn't a long-distance commuter, so he doesn't have a car of his own.
5. Don't come over to see us if you don't have enough time to spare.
6. Mark wasn't appointed for the job because he didn't have good references.
7. Don't be silent about the points you don't want to remain secret.
8. The fact that you haven't reported these incidents to the police doesn't do you credit.
9. We weren't convinced that the door hadn't been forced open before.
10. I didn't do all the exercises as I wasn't preparing for an important exam.

5.3. The modal auxiliaries

Sections 483–485; 736

Task **

1. You needn't come back until the end of this week.
   You don't need to come back until the end of this week.
2. Sandra didn't use to send postcards when she was abroad.
   Sandra usedn't to send postcards when she was abroad.
3. Do you dare to call me a selfish person?
   Dare you call me a selfish person?
4. I don't dare to think how disastrous such a policy might be.
   I daren't think how disastrous such a policy might be.
5. Did Mrs Barnes use to give money to charity?
6. Need I write more than thirty lines, sir?
   Do I need to write more than thirty lines, sir?
7. The PM doesn't dare to call an election yet.
   The PM daren't call an election yet.
8. We didn't use to condemn such eccentric behaviour.
   We usedn't to condemn such eccentric behaviour.

9. Doesn't John need to have his passport renewed?

Needn't John have his passport renewed?

10. Didn't people use to be afraid of ghosts in those days?

5.4. Meanings and forms

Sections **113–115**; **573–578**; **740–741**

Task one **

is (× 2): state; simple present

gave: event; simple past

started: event; simple past

has . . . spread: event; present perfect

has turned around: event; present perfect

has: state; simple present

are moving: temporary; present progressive

is: state; simple present

draw: habit; simple present

are thriving: temporary; present progressive

is: state; simple present

says: event; simple present

Task two (suggested answers) ***

1. Fiona doesn't eat meat. /Fiona never eats meat.
2. Sibyl plays the piano.
3. Winston Churchill smoked cigars.
4. We regularly went to church in those days.
5. Mr Hazelhurst taught Russian for twenty years.
6. Dr Winter operates on people's brains.
7. Davy asks people for food and money.
8. Ms Booth defends people in court.
9. Alan Sparke sets fire to buildings.
10. My cousin refuses to join the military on moral grounds.
11. This convict has killed several people.
12. Ben Jonson acted on the stage and wrote several plays.

5.5. Present time

Sections 116–121

Task one **

1a. temporary present habit; 1b. present state; 2a. present habit; 2b. present habit; 3a. temporary present habit; 3b. present habit; 4a. present habit; 4b. present habit; 5a. persistent habit; 5b. present state; 6a. present state; 6b. present (complete) event; 7a. temporary present event; 7b. present (complete) event; 8a. present state; 8b. present habit; 9a. present state; 9b. present state; 10. present state (tactfully expressed)

Task two **

1. My car is still being repaired so I'm commuting by train this week.
2. I assure you the situation is getting out of hand very quickly.
3. Lions hunt by night and feed on any animals they can pull down.
4. Bob, you are (being) very rude again to the very person who loves you most.
5. It says in the newspaper that new measures are being considered to fight organized crime.
6. Why are you continually interrupting the speaker? He deserves your undivided attention, you know.
7. I wonder if you could possibly help me. I'm trying to fix the ventilator but it isn't working yet.
8. Millions of people in Britain get their paper early in the morning because many newsagents organize 'paper rounds'.
9. I'm making a mess of this job but I promise to do better next time.
10. Are you still thinking of moving to the Seychelles or do you prefer to stay in our northern hemisphere after all?
11. Dad keeps telling me that the early bird catches the worm.
12. This tropical disease is spreading fast in Central Africa, where people don't earn enough to buy expensive medicines.

5.6. Past time 1

Sections 122–127; 550–572

Task one **

– *was shot*: definite time in the past; simple past
– *has been awarded*: past indefinite event; simple present perfect

– *was seriously injured*: definite time in the past; simple past
– *disturbed*: definite time in the past; simple past
– *was staying*: past activity in progress; past progressive
– *lost*: definite time in the past; simple past
– *needed*: definite time in the past; simple past
– *had perforated*: time in the past as seen from a definite time in the past; past perfect
– *(.....) nicked*: time in the past as seen from a definite time in the past; past perfect

Task two **

1a. has died; 1b. became; 2a. elected; 2b. has had; 3a. was; 3b. has spent; 4a. was founded; 4b. has helped; 5a. have risen; 5b. warned; 6a. thought; 6b. were created; 6c. struck; 7a. have made; 7b. have even succeeded; 8a. have been known / were known; 8b. contracted / had contracted; 9a. escaped; 9b. were sent; 10a. has been; 10b. (has) shed; 10c. (have) had

Task three **

1. Rural communities felt their traditions were threatened as English people bought property at prices that were out of the reach of locals.

2. Police officers approaching retirement were to be offered more money to stay on for a further five years under new Home Office plans to retain experienced staff.

   Supporters of the proposals hoped they would encourage long-serving constables and sergeants in their 50s to stay on. Under the rules existing then, police in the lower ranks had to retire at 55, and many chose to take their pension after 30 years' service. As a result, forces across the country were facing a retirement "timebomb", with many officers due to leave the following decade.

3. Top scientists believed that global warming had caused an unexpected collapse in the number of the world's most hunted whale.

   They thought that a sharp contraction in sea ice in the Antarctic was the likeliest explanation behind findings which suggested that the numbers of minke whales in the surrounding seas had fallen by half in less than a decade. The findings greatly strengthened the arguments of conservationists who were resisting moves to lift a 15-year-old official ban on the hunt. (. . .)

   Commercial whaling had been banned officially since 1986, but Japan and Norway each continued to kill about 500 minke whales a year. Japan did so under the guise of "scientific research", allowed under the IWC's treaty; Norway by exempting itself from the ban, which was also permitted under the agreement.

Task four *

1. has been raining; 2. Have you seen; 3. have written; 4. You've been drinking; 5. have known; 6. have you been waiting; 7a. have been studying; 7b. have not drawn; 8a. has become; 8b. have been crossing; 9a. have never witnessed; 9b. have flown / have been flying; 10a. has been cheating; 10b. has decided; 11a. has just told; 11b. have been constantly arguing; 12a. has been working; 12b. has still not finished

Task five ***

Stella: Kevin has just died in hospital. He fell off his horse a week ago and broke a leg and several ribs. Instead of recovering after the operation, however, he suffered a stroke and lay in a coma for three or four days from which he didn't wake up again.

I've already fixed a date for the funeral but haven't contacted my husband's brother and sister yet as I've been out of touch with them for years. Kevin was a wonderful man and I've never regretted marrying him. Did you know about Kevin's recent conversion to Buddhism?

Speaker: I heard some rumours about it at the local pub and I have considered converting to it myself lately. I've always believed in an afterlife, but (I've) kept it to myself until now.

Stella: Thank you. You have, at least, offered me the prospect of one day meeting Kevin again.

5.7. Past time 2

Sections 128–131

Task one ***

1. Harry Trotter is suspected of having killed his aunt.

2. 60 per cent of viewers appear to have watched the Cup Final yesterday.

3. Edith is very pleased to have been given a second chance.

4. Millions of euros are rumoured to have been stolen from a local bank last night.

5. The police are unlikely to have identified the culprits.

6. I'm so sorry to have drawn everyone's attention to the flaws in your project.

7. We are very much aware of the authorities having been forced to accept this questionable deal.

8. All three candidates are certain to have been screened.

9. Some people are worried about not having been informed at all.

10. Mr Bunker is the first man to have swum across the lake in winter.

11. Some politicians are alleged to have accepted bribes from lobbyists in the early 90s.

12. Dozens of drivers were fined for having exceeded the speed limit.

Task two **

1. caught; 2. lay; 3. Have you taught; 4. crept; 5. have spent; 6. has not risen; 7. chose; 8. tore up; 9. struck; 10a. burst; 10b. have had; 11a. Have you fed; 11b. has already eaten; 12a. has borne; 12b. beat

Task three **

1. used to be; 2a. would tinkle; 2b. would open; 2c. would kiss; 3. used to send; 4. used to hate; 5a. wouldn't stop; 5b. wouldn't ask; 5c. would work; 5d. would be working; 5e. would be doing; 5f. would be doing; 5g. would ask; 5h. would have to set

5.8. The progressive aspect

Sections 132–139

Task one **

1a. were having; 1b. burst in; 2a. have been searching; 2b. have only found; 3a. are you still considering; 3b. do you want; 4a. came in; 4b. were punching; 5a. are getting; 5b. is handling; 6a. do you normally react/did you normally react/have you normally reacted; 6b. calls/called/has called; 7a. were you whispering; 7b. saw; 8a. Have you finished; 8b. have been working; 9a. are you complaining; 9b. have eaten; 10a. were fast running; 10b. came; 11a. sent; 11b. are still waiting; 12a. has risen; 12b. took over; 12c. stabilised

Task two **

know; vividly remember; consists of; contains; had belonged to; loved; looked like; owed; remained; William understood; depended; resembled; believed; lacked; required

Task three **

1. have been hearing; 2a. tastes; 2b. tastes/tasted; 3. was still feeling; 4a. see; 4b. are (being) / have been / were; 5a. was smelling; 5b. saw; 5c. smelt; 6. was tasting; 7a. hear; 7b. are; 8a. are (being); 8b. feel; 9. have been seeing; 10a. heard; 10b. felt

5.9. Future time 1

Sections 140–146

Task one *

1a. *It's not going to start*: future resulting from present cause; 1b. *I'll drive you home*: element of intention with personal subject; 1c. *we'll phone someone*: element of intention with personal subject.

2a. *I shall be an embarrassing flat mate*: element of intention with personal subject; 2b. *How will you explain me*: neutral future of prediction; 2c. *We shan't be seeing*: future event which will take place 'as a matter of course'; 2d. *If we do run into them*: future in conditional clause; 2e. *I shall explain*: element of intention with personal subject.

3a. *Helen is about to celebrate*: imminent future (= less common expression); 3b. *She and Daniel will . . . be going out tonight*: future event which will take place 'as a matter of course'.

4a. *Encouraging news will reach you*: neutral future of prediction; 4b. *before you've been*: future in time clause; 4c. *it will soon pass*: neutral future of prediction.

5a. *she's starting*: future event arising from present plan; 5b. *what will she do*: element of intention with personal subject; 5c. *when school finishes*: future in time clause.

Task two **

1. is; 2. Will you be staying; 3a. doesn't take; 3b. she'll get; 4. I'm going to throw up; 5. I'm seeing; 6. will be cruising; 7. We're going to win; 8. begins; 9. Are you going to buy; 10a. We're leaving; 10b. will probably return; 11a. doesn't last; 11b. it will take; 12. It's going to blow up; 13a. are coming; 13b. shall be; 14a. enters; 14b. you will see; 15. will be complaining / are going to complain.

Task three **

Sue: are leaving; will be; takes off.
Pat: are you spending; don't get
Sue: we're flying; we'll get
Pat: Will you be lying
Sue: we're going to tour; we're definitely going to visit; we'll also go
Pat: you're going to enjoy yourselves; you'll never get; I go

5.10. Future time 2

Sections **147–148**

Task **

1. will have been; 2. weren't going to; 3. were to rescue / would rescue; 4. will have been delivered; 5. was going to jump; 6. was never going to see; 7. was going to come; 8. would haunt; 9a. have read; 9b. will have died; 10. was going to cry; 11. would regret; 12. were just about to leave

5.11. Summary

Sections **149–150**

Task one **

- *resembles*: simple present – A1
- *stretch*: simple present – A1
- *are hoping*: present progressive – A4
- *will . . . grow*: neutral future – C15
- *will stay*: neutral future – C15
- *are getting*: present progressive – A5
- *says*: simple present – A2
- *are saying*: present progressive – A5
- *don't have*: simple present – A1
- *imposed*: simple past – B10
- *ended*: simple past – B9
- *was*: simple past – B8
- *have risen*: present perfect – B4
- *doubled*: simple past – B9
- *is seeking*: present progressive – A4
- *is encouraging*: present progressive – A5
- *have . . . seen*: present perfect – B1
- *are expected*: simple present – A1
- *have . . . stopped*: present perfect – B4
- *are*: simple present – A1
- *has risen*: present perfect – B4
- *represents*: simple present – A1
- *spend*: simple present – A3

Task two ***

1a. are you going to tell; 1b. are leaving; 1c. gets; 1d. bet; 1e. is; 1f. will be; 1g. do you want

2a. is being rapidly reduced; 2b. reveals; 2c. concludes; 2d. has been cut; 2e. are beginning; 2f. promises

3a. do the natives in the Amazon Rainforest live; 3b. is discovering; 3c. have traditionally relied; 3d. have been used; 3e. started; 3f. have not been; 3g. am

4a. was; 4b. were; 4c. was; 4d. followed; 4e. passed; 4f. had been; 4g. spent; 4h. earned; 4i. were; 4j. was; 4k. had loved; 4l.has ever featured; 4m. was experiencing; 4n. turned; 4o. was struggling; 4p. appeared

5a. constitutes; 5b. have already travelled; 5c. is; 5d. recognise; 5e. requires; 5f. has been; 5g. is; 5h. will put; 5i. will never forget; 5j. have listed; 5k. has been; 5l. are providing

Task three (suggested answers) ***

Vivien asked Pearl, as she was a social worker running a project for single mothers, if it was possible for them to keep their babies.

Pearl replied that, in some parts of her country, those women were still experiencing problems. She said that often the family couldn't afford to feed an extra mouth, but she had found that, if a woman and her baby got some support, they were accepted into the family.

Vivien asked what happened if they were not accepted.

Pearl said that the less fortunate women were told that there were support services at several refuges. She added that over two hundred single mothers had passed through them since 1998 and most were coping well on their own.

Vivien suggested that, in spite of all their efforts, they didn't always reach those who needed to be helped most.

Pearl agreed. She said she knew dozens of women who had given up their babies, but she felt sure their numbers would keep going down, as they had over the past few years.

Adjectives

6.1. Adjectives

Sections **440–444**

Task one **

Used **attributively**: 1. *medical – vegetable – chief*; 2. *sheer – main – utter*;
4. *mere* 5. *live*
Used **predicatively**: 2. *afraid*; 4. *alive and kicking*; 5. *asleep – awake*
Used **attributively** & **predicatively**: 1. *obvious – healthy*; 2. *lazy – clumsy*;
3. *bright – cloudier – odd – late*; 4. *ill – deadly – complete*; 5. *shocking – clear
– heinous – evil – unpunished*

Task two *

1. *quite*; 2. *extremely*; *a little*; 3. *mainly*; 4. *really*; 5. *wide – abundantly*

Task three (suggested answers) ***

1a. the worried parents; 1b. the parents involved

2a. the people on the board now; 2b. the members who are there at this
moment

3a. five times one square metre; 3b. five metres times five metres

4a. the complicated calculations; 4b. the calculations that had to be done

5a. proper = correct; 5b. London proper = within the real boundaries of
London

Task four ***

1. (b) reduced present progressive ('to be' is understood, and an object
governed by a preposition follows).

2. (a) preceded by premodifying degree adverb

3. (a) preceded by degree adverb

4. (b) present progressive ('is ... ing' is followed by direct object)

5. (a) preceded by degree adverb

6. (a) preceded by degree adverb

7. (a) is synonym for another adjective, e.g. 'positive'

8. (a) preceded by degree adverb

9. (b) passive construction; (b) followed by direct object

10. (a) is a synonym for another adjective, e.g. 'difficult'; (b) followed by direct object

11. (b) passive construction; (a) preceded by degree adverb

12. (a) is a synonym for another adjective, e.g. 'furious'; (a) is a synonym for another adjective, e.g. 'very strong'; (b) reduced passive: 'which was voiced by ...'

Task five **

towering; spongy; former; wiry; sharp; prickly; dressed; oily; rear; sure; working; useful; plastic; squeaky

6.2. Adjective or adverb?

Sections 445–447

Task one **

1. angrily; 2. angry; 3. courageous; 4. courageously; 5. marvellous; 6. marvellously; 7. deliciously; 8. delicous; 9. fatal; 10. fatally; 11. hazy; 12. hazily

Task two **

1. direct; 2. highly; 3. close; 4. bare; 5. short; 6. lately; 7. barely; 8. strong; 9. directly 10. loud and clear; 11. shortly; 12. high; 13. hard; 14. loudly and clearly; 15. late; 16. closely; 17. rightly; 18. hardly; 19. strongly; 20. right

6.3. Adjectives as heads

Section 448; 90; 579–580

Task one *

1. the unemployed; 2. the disabled; 3. the rich/well-off/wealthy; 4. the faithful/religious; 5. the oppressed; 6. the homeless; 7. the British; 8. the Welsh; 9. the Irish; 10. the Spanish; 11. the French; 12. the Dutch

Task two ***

> 1. the supernatural; 2. the obvious; 3. the absurd; 4. the impossible; 5. the insane; 5. (all) the necessary; 7a. the eternal; 7b. the temporary; 8. the unimaginable/unthinkable

6.4. Adjective patterns

Sections **436–438**

Task one **

> 1. on; 2. of; 3. for; 4. with; 5. with; 6. in; 7. to; 8. of/for/about; 9.with; 10. at; 11. on; 12. for

Task two **

> 1. I am shocked that / It is shocking that so many people are using drugs these days.
> 2. It is essential that the government forms / should form a Royal Commission.
> 3. I am grateful that you are offering me this unique opportunity.
> 4. I was proud that I had helped in the attempt to fight poverty.
> 5. It is shameful that we have not learned any lessons from this bloody conflict.
> 6. It is/was outrageous that *Titanic* beat *Star Wars* at the box office.
> 7. I am confident that the scheme will be very successful.
> 8. I am not surprised / It is not surprising that Mr Welsh offers useful advice on how to deal with the war on drugs.
> 9. I am/was alarmed / It is/was alarming that Peter tried to deny the gravity of the problem.
> 10. I was convinced that I was watching another movie altogether.
> 11. It is evident that we should move forward in positive and productive ways.
> 12. I am hopeful that I will begin to get some real answers at last.

6.5. Adjective patterns with a *to*-infinitive

Section **439**

Task one **

> 1. The doctor slowly realised the seriousness of his patient's condition.
> 2. It was wise of Susan to ditch her boyfriend. / Susan wisely ditched her boyfriend.

3. It is almost impossible to come by manual typewriters these days.

4. It made the Queen (feel) astonished to see so many well-wishers.

5. It is likely that such vicious attacks will recur in the next few months.

6. It can be very pleasant to teach sixteen-year-olds.

7. It is certain that the 6 o'clock plane for Tokyo will arrive on time.

8. It was foolish of you to accept a bribe from that man.

9. It is increasingly hard to catch some species of fish.

10. It made the couple next door (feel) relieved to get news of their son.

11. It was clever of Bob to write a letter of apology to the headmaster.

12. It made me (feel) happy to be invited to the Prime Minister's birthday party.

Task two **

1. *slow*: type 4 (quick)

2. *wise*: type 1 (clever, foolish, silly, stupid, unwise)

3. *impossible*: type 2 (hard, difficult, easy)

4. *astonished*: type 3 (amazed, surprised)

5. *likely*: type 5 (unlikely, certain)

6. *pleasant*: type 2 (easy, hard)

7. *certain*: type 5 (uncertain)

8. *foolish*: type 1 (silly, stupid, unwise, clever, wise)

9. *hard*: type 2 (difficult, easy)

10. *relieved*: type 3 (glad, amazed, astonished)

11. *clever*: type 1 (wise, foolish, silly, stupid, unwise)

12. *happy*: type 3 (glad, sad)

Adverbs, adverbials and prepositions

7.1. Adverbs

Sections **464–469**

Task one *

too; *effectively*; *largely*; *directly*; *otherwise*; *fully*; *even*; *so*; *right*; *why*; *else*; *back*

Task two **

too: pre-modifier of adjective; *effectively*: adverbial in sentence;
largely: adverbial in sentence; *directly*: adverbial in sentence;
otherwise: adverbial in sentence; *fully*: pre-modifier of noun phrase;
even: pre-modifier of adverb; *so*: adverbial in sentence; *right*: adverbial in sentence;
why: adverbial in sentence; *else*: post-modifier; *back*: pre-modifier of preposition

Task three **

far; just; still; normally; beautifully; well; still; mainly; almost/nearly; nearly/almost; only; certainly; more; ago; however; never; never

Task four (suggested answers) **

1. somewhere else/elsewhere; 2. powerful enough; 3. how impertinent a young man; 4. hardly any; 5. sufficiently familiar; 6. what a ludicrous; 7. very little; 8. no-one else; 9. not an experienced enough pilot; 10. too honest a stockbroker ever to cheat

7.2. Adverbials – Introduction

Sections **449–452**

Task one **

In the last 50 years; in Newfoundland economics; although the fishing indus-tries are still the largest employers; still; no longer; exclusively; for its livelihood; In recent years; off the coast of the island and off Labrador; just off the east coast of St John's; If plans are realized; by the millennium

Task two **

(a) adverbs: *still* (MP); *exclusively* (EP)
   adverb phrases: *no longer* (MP)
   prepositional phrases: *In the last 50 years* (FP); *in Newfoundland economics* (EP); *for its livelihood* (EP); *In recent years* (FP); *off the coast of the island and off Labrador* (EP); *just off the coast of St John's* (EP); *by the millennium* (EP)
   finite subclause: *Although the fishing industries are still the largest employers* (FP); *If plans are realized* (FP)
(b) Short adverbials (adverbs and adverb phrases) have MP, except for *'exclusively'*, which has EP here (still followed by a longer adverbial). Long adverbials (prepositional phrases and subclauses) all have FP or EP.

Task three **

1a. General elections always take place on a Thursday.

1b. They are not public holidays. People have to work in the normal way, so polling stations are open from seven in the morning till ten at night to give everybody the opportunity to vote.

2a. Not long ago, Andrew Nugée would pack an SLR film camera and about 30 rolls of film when he went on vacation.

2b. Now he simply takes a digital camcorder for capturing both moving and still images.

2c. Nugée is just one of many who have been bitten by the digital-imaging bug. "It's completely changed my approach to photography. I take my camcorder everywhere," he says.

7.3. Time-when 1

Sections **151–155**; **455–456**

Task one *

1. in the 1960s; 2. in 2000, on 5 August; 3. last Friday; 4. in the 19th century; 5. by/at night; 6. at midnight; 7. during a recession;

8. next week; 9. at 10.45 a.m.; 10. early autumn/in the early autumn; 11. Tuesday morning / on Tuesday morning; 12. in 1918, at 11 a.m. on 11 November.

Task two (possible answers) **

1. in 1962 / on 1 May / at 3 a.m.; 2. in 1967 / in September 1967; 3. two years ago; 4. at university between 1985 and 1988; 5. at half-past six .... at midnight; 6. now; 7. in the dark; 8. after the evening meal; 9. next week; 10. in June

Task three **

1a. at 3.30 a.m.; 1b. at half-past nine; 2a. in July; 2b. again; 2c. in August; 3a. on 11 May 1926; 3b. on 14 May; 3c. three years later; 4a. when I get back indoors; 4b. this autumn

7.4. Time-when 2

Sections 156–160

Task one **

1. I decided to talk to my wife first and see my solicitor afterwards.

2. Over 170 nations had already signed the non-proliferation treaty by the end of 1999.

3. The European Union may well consist of about twenty-five member states a few years from now.

4. George Bush Sr. was President of the United States before he was succeeded by Bill Clinton.

5. The missing girl left home two weeks ago and has not been seen since.

6. The Boeing 747 took off from Dubai Airport hours ago, so it should have landed in Delhi by now.

7. The situation in Eastern Europe began to change very fast after the collapse of communism.

8. I still don't know whether a solution has yet been found.

9. Hostilities had resumed earlier that month, but fortunately things quietened down after a while.

10. We were soon to learn that the suspect had previously been convicted of drugs trafficking.

Task two **

1. I met Sheila when I was 17 years old.
2. The tourists picnicked in the city's main park before visiting a local museum.
3. Two wings of the castle were destroyed by fire after it was struck by lightning.
4. I will phone you as soon as I have finished this repair work.
5. The car crash happened while it was raining heavily.
6. We can all heave a sigh of relief now that the worst of the storm is over.
7. Steering a canoe is relatively easy once you get the hang of it.
8. The patient's condition seemed to stabilize as time passed.
9. I do not want to fly to Canada until the international situation has improved.
10. There has only been one single burglary since a security camera was installed.

7.5. Duration

Sections 161–165; 457

Task one **

1. for millennia; 2. briefly; 3. up to now; 4. all winter long; 5. for several years now; 6. until his grasp loosened; 7. ever since I've known about the health risks involved; 8. for ever; 9. from 1837 to 1901; 10. temporarily

Task two **

1. for four years; 2. for the rest of this century; 3. forever; 4. for a few weeks now; 5. up to Easter; 6. the whole day; 7. for a short time now; 8. at the week-end; 9. The heatwave continued throughout the summer; 10. . . . while police officers were (simultaneously) combing the woods for the missing girl.

7.6. Frequency

Sections 166–169; 458

Task one **

1. I've often met this famous comedian.
2. I used to see Mum every other day.

3. Even hardened soldiers occasionally become sentimental. / Even hardened soldiers become sentimental from time to time.

4. I go to the sauna monthly.

5. I've frequently been to the United States.

6. Our neighbours have a barbecue nearly every weekend.

7. Mr Sweethome seldom/rarely travels abroad.

8. Some people go for a walk daily.

9. We have breakfast at 7.30 most days.

10. My elder brother is rarely/seldom at home.

11. I borrow books from the library every fortnight.

12. Bossy people are frequently difficult to communicate with.

Task two ***

1. True vegetarians NEVER eat meat.

2. A footballer performing a hat-trick is a player who scores THREE TIMES.

3. Gypsies are people who are ALWAYS/CONSTANTLY on the move.

4. Bill Clinton was TWICE elected President of the United States.

5. Drink-driving is ALWAYS a serious offence.

6. The Olympic Games take place ONCE EVERY FOUR YEARS.

7. Even the best actors SOMETIMES forget their lines.

8. A bimonthly journal is published EVERY TWO MONTHS.

9. Most adults NORMALLY go to bed between 10 p.m. and midnight.

10. Astronauts have orbited our planet MANY TIMES.

11. People aged over 100 HARDLY EVER live on their own.

12. Commuters ALWAYS travel to work. / Commuters travel to work DAILY.

7.7. Place, direction and distance

Section 170; 454

Task one **

1. *Nowhere in Chester; of the River Dee; on the north bank; there; on the Dee; on the Groves; past Eaton Estate; of Westminster.*

2. *Australia; from north; to south; east; back to the Pacific coast; on to New Zealand; the most southerly landfall; on this side of the Rim; across flat plains; past Broken Hill; where; anywhere in the world; through the Blue Mountains; into Sydney*

Task two **

a. *of the River Dee; of Westminster; Australia; the most southerly landfall; on this side of the Rim*

b. adverbs and adverb phrases: *Nowhere in Chester; there; east; where; anywhere in the world*
   prepositional phrases: *on the north bank; on the Dee; on the Groves; past Eaton Estate; from north; to south; back to the Pacific coast; on to New Zealand; across flat plains; past Broken Hill; through the Blue Mountains; into Sydney*

7.8. Prepositions of place

Sections 171–178

Task one **

1a. at/in; 1b. outside; 2a. off; 2b. into; 3a. from; 3b. to; 3c. through; 4a. through; 4b. on; 5a. to/into; 5b. from/out of; 5c. to; 6a. from; 6b. across/over; 6c. on; 7a. across; 7b. through; 7c. along; 8a. in/inside; 8b. away from; 9a. at; 9b. off/out of; 9c. on to; 9d. into; 9e. to; 9f. on; 10a. at; 10b. to; 10c. in; 10d. to; 10e. in; 10f. through; 10g. within (or: to/by/along)

Task two (suggested answers) **

1. off his horse; 2. out of it; 3. out of / into the station; 4. on the statue; 5. over the bridge; 6. in the bus; 7. close to the shore; 8. over the wall; 9. on to the next town; 10. from Western Docks; 11. on her finger; 12. in a bar

7.9. Overlap between types of prepositions

Sections 179–183

Task **

1. on; 2. at; 3. in; 4. at; 5. on; 6. at; 7. in; 8. at; 9. to; 10. into; 11. at; 12. in

7.10. Various positions

Sections 184–186

Task one (suggested answers) ***

1. above the eyes; 2. below street-level / underneath the house; 3. by the fire; 4. between two countries; 5. under his shirt; 6. behind each other; 7. in front of you; 8. behind him; 9. opposite yours; 10. among colleagues; 11. round the walls; 12. on top of the pile

Task two **

1. Most of the divers had resurfaced but one or two were still trapped BELOW.

2. During the occupation of the area only the old and sick stayed BEHIND.

3. Dozens of B-52s and other warplanes were flying OVERHEAD that morning.

4. Young children travelling in cars are not normally allowed to sit IN FRONT.

5. I was awakened by a persistent stamping of feet produced by the people living ABOVE.

6. Before putting the pizza in the oven just sprinkle some Parmesan ON TOP.

7. The man sitting OPPOSITE leaned forward and suddenly grabbed me by the shoulders.

8. I lifted the carpet to find out what had been hidden UNDERNEATH.

9. Hours after the tragedy groups of relatives and friends were still standing AROUND.

10. On this side of the road are several detached houses, with a few remaining plots of land IN BETWEEN.

7.11. Motion

Sections 187–189

Task ***

1. came/went into; 2. came down; 3. went round; 4. coming towards; 5. get out of/away from; 6. went by; 7. going up; 8. got through; 9. went along; 10. drive over; 11. get on; 12. get over

7.12. Space and motion

Sections **190–192**

Task one **

1. up; 2. across; 3. beyond; 4. through; 5. down; 6. round; 7. throughout; 8. all over the; 9. are out of; 10. be away from

Task two **

1. beyond; 2. under; 3. behind; 4. below; 5. out of; 6. into; 7. along; 8. past; 9. on top of; 10. amid; 11. over 12. beneath

Task three ***

1. walked in; 2. sailed over; 3. drove away; 4. came up; 5. moved out / went away; 6. carried on; 7. dropped by/in; 8. broke/split up

7.13. Distance

Section **193**

Task **

1. thousands of miles away; 2. thousands of miles; 3. about two hundred yards from here; 4. five thousand feet below; 5. six hundred miles; 6. a few hundred yards; 7. just inches from my head; 8. a hundred feet above our heads; 9. miles away; 10. two inches

7.14. Manner, means and instrument

Sections **194–197; 453**

Task one **

1. *extremely carefully*: adverb phrase; *at a slow speed*: prepositional phrase; *in as high a gear as possible*: prepositional phrase; *very gently*: adverb phrase; *particularly slowly*: adverb phrase; *progressively*: adverb; *smoothly*: adverb; *by choosing a safe place to brake gently*: adverbial clause; *gently*: adverb

2. *like a soldier*: prepositional phrase; *at a fast cat-like crouch*: prepositional phrase; *weaving and ducking and using the river bed for cover*: adverbial clause

Task two **

1. The trade unions protested VIGOROUSLY (or: IN A VIGOROUS MANNER / WITH VIGOUR) against the government's measures.
2. The new proposal was ENTHUSIASTICALLY received / The new proposal was received ENTHUSIASTICALLY.
3. The losing team COURAGEOUSLY fought back / The losing team fought back COURAGEOUSLY.
4. The local tribes were treated CRUELLY AND UNJUSTLY.
5. I was dressing the patient's wounds LIKE A QUALIFIED NURSE.
6. Mr Pym was behaving LIKE A SIXTEEN-YEAR-OLD towards the new trainee.
7. The front gate was locked, so I tried to get in BY THE BACKDOOR.
8. Fortunately, we were able to communicate BY MOBILE PHONE.
9. The employers sought to win over the workers WITH A PAY RISE.
10. Why don't we resolve the problem WITH A CHANGE OF TACTICS.
11. The burglars knocked the night porter unconscious WITH A BASE-BALL BAT.
12. We cannot reduce the flood risk WITHOUT PROPER SEA DEFENCES.

Task three **

1. using an old-fashioned fountain pen; 2. with great difficulty; 3. by the path we always used; 4. so slowly; 5. with a crowbar; 6. with fond approval; 7. by road or by rail; 8. like an Arctic explorer; 9. as if it were your last day on earth; 10. by sounding your horn; 11. by a perilously slim extending ladder, with a little piece of rope for support; 12. clearly and accurately, by the use of symbols

7.15. Prepositions (general)

Sections 657–660

Task one **

1. in; 2. in; 3. at; 4. in; 5. before; 6. on; 7. of; 8. between; 9. along; 10. in; 11. for; 12. to; 13. in; 14. of; 15. in; 16. to; 17. into; 18. for; 19. about (or: on); 20. with; 21. of; 22. with; 23. out; 24. about

Task two **

1. P; 2. PA; 3. PA; 4. PA; 5. PA; 6. PA; 7. P; 8. P; 9. PA; 10. P

7.16. Two or more adverbials

Section **460**

Task **

> 1. in Iceland in fifty years; 2. into the small colonial room at the front of the building; 3. in an armchair with a magazine in her lap; 4. among the boulders by the tower; 5. on Stella's door at ten past four; 6. eastward on the Transsiberian Express; 7. intimidatingly in my direction; 8. in the penal colony in 1840 after a career of crimes, arrests and escapes; 9. extensively in the North for several years; 10. in his office on the fourth floor of a supermarket in Hong Kong; 11. fixedly at the paving stone under her feet; 12. to starboard about 1 o'clock in the afternoon.

7.17. Degree

Section **215**; **459**

Task *

> 1. *particularly*: H, M; 2. *simply*: L, A; 3a. *Just*: L, A; 3b. *monumentally*: H, M; 4. *quite*: H, M; 5a. *pretty*: H, M; 5b. *much*: H, A; 6. *almost*: L, M; 7. *deeply*: H, A; 8. *ill*: L, A; 9. *totally*: H, A; 10. *all but*: L, M; 11. *a little*: L, M; 12. *terribly*: H, M; 13a. *really*: H, A; 13b. *right*: H, M; 14a. *piercingly*: H. M; 14b. *only*: L, M; 14c. *partly*: L, A; 15a. *rather*: H, M; 15b. *barely*: L, M; 15c. *fully*: H, M

7.18. Gradable words and degree 1

Sections **216–218**

Task one **

> 1. The situation in the border area is getting PRETTY desperate.
>
> 2. High Street spending has increased CONSIDERABLY over the last two months.
>
> 3. Teachers are complaining about class sizes A GREAT DEAL these days.
>
> 4. In her early nineties now, Mrs Wilson is beginning to look VERY frail.
>
> 5. Ricky's mood swings are making me feel A LITTLE uncomfortable.
>
> 6. On the whole, I QUITE like these after-dinner speeches.
>
> 7. Careful, that wooden chest is RATHER heavy!
>
> 8. Aren't you getting A BIT worried about Mandy's recent behaviour?
>
> 9. Teenagers tend to admire pop stars VERY MUCH.

10. I think we should reword this letter SLIGHTLY.

11. We were given a FAIRLY accurate description of the situation.

12. Dear Kenny, I'm looking forward to your visit A LOT.

Task two *

1. rather; 2. exactly; 3. too; 4. strictly; 5. utterly; 6. a great deal; 7. in the least; 8. slightly; 9. altogether; 10. quite; 11. a little; 12a. almost; 12b. extremely

7.19. Gradable words and degree 2

Sections 219–221

Task one **

1. much; 2. very much; 3. altogether; 4. very; 5. very much; 6. much; 7. very; 8. a lot; 9. altogether; 10a. very; 10b. very much

Task two **

1. Jimmy looked RATHER pathetic standing in the rain outside.

2. Joan seemed ENTIRELY at ease in this new environment.

3. It's QUITE a pleasant walk now that the heather is in full bloom.

4. The information we received was FAIRLY accurate.

5. The next of kin were UTTERLY devastated by the news.

6. I'm not AT ALL convinced that this is the ideal approach.

7. For thirty years Mr Lee made a FAIRLY easy living as a fisherman.

8. I've been A BIT worried about my health lately.

9. What you were saying is COMPLETELY beside the point.

10. It would be EXTREMELY foolish to support such a stupid idea.

7.20. Other aspects of degree adverbs

Sections 222–223

Task one ***

1. absolutely unique; 2. literally starving; 3. absolutely desperate; 4. absolutely livid; 5. almost impossible; 6. absolutely fascinating; 7. absolutely amazing; 8. absolutely superb; 9. utterly crazy. 10. completely wrong

Task two **

An old ruler was complaining that he was not AT ALL loved by his subjects. However HARD he tried to convince them of HIS love for THEM, it was all to no avail. The old man UTTERLY failed to realize that people THOROUGHLY disapproved of the way he managed the finances of the realm.

Years of excessive spending had left his country with ABSOLUTELY no money / no money AT ALL. Endless military campaigns had been draining it of funds BADLY needed elsewhere.

Was it AT ALL possible to make the ruler change his policies? It HARDLY seemed so. Even though his subjects BADLY wanted reform, he THOROUGHLY disagreed with even the suggestion of change.

7.21. Role, standard and point of view

Section 224

Task one *

1. *In theory*: point of view; 2. *at dealing with extreme weather conditions*: role; 3. *technically*: point of view; 4. *For a man over sixty*: standard; 5. *at solving problems*: role; 6. *As a football player*: role; 7. *In a political sense*: point of view; 8. *for such a young team*: standard; 9. *on paper*: point of view; 10. *for a beginner*: standard; 11. *as a teacher and trainer*: role; 12. *Objectively . . . Subjectively*: point of view

Task two **

1. THEORETICALLY, most of our environmental problems can be solved.

2. Britain DEALS BADLY with extreme weather conditions.

3. If you inadvertently wander off the footpath, IN A TECHNICAL SENSE, you are trespassing.

4. CONSIDERING THAT HE IS a man aged over sixty, running such a distance was quite an achievement.

5. We have become successful AS PROBLEM-SOLVING EXPERTS.

6. David Beckham is UNBEATABLE AT FOOTBALL.

7. POLITICALLY, the uninsured hardly formed a group at all.

8. The coach said we did well CONSIDERING THAT WE WERE such a young team.

9. AS THEY ARE FORMULATED, this set of rules looks impressive.

10. Six out of ten is not too bad CONSIDERING THAT HE IS a beginner.

11. Ms Carpenter is excellent AT TEACHING AND TRAINING.

12. FROM AN OBJECTIVE POINT OF VIEW, this war is terrifying. IF WE LOOK AT IT SUBJECTIVELY, it remains strangely uninvolving.

7.22. Sentence adverbials

Sections **461–463**

Task one *

1. Oddly (enough); 2. Clearly; 3. Frankly; 4. Hopefully; 5. As an expert; 6. Admittedly; 7. Unfortunately; 8. Honestly; 9. Surprisingly; 10. Characteristically; 11. Undoubtedly; 12. Superficially / On the surface

Task two **

1. The Prime Minister is suffering from a hernia. AS A RESULT, he will not be able to attend the European summit.

2. The peace process is in deep trouble. HOWEVER, the various parties involved are prepared to continue their efforts.

3. Nursery education has been transferred to community colleges. SIMILARLY, teacher training has been shifted to colleges and universities.

4. We could travel by train. ALTERNATIVELY, we could travel by plane.

5. I did not feel put off by this unexpected confrontation. ON THE CONTRARY, I was already looking forward to the next challenge.

6. We are not going to buy a sunbed as it is too expensive. MOREOVER, someone told me UV-radiation can cause skin cancer.

7. I think we should show some more understanding for Susan's behaviour. AFTER ALL, she's been through a lot lately.

8. Is there a cheaper solution? IN OTHER WORDS, can you make a cheaper device?

9. Don't forget to tell the boss. OTHERWISE, you will get into a lot of trouble.

10. The suspect did not answer any of my questions. INSTEAD, he kept staring into the distance.

Clause types

8.1. Cause, result, purpose and reason

Sections **198–206**; 323; 365; 613–615

Task one **

1. *so I had to get to work by car*: consequence
2. *Because I set off early*: reason
3. *on account of the strike*: reason
4. *that there were long queues of traffic*: result
5. *with the result that nothing was moving*: result
6. *Since I had been stuck for so long*: cause
7. *so I decided to stay in a hotel that night*: consequence
8. *Because so many people had the same idea*: cause
9. *As I still didn't want to drive home in all the traffic*: reason
10. *so I was woken at five o'clock in the morning when the cleaners came in*: result

Task two ***

1. The weather was very stormy, so people were advised not to travel.
2. A full survey of the house wasn't done, so that many faults were discovered later.
3. As the Post Office lost over £2m last year, some postal deliveries must be curtailed.
4. A virus was sent through the e-mail, with the result that whole programs were lost on the computer.
5. Since public services need more investment, taxes will have to be raised.
6. Because of a sudden death in the family, his trip to Hungary was cancelled.

7. Because of his sedentary life, Gabor was very overweight.

8. His doctor told him to do more exercise (in order) to lose weight.

9. The ski resorts lost a lot of money last year because there was very little snow.

10. The trains were running late and consequently the meeting was postponed.

Task three *** (some possible sentences)

– It is surprising that British people are becoming dangerously overweight because there is so much information about healthy life-styles.

– Our eating habits need to change, so people should dedicate time to sit down and eat properly.

– Some experts say there is an epidemic of obesity because we take in more calories than we burn off.

– People get anxious about work so they eat to cheer themselves up.

– Since many people try diets but then fall back we also need to do more exercise.

– Diets often leave us feeling hungry and miserable, consequently it gets harder to shed weight each time we diet.

Task four **

1. as; 2. resulted in; 3. so . . . that; 4. because; 5. so that ; 6. as a result of; 7. (in order) to; 8. seeing that; 9. (so as) to; 10. as a result; 11. for

Task five **

1. reason; 2. result ; 3. result; 4. reason; 5. result; 6. result; 7. purpose; 8. reason; 9. purpose; 10. result; 11. reason

8.2. Concession and contrast

Sections 211–212; 361; 462

Task one **

1. Although it was raining heavily last Sunday, we (still) went out for a walk after lunch.

2. In spite of the fact that he lost all his money (or: In spite of losing all his money), he maintained an air of calm reassurance.

3. Much as I admire his paintings, I doubt if he is a major artist.

4. Whereas film directors in Hollywood have a long training, young British directors can go straight into making major films.

5. For all the hard work he puts in, he never gets any promotion.

6. The administration maintains an aggressive stance. Nevertheless there are signs of compromise among some of its members.

7. Notwithstanding these favourable weather conditions, the rough terrain should persuade them not to make the trip.

8. Some critics had written some very bad notices. Even so the play was sold out for all performances.

9. While the evidence points strongly towards a conviction, the defence still believes the woman will be found not guilty.

10. The ruined abbey is in a very beautiful setting. All the same, I'm not sure I want to see it.

Task two ***

1. although; 2. despite; 3. while; 4. whereas; 5. in spite of; 6. so; 7. though; 8. however; 9. nevertheless; 10. yet

Linking

9.1. Linking signals

Sections **351–359**; 238; 470–472

Task ★★

1. well; 2. in other words; 3. by the way; 4. for example; 5. now; 6. well; 7. first; 8. second; 9. third; 10. altogether; 11. that is; 12. for instance; 13. in short; 14. moreover; 15. that is to say; 16. in a word; 17. in fact; 18. incidentally; 19. namely; 20. in fact (or: on the contrary)

9.2. 'General purpose' links

Sections **371–374**; 110–111; 493–494; 686–694

Task one ★★

1. They won't finish the work today and (consequently) this causes a problem.
2. I don't like mobile phones because they have a musical repetitive tone.
3. He was always late, with the result that he lost his job.
4. When (or: If) you buy a savings bond, make sure it gives you a good return on your investment.
5. The books were badly stacked so that they fell across the floor.
6. They have problems with their neighbours because they are very noisy.
7. Many people found themselves always playing 'Solitaire' on their computer and have therefore had the game removed.
8. People shouldn't ski off-piste, as it is dangerous.
9. The arrangements for the conference angered him because they were very bad.
10. He fell madly in love with Barbara, and she was directing the play.

Task two **

1. B (reason); 2. G (purpose); 3. I (reason); 4. E (result); 5. H (condition); 6. C (negative condition); 7. A (reason); 8. J (cause); 9. D (reason); 10. F (reason)

Task three **

– Knowing it was time to go, . . .
– Not wanting to leave, he . . .
– Now empty of all his books and papers, . . .
– Just looking round the room, he . . .
– Feeling proud, he had determined to . . .
– If seen to be a keen and co-operative worker, . . .
– Not understanding the corporate culture, . . .
– Having grown tired of this, they . . .
– Soon failing to get things done on time, he . . .
– Knowing there was nothing to do, he . . .

9.3. Cross-reference to noun phrases and substitutes for a noun phrase

Sections **375–382**; 510; 529; 597–601; 619–622; 675–680

Task one **

1. it; 2. him; 3. its; 4. he – his – his; 5. them; 6. their; 7. them; 8. our; 9. this – it; 10. we

Task two **

1. them; 2. those; 3. those; 4. none; 5. himself; 6. one; 7. ones; 8. they; 9. one – another; 10. some – them; 11. one; 12. this; 13. one; 14. one; 15. some – some

9.4. Substitutes for structures containing a verb

Sections **383–385**; 479; 482

Task one *

1. do – don't; 2. did; 3. have/have done/did; 4. o – may; 5. didn't; 6. will; 7. have; 8. don't; 9. was; 10. can

Task two **

1. ...if Susan will; 2. ...but I don't think he will; 3. ...but he can; 4. Yes, he is; 5. I know I should have; 6. Why should I?; 7. It might be; 8. ..., but not the one for those in Singapore; 9. ...you should have; 10. I could but I don't want to.

Task three **

1. do that; 2. do it; 3. do that; 4. do that; 5. does so; 6. do so; 7. do that; 8. do that; 9. do that; 10. do so

9.5. Substitutes for wh-clauses and to-infinitive clauses

Sections 387–389; 94; 99; 376

Task **

1. I don't know where; 2. I'd love to; 3. I don't know when; 4. if you want to; 5. it; 6. that; 7. this; 8. if you want me to; 9. I don't want to; 10. How do you know that?; 11. I can't bear to; 12. this

9.6. Omission with non-finite and verbless clauses

Sections 392–394; 493–494

Task one **

1. This man, well-known to me, caused all the problems in the department.

2. I expect to see you while I'm in London.

3. Next month is the time to visit Italy.

4. A born leader, James soon attracted the attention of the company management.

5. Having retired from the army, he gave up his title of General.

6. Doubting that she would come, he made plans to go with another woman.

7. Knowing how you behaved in the past, I cannot accept you as a member of the group.

8. Ian had thought of seeing a film that evening.

9. Having been given so much time, he should have completed the work.

10. Please get me a taxi. Having drunk so much, I mustn't drive my car tonight.

Task two *

1. While knowing Maria had cheated in the exam, Tom, nonetheless, congratulated her warmly.

2. Going to Sweden for his job, he decided to wait until he was there before buying a new winter coat.

3. Since living here, I've not made any real friends.

4. Whether rich or poor, Joe always organized a good party on his birthday.

5. After reading that best-seller about an old woman, Mary felt she was able to cope with old age.

6. When meeting her after several years; he felt very sorry they had not become close friends.

7. After retiring, he lived in Tasmania.

8. Not knowing the way, I'd rather you drove.

9. Since knowing the truth about them, he has become very wary of them.

10. Though unsuccessful in their last business, they are determined to start again.

Conditions

10.1. Open and hypothetical conditions

Sections **207–210**; 275; 366–367

Task one *

1. Type 2; 2. Type 1 – *'provided that'* can be replaced with 'if'; 3. Type 3 – *'supposing'* can be replaced with 'if'; 4. Type 1 – *'so long as'* can be replaced with 'if'; 5. Type 1 – a general truth, *'unless'* can be replaced with 'if . . . not'; 6. Both Type 1 – general truths, *'slowing down if necessary'* = 'you should slow down if it is necessary'; 7. Type 1 – *'provided that'* can be replaced with 'if'; 8. Type 1 – general truth, *'unless'* can be replaced with 'if . . . not'; 9. Type 2 – *'if given'* = 'if they were given'; 10. Type 1 – general truth, *'in case of burglary'* = 'if you are burgled'; 11. Type 2 – *'in the event of renewed terrorist attacks'* = 'if there were renewed terrorist attacks'; 12. Type 3 – *'without the official sanction of the Nazi regime'* = 'if the Nazi regime hadn't sanctioned it'.

Task two **

1. *Given the opportunity* = If it is given / If there is the opportunity; 2. *Without fear* = If people weren't afraid; 3. *In case of anticipated payment* = If you have already paid; 4. *Giving people confidence* = If you give people confidence; 5. *In the case of the latter's death, removal from office or disability* = If the governor dies, is removed from office or is disabled; 6. *Don't drive so fast or* = If you drive so fast; 7. If you don't comply with the rules, one point will be deducted or you will be disqualified; 8. *In the event of my not being elected* = If I am not elected; 9. *But for the protesters* = If there hadn't been any protesters; 10. *in case of a conflict* = if there was a conflict; 11. *By a proper freedom of information bill* = If there had been a proper freedom of information bill; 12. *Without reform and better relations with the United States* = If there isn't any reform or there aren't better relations with the United States; 13. *Cling too long to yesterday's strategy and* = If you cling too

long to yesterday's strategy; 14. If the violence intensified, it would be difficult to reach a negotiated settlement.

Task three **

1. ever visit – don't miss; 2. send / would send – strike/struck; 3. rose – would be; 4. will cause – are; 5. would probably have developed – had not moved; 6. were (or: would be) – could; 7. would never have paid – hadn't lent; 8. had not taught – would almost certainly have drowned; 9. wouldn't have – had chosen; 10. had made – would still survive; 11. will have – arise; 12. had caught – would have sent

Task four (suggested answers) **

1. ...., tell him the game starts at 7 o'clock.
2. ...., would you accept his apologies?
3. .... if I can return it by Friday.
4. If you'd seen so many extra charges, ...
5. .... if I had known it was going to be in the papers.
6. .... you explained everything, ...
7. ...., you would have been very angry.
8. .... you had thought he would have behaved in that way.
9. They're not going to support you, ...
10. ...., get help.
11. If I misbehaved, ...
12. .... they had managed to conquer Everest with such poor equipment.
13. ...., I would raise taxes and have better public services.
14. .... Hitler hadn't fought on two fronts in 1943.
15. .... hadn't conquered Britain, the British would have remained a very closed society.

Task five ***

1. 20 January: A leading official in Germany WOULDN'T HAVE HANGED himself IF a parliamentary group HAD NOT BEGUN an investigation into illicit payments to his party in the 1990s.
2. 27 February: The Limpopo River in southern Africa WOULDN'T HAVE OVERFLOWED its banks IF THERE HADN'T BEEN weeks of heavy rain and flooding.
3. 10 March: IF a dam in a Romanian mine HADN'T BROKEN, THERE WOULDN'T HAVE BEEN a spillage of toxic metals into nearby rivers.

4. 5 April: IF THERE HADN'T BEEN A computer glitch, the London Stock Exchange WOULDN'T HAVE CLOSED DOWN for nearly eight hours on the last day of Great Britain's fiscal year.

5. 12 May: UN Secretary-General Kofi Annan WOULDN'T HAVE CRITICIZED the US IF IT HAD PARTICIPATED fully in peacekeeping operations in Africa.

6. 9 June: Buenos Aires WOULDN'T HAVE BEEN BROUGHT to a virtual standstill IF workers HADN'T STAGED a one-day strike to protest the Argentine government's austerity plan.

7. 2 July: The former communist rulers in Mongolia WOULDN'T HAVE BEEN RETURNED to power IF they HADN'T WON a landslide victory in the general election.

8. 12 August: The Russian nuclear submarine *Kursk* WOULDN'T HAVE SUNK in the Barents Sea IF the hull HADN'T BEEN DAMAGED by a series of explosions.

9. 16 September: Public transportation in Los Angeles WOULDN'T HAVE SHUT DOWN IF the United Transportation Union HADN'T GONE on strike.

10. 5 October: IF THERE HADN'T BEEN a challenge from Germany, the European Court of Justice WOULDN'T HAVE HALTED a proposed European Union-wide ban on tobacco advertising.

11. 30 November: The city of Bethlehem WOULDN'T HAVE CANCELLED its traditional Christmas celebration IF THERE HADN'T BEEN ongoing violence between Israelis and Palestinians.

12. 7 December: Officials in California WOULDN'T HAVE DECLARED a stage-three power alert IF electricity reserves HADN'T DROPPED to dangerous levels.

Task six ***

Tom: The world WILL BE like paradise twenty years from now IF ever more robots RELIEVE us of all sorts of boring tasks.

Daisy: I don't agree. Life on earth MIGHT BE be hell IF these robots WERE BECOMING more intelligent than humans. Some of them COULD even DEVELOP into monsters IF scientists DECIDED to fit them with brains.

Tom: What? IF scientists BEHAVED like modern Frankensteins, there WOULD BE every reason to worry. No, IF they INTRODUCE very strict guidelines, everything WILL BE be under control.

Daisy: And what about cloning? It WOULD BE terrible IF a few nutty professors REPRODUCED themselves. IF we DON'T LOCK them up, things WILL GET out of hand.

Tom: You sound like one of those latter-day Luddites. IF we PUT a few of them in charge, we'RE back in the Stone Age.

10.2. Other ways of expressing hypothetical meaning

Sections 277–278

Task *

1. Had we known ....; 2. Were this to be true ....; 3. Should you have ....; 4. Had we realized ....; 5. .... were such an incident to happen; 6. Had this man been assisted ....; 7. Should this not be ....; 8. Were they ever to build ....; 9. .... should anything go wrong.; 10. Were a solution to be ....; 11. Had the women been given ....; 12. .... were someone to find . . .

10.3. Condition and contrast

Sections 213–214; 368

Task ***

1. This pup will win your heart, EVEN IF you don't like dogs.

2. Your panoramic view of the lake is breathtaking WHENEVER / NO MATTER WHEN you choose to come.

3. EVEN IF your home is only temporary, you can STILL decorate with style.

4. WHETHER you have good credit OR a past history of credit problems, our experts will help you every step of the way.

5. Every child has a legal right to financial support EVEN IF they are children of divorced parents.

6. HOWEVER far away you may be, I will always love you.

7. WHEREVER you are travelling, you'll find a familiar place where you can relax.

8. WHETHER OR NOT you are advanced, there's one more trick for you to consider.

9. WHATEVER people are saying, just do your own thing.

10. EVEN IF you are not an art lover, I still think this collection is something for you.

11. You are going to have fun WHETHER you like it OR NOT.

12. The US appeals court has made the right ruling EVEN IF it is difficult to enforce.

Comparison

11.1. Comparison 1

Section **227**; 500–504

Task one **

1. most serious – older/elder; 2. ablest / most able – further; 3. worse – more drastic; 4. unhappiest – more wrong; 5. cleverer – shallowest; 6. most carefully – more disastrously; 7. hardest – most densely; 8. more highly – best; 9. more acutely – most autocratically; 10. less – more widely – more/most truly; 11. older – more closely; 12. more heavily – nearest; 13. more/most thorough – most hotly; 14. most emphatically – least; 15. longest – greatest – more delicious.

Task two **

a. latest = the most recent; b. last = opposite to first/Germany is at the bottom of the list.

Task three **

1. The Red Bull is the best pub in the Northern Hemisphere.

2. Winnie is the most attractive of the three girls.

3. Religious fundamentalism is the worst of our enemies.

4. The Ibans are the fiercest tribe in Borneo.

5. The moon landing was the most exciting event in the 1960s.

6. Gregory is the toughest of Sam's opponents.

7. Shirley is the most competent secretary in the department.

8. The Thirty Years' War was the bloodiest conflict in 17th century Europe.

9. David is the brightest of my overseas students.

10. Malaria is the most common of present-day tropical diseases.

11. Bologna is the oldest university in the world.

12. Nero was the most ruthless of the Roman emperors.

11.2. Comparison 2

Sections 225–226; 505–507

Task one (suggested answers) **

1. Angela's skin is lighter than mine. / My skin isn't as light as Angela's.

2. Most voters are not as optimistic as our politicians. / Our politicians aren't so pessimistic as most voters.

3. I was feeling worse than Cynthia. / Cynthia wasn't feeling as bad as me.

4. I don't look as healthy as Boris. / I look less healthy than Boris.

5. There were more casualties in the coach than there were in the train. / There were fewer casualties in the train than there were in the coach.

6. Adrian arrived earlier than me. / I didn't arrive as early as Adrian.

7. The anti-globalists weren't dealt with as leniently as the hooligans. / The anti-globalists were dealt with less leniently than the hooligans.

8. Assertive children speak more loudly than shy ones. / Shy children don't speak as loudly as assertive ones.

9. Madonna's home is decorated more lavishly than mine. / My home is decorated less lavishly than Madonna's.

10. The British athletes were running more slowly than their Ethiopian counterparts. / The Ethiopian athletes were running faster than their British counterparts.

Task two ***

1. South Africa is more populous than IRELAND, CANADA and AUSTRALIA / less populous than the UNITED KINGDOM. // The UNITED KINGDOM is the most populous / Ireland is the least populous of the five countries.

2. Canada is more sparsely populated than the UNITED KINGDOM, IRELAND and SOUTH AFRICA / more densely populated than AUSTRALIA. // The UNITED KINGDOM is the most densely / AUSTRALIA is the most sparsely populated country.

3. The UNITED KINGDOM has a lower birth rate than IRELAND, AUSTRALIA and SOUTH AFRICA / a higher birth rate than CANADA. // SOUTH AFRICA has the highest / CANADA has the lowest birth rate.

4. IRELAND has a younger population than the UNITED KINGDOM, CANADA and AUSTRALIA / an older population than SOUTH AFRICA.

// SOUTH AFRICA has the youngest / the UNITED KINGDOM has the oldest population.

5. CANADIANS live longer than BRITISH, IRISH and SOUTH AFRICAN people / shorter than CANADIANS. // CANADIANS LIVE longest / SOUTH AFRICANS live shortest.

6. IRELAND has a wider gender gap than . . . / a narrower gender gap than . . . // CANADA has the widest / SOUTH AFRICA has the narrowest gender gap.

7. AUSTRALIA is richer than . . . / poorer than . . . // The UNITED KINGDOM is the richest . . . / SOUTH AFRICA is the poorest . . .

8. CANADA is wetter than . . . / drier than . . . // AUSTRALIA is the wettest . . . / The UNITED KINGDOM is the driest . . .

9. SOUTH AFRICA has a warmer climate than . . . / a colder climate than . . . // AUSTRALIA has the warmest . . . / CANADA has the coldest climate.

10. SOUTH AFRICA is further/farther away from the UNITED KINGDOM than . . . / closer to the the UNITED KINGDOM than . . . // AUSTRALIA is furthest/farthest away . . . / IRELAND is closest to the UNITED KINGDOM . . .

Task three (suggested answers) **

1. Simpson writes more elegantly than Williams.
2. Pete plays baseball better than Chuck.
3. Lady Carcrash drives more recklessly than Lord Slowlane.
4. Americans support euthanasia less ardently than Europeans.
5. Sarah believes as firmly in life after death as Monica.
6. Keith Michell didn't act as brilliantly as John Gielgud.
7. Barbara protested less peacefully than Sarah.
8. Andrikos doesn't speak English as fluently as Conchita.
9. Arthur works much harder than Hyacinth.
10. Sybil swims more energetically than Dorothy.

11.3. Comparison 3

Sections **228–229**; 233

Task *

got worse and worse; more and more worried; the longer they waited; the greater the risk; angrier and angrier / more and more angry; as food got scarcer and scarcer / more and more scarce; the louder their complaints; the sooner their plight; more and more aware; more and more speedily.

11.4. Comparison 4

Sections 230–232

Task one (suggested answers) ***

1. to go on holiday in Australia; 2. to be left to work on their own; 3. I don't think I should drive to work; 4. that he would even believe his own lies; 5. to give evidence; 6. that I'll have to get a porter to help me; 7. to be moved; 8. that I won't bother to attend his lectures; 9. to understand our strengths and weaknesses; 10. that I just stayed indoors all day; 11. to ask any questions about the job; 12. that she's certain to be promoted next time; 13. to accept that there can be peace with that group; 14. as his decision to get married last year; 15. than she thinks.

Task two ***

1. Anne is earning so little that she can't afford to go on holiday in Australia.

   Anne is earning too little to be able to go on holiday in Australia.

2. The trainees weren't experienced enough to be left to work on their own.

   The trainees were so inexperienced that they couldn't be left to work on their own.

3. The fog is too dense for me to drive to work.

   The fog isn't thin enough for me to drive to work.

4. Tony is so foolish as to believe his own lies.

   Tony is foolish enough to believe his own lies.

5. The witness was so afraid that she couldn't give evidence.

   The witness wasn't calm enough to give evidence.

6. The suitcase isn't light enough for me to carry alone.

   The suitcase is too heavy for me to carry alone.

7. The patient was so weak that she couldn't be moved.

   The patient wasn't strong enough to be moved.

8. Professor Puniverse is too boring for me to bother to attend his lectures.

   Professor Puniverse isn't interesting enough for me to bother to attend his lectures.

9. We had been practising so long that we understood our strengths and weaknesses.

   We had been practising too long not to understand our strengths and weaknesses.

10. It had been snowing too heavily for me to leave the house.

    It had been snowing heavily enough for me to stay indoors.

11. Some of the interviewees were so nervous that they didn't ask any questions about the job.

    Some of the interviewees weren't calm enough to ask questions about the job.

12. Ms Lovelace works so hard that she's certain to be promoted next time.

    Ms Lovelace works hard enough to be promoted next time.

13. The President is realist enough not to accept that there can be peace with that group.

    The President is so realistic that he won't accept that there can be peace with that group.

14. Ted's sudden departure was as surprising as his decision to get married last year.

    Ted departed so suddenly that we were as surprised as when he got married last year.

15. Tracy's poor marks at school aren't as worrying as she thinks.

    Tracy's poor marks at school cause her to worry more than she needs to.

Addition, exception and restriction

12.1. Addition

Sections **234–235**

Task one ***

1. The play was far too long; it was also badly acted.

2. At the party Bianca sang and danced too.

3. The department offers a BA in political science. In addition, it serves the community in various ways.

4. Besides speaking English and Russian, Jane spoke fluent Arabic.

5. In addition to building the South, slaves created the wealth of the North.

6. As well as being a frequent guest on NBC's *Weekend Today*, Ms Moore has done more than 200 television interviews.

7. In addition to having hundreds of hotels and motels, Arkansas has more than 170 bed and breakfast inns.

8. As well as being absolutely necessary, a good guide is very affordable.

9. The Amazon rain forest faces peril, and another Brazilian jewel too.

10. Not only do we have a tradition of sparkling wine, but we have also just begun brewing beer.

11. Prisoners of war received the same rations and supplies, and comparable medical care as well.

12. Healthy aging depends not only on physical activity but also on social activity.

Task two **

Tess: So was mine; Nor/Neither did I; So have lots of other people;
Nor/Neither can I; Nor/Neither do some people sitting behind desks;
Nor/Neither should lorry drivers

Ron: So would I; So did most of their generation; So are cyclists and
pedestrians . . . and even animals crossing roads; So do I

12.2. Exception

Section 236

Task **

1. otherwise; 2. bar; 3. except for; 4. but; 5. apart from; 6. except that;
7. else; 8. except; 9. even; 10. except for; 11. otherwise; 12a. apart from;
12b. else

12.3. Restriction

Sections 237–238

Task (suggested answers) ***

1a. . . . only underlined interviewed . . . , they didn't photograph him / they didn't
take pictures of him.

1b. . . . only . . . the Prime Minister, they didn't interview any other
members of the government (or: . . . , not any other members of the
government).

2a. . . . isn't just a keen tennis player, she's also a very talented player.

2b. . . . isn't just a keen tennis player, but also a keen chess player.

3a. . . . merely suggested changing . . . , he didn't insist on changing them.

3b. . . . changing priorities, not changing the party programme.

4a. . . . didn't even try to deal . . . , let alone succeed in dealing with them.

4b. . . . with the worst types of crime, let alone petty crime.

5a. . . . also had to underline the adjectives, in addition to classifying
them.

5b. . . . to underline the adjectives, not only the adverbs.

6a. . . . isn't merely against modern music, she's against classical music
as well.

6b. . . . against modern music, but also against modern painting and
modern architecture.

7a. . . . not only <u>envied</u> his cousin but also <u>despised</u> him.

7b. . . . not only envied his <u>cousin</u> but also his only <u>sister</u>.

8a. . . . couldn't even <u>understand</u> simple questions, let alone <u>answer</u> them.

8b. . . . couldn't even understand <u>simple</u> questions, let alone <u>difficult</u> ones.

9a. . . . didn't just go to <u>Arizona</u> to meet . . . but also to <u>Oregon</u> and <u>Utah</u>.

9b. . . . to meet Native <u>Americans</u>, but also local <u>business</u> people.

10a. . . . also <u>fined</u> for not wearing . . . , not just <u>reprimanded</u>.

10b. . . . for not wearing his <u>safety</u> belt, not only for <u>speeding</u>.

Information, reality and belief

13.1. Questions and answers 1

Sections **240–242**; **536–541**; **609–612**; **681–683**

Task one *

1. Are they going to build a new bridge across the river?
2. Can motorists park in the town square on Sundays?
3. Has Arthur lived in South Africa all his life?
4. Were two gunmen killed by the security forces yesterday?
5. Will inflation start rising again in the next few months?
6. Did Charlotte catch pneumonia last winter?
7. Is skin-diving Uncle Toby's favourite pastime?
8. Had patients been waiting for hours before seeing a doctor?
9. Should these measures have been taken years ago?
10. Does the postman always ring twice?
11. Was Susan disappointed after the job interview?
12. Does the principal have a fourteen-year-old daughter?

Task two **

1. Who; 2. Which; 3. What/Which; 4. Who; 5. What; 6. Which; 7.What; 8. Whose; 9. Who; 10. Which; 11. Why; 12. How; 13. Where; 14. When; 15. How

Task three **

1a. Yes, he will try to get in touch with one of our senior staff.
1b. Yes, he will.

2a. (I think) it will be declared at midnight.

2b. At midnight.

3a. I think we should buy a new car.

3b. A new car.

4a. The second candidate is the most suitable for the job.

4b. The second candidate.

5a. No, they didn't catch any of them./ Yes, they caught one of them.

5b. No, they didn't./ Yes, they did.

6a. I think we should cancel the cruise.

6b. Cancel the cruise.

7a. We have to read at least five of them.

7b. At least five.

8a. Yes, all the necessary precautions have been taken.

8b. Yes, they have.

9a. Yes, they taught us how to pronounce "thoroughly".

9b. Yes, they did.

10a. They eat junk food because it's cheap and tastes good.

10b. Because it's cheap and tastes good.

11a. I'd prefer a house in the country.

11b. A house in the country.

12a. Herman Melville wrote *Moby Dick*.

12b. Herman Melville.

Task four ***

What is the name of one of Africa's most active volcanoes?

How many volcanoes are there along the borders of Rwanda, Congo and Uganda?

When was Nyiragongo last active?

What happened in its summit crater?

How serious is the latest eruption compared with the one in 1994?

How fast can lava from Nyiragongo travel?

How far might the lava go and what might happen?

Who said lava could react with gas in the lake?

What did Bill Evans of the US Geological Survey say?

What is the gas composed of?

How could it affect local people living around the lake?

Where are Nyiragongo and another active volcano located?

Which border does the Virunga mountain range straddle?

How many of Africa's historical eruptions are the pair responsible for?

Task five ***

What is your name?

Where and when were you born?

Did you always live in Cape Town?

Did you go to school in Durban?

Did you go to university in South Africa?

Why did they do that?

Which university did you go to?

Do you have any foreign languages?

How did you pay for that?

Are you looking for a full-time job now?

How much do you want?

Do you have / Have you (got) any references?

13.2. Questions and answers 2

Sections 243–244

Task ***

1. Are some of the candidates unsuitable for the job?
2. Did you see all of the candidates?
3. It won't make any difference?
4. Have they ever been successful?
5. Are any of them being taken care of?
6. Not many people knew about it?
7. You had already met all of them?
8. Have you written to any of them?
9. They protest sometimes?
10. There's no one on earth who can?
11. It's not going to get better at all?
12. Couldn't it make a big difference for some of them?

13.3. Questions and answers 3

Sections **245–248**; 612; 684

Task one *

1. isn't he; 2. did they; 3. can you; 4. don't they; 5. won't it; 6. is it;
7. haven't there; 8. shouldn't they; 9. doesn't she; 10. have they;
11. aren't they; 12. would they

Task two ***

1. Who wants to visit what?

2. Who did you give it away to, and why?

3. Who is going where?

4. How did you kill it, and when?

5. How many did she order, and for when?

6. Who is who?

7. Where have you put what?

8. Who was driving how fast?

9. Where and when is it going to take place?

10. Who stayed on to do what?

13.4. Responses

Sections **249–252**; 22–23

Task one (suggested answers) **

I see; Yeah; That's right; No; Really; Sure; Uhuh; Of course; Thank you;
Indeed

Task two **

1a. Where? 1b. In Birmingham.

2a. What about? 2b. The possible merger.

3a. How many? 3b. Ten.

4a. Why not? 4b. It's too far from the family.

5a. When? 5b. Three o'clock yesterday.

6a. Which ones? 6b. To Düsseldorf and Brussels.

7a. How often? 7b. Every afternoon.

8a. How long? 8b. Three days.

9a. How? 9b. I'll take her to dinner.

10a. What stuff? 10b. Over there, by the gate.

11a. How? 11b. By a motorbike.

12a. Who for? 12b. Caroline.

Task three **

1. What did you lose? / You lost what?

2. He considers himself an excellent driver? / An excellent driver?

3. He should have his head examined? / His head examined?

4. What did she become? / Became what?

5. Where did you spend two months? / Spent two months where?

6. You're going to buy a speedboat next summer? / Buy a speedboat?

7. How much did he earn? / He earned how much?

8. You admire body builders for their big muscles? / Body builders for their big muscles?

9. When was she born? / She was born when?

10. The government wants to privatise the prison system? / Privatise the prison system?

11. Who's a specialist in medieval manuscripts? / Brother who?

12. Why did they kill the hamsters? / Killed them for what?

13.5. Omission of information

Sections 253–255

Task one (suggested answers) ***

There certainly is.; True enough.; Oh, no.; You can't do that.; Excellent.; They are?; I suppose they could.; Not sure about that.; You mean that?; Rubbish.

Task two **

1. Not so fast! 2. Some more? 3. Not fair. 4. Want a drink? 5. Can't understand you. 6. Help! 7. Well done! 8. Oh God! 9. Democrats forever. 10. Sorry! 11. (Beg your) pardon? 12. Excuse me!

13.6. Reported statements

Sections 256–258

Task one **

1. Edith said that she was leaving for Thailand that evening.
2. A spokesman declared that two suspects had been caught by the police the day before.
3. Helen confided to her friends that she didn't want to stay there for the rest of her life.
4. The weatherman added that there would also be widespread frost the next day.
5. The drunken driver claimed that he hadn't touched a drop of alcohol since the previous week-end.
6. The chairman told his audience that they couldn't imagine what the situation had been like two years before.
7. Replying to the detective, Tom refused to reveal the truth then because he was being blackmailed.
8. Susan promised Mark that, if he lent her his sportscar for a day or two, she would invite him to her party.
9. The old couple explained to the social worker that they hadn't realised he/she was taking care of those problems.
10. The Secretary-General emphasised that the United Nations must become more active if the organisation was to keep its credibility.
11. The doctor warned his patient that he/she might be in pain for a few days, but he/she would definitely feel better by the end of that week.
12. The principal told the parents that it was regrettable that children watched so many violent programmes on TV these days.

Task two (a) *

CARE CUTS PUT OAPs' 'LIVES AT RISK'
The government is putting the lives of elderly people at risk and is jeopardizing its own plans to reform the health service, according to a report published on Thursday, 31 January 2002.
It says residential care and support in people's own homes is being rationed and more than a million old people are suffering as a result.
A spokesperson stresses that the report was compiled by 21 organizations, including Help the Aged, Age Concern and the Alzheimer's Society.
It suggests that, while the National Health Service might grab the headlines and the lion share of resources, social care is in crisis.
There are more old people than ever, yet the number receiving support in their own homes is actually falling with only the most needy qualifying for help, the document says.

•

Some 35,000 residential care beds have been lost in the past three years, it adds.

The organizations claim that many elderly people do not receive the help they need with washing, dressing and other forms of personal care.

Others have to wait, sometimes in NHS hospital beds, because they cannot be discharged anywhere else.

Ministers acknowledge that funding for social care has not kept up with the health service.

The report suggests that, without substantial investment, the problems in this area could jeopardize attempts to modernize the NHS.

(slightly adapted from *www.bbc.co.uk*, 31 January 2002)

Task two (b) ★★★

CARE CUTS PUT OAPs' 'LIVES AT RISK'

A report published on Thursday 31 January 2002 said that the government was putting the lives of elderly people at risk and was jeopardising its own plans to reform the health service.

It said that residential care and support in people's own homes was being rationed and more than a million old people were suffering as a result.

A spokesman stressed that the report had been compiled by 21 organisations, including Help the Aged, Age Concern and the Alzheimer's Society.

It suggested that, while the National Health Service might have grabbed the headlines and the lion share of resources, social care was in crisis.

The document said that there were more old people than ever, yet the number receiving support in their own homes was actually falling with only the most needy qualifying for help.

It added that some 35,000 residential care beds had been lost in the previous three years.

The organisations claimed that many elderly people did not receive the help they needed with washing, dressing and other forms of personal care.

They also claimed that others (had) had to wait, sometimes in NHS hospital beds, because they couldn't be discharged anywhere else.

Ministers acknowledged that funding for social care had not kept up with the health service.

The report suggested that, without substantial investment, the problems in this area could jeopardise attempts to modernise the NHS.

(slightly adapted from *www.bbc.co.uk*, 31 January 2002)

13.7. Indirect questions

Sections 259–260; 681

Task ★★

1. Margaret suddenly asked her roommate if she was right-handed or left-handed.

2. The consultant asked the personnel manager which of those candidates he/she preferred.

3. Mr Patten kept wondering why the council couldn't put off the meeting until the next day.

4. The talk show host asked the superstar if he/she had ever suffered from stage fright.

5. The insurance man asked what had caused the car crash on the railway bridge two days before.

6. The nurse wanted to know if he/she might/could give the patient two pills instead of one.

7. The inquisitive woman asked the shop assistant where exactly they stored the yoghurt.

8. The 10-year old wondered if parents had taught their children good manners in the 1970s.

9. I wanted to know which platform the number 17 bus left from.

10. The PR woman inquired whether the foreign delegation would start arriving that afternoon.

11. The learner driver asked the instructor how he/she should reverse the car. (or: . . . how to reverse the car)

12. I wondered if I should send a card or a bunch of flowers. (or: . . . whether to send a card or a bunch of flowers)

13.8. Denial and affirmation 1

Sections **261–262**; **581–585**; **610–611**; **697–699**

Task one *

1. I have not been here before. / I haven't been here before.

2. We will not be running out of money shortly. / We won't be running out of money shortly.

3. Charles does not teach English to Asian immigrants. / Charles doesn't teach English to Asian immigrants.

4. We had not received an invitation from the local council. / We hadn't received an invitation from the local council.

5. Some people do not like watching soap operas. / Some people don't like watching soap operas.

6. I would not buy a holiday cottage if I were you. / I wouldn't buy a holiday cottage if I were you.

7. Jessica is not being stalked by her ex-boyfriend. / Jessica isn't being stalked by her ex-boyfriend.

8. Bill has not been listening to the concert. / Bill hasn't been listening to the concert.

9. David did not strike me as a very dedicated young man. / David didn't strike me as a very dedicated young man.

10. They did not build a new tunnel to link the two islands. / They didn't build a new tunnel to link the two islands.

11. I shall not see the leading actress after the performance. / I shan't see the leading actress after the performance.

12. Our gardener did not cut down the big chestnut trees. / Our gardener didn't cut down the big chestnut trees.

Task two **

1a. I absolutely don't believe what happened last night.

1b. I can't completely believe what happened last night, but it might be true.

2a. The things Jim doesn't like most are the fruit-cakes.

2b. Jim doesn't like the fruit-cakes very much.

3a. It is obvious that smoking isn't forbidden.

3b. It isn't obvious if smoking is forbidden.

4a. It is true that Frank doesn't know why Paula is upset.

4b. Frank doesn't know everything about why Paula is upset.

5a. We may be able to come tomorrow, but it's not certain.

5b. It is absolutely certain that we can't come tomorrow.

Task three ***

1a. The applicants were (probably) not interviewed at all. (scope of 'not': interviewed)

1b. The applicants were interviewed by someone else. (scope of 'not': interviewed by the human resources officer)

2a. I (probably) haven't discussed the children's future with anyone at all. (scope: discussed the children's future)

2b. I have discussed the children's future with someone else. (scope: discussed the children's future with my wife)

3a. There (probably) isn't going to be a demonstration at all. (scope: going to stage a demonstration)

3b. There's going to be a demonstration at another time. (scope: going to stage a demonstration next week)

4a. I (probably) didn't offend Patricia at all. (scope: offend Patricia)

4b. I offended Patricia in some other way. (scope: offend Patricia by telling her she looked a bit under the weather)

5a. I don't vote for them and the reason is that I want to please my dad. (scope: vote for the New Democrats)

5b. I vote for them but the reason is not that I want to please my dad. (scope: vote for the New Democrats to please my dad)

6a. The patient (probably) didn't suffer any pain anywhere. (scope: suffer any pain)

6b. She suffered pain while she was somewhere else. (scope: suffer any pain while she was in hospital)

7a. The party leader was not re-elected and the reason was the smear campaign. (scope: re-elected)

7b. The party leader was re-elected but the smear campaign was not the reason. (scope: re-elected as a result of a smear campaign)

8a. Monica collided with the van but she didn't get injured. (scope: get injured)

8b. Monica was injured by something else. (scope: get injured when she collided with the van)

9a. I (probably) haven't been able to contact Jack at all. (scope: been able to contact Jack)

9b. I've been able to contact Jack by some other means. (scope: been able to contact Jack on my mobile phone)

10a. I didn't want to see Sylvia and the reason was that I felt depressed. (scope: want to see Sylvia).

10b. I wanted to see Sylvia but the reason was not that I felt depressed. (scope: want to see Sylvia because I felt depressed)

Task four ***

1a. outside; 1b. I have seen some of the famous Walt Disney films, but not all.

2a. inside; 2b. Alice hasn't visited the Taj Mahal up to now, but she may in the future.

3a. inside; 3b. We'd never been notified of the health risks involved.

4a. outside; 4b. Young Mr Plimsoll sometimes attends Professor Barnaby's lectures, but not always.

5a. inside; 5b. Nobody was around to show me the way to the boardroom.

6a. outside; 6b. Look, we've already got enough problems.

7a. outside; 7b. The problem with Terry is that there are times when he doesn't listen to what I'm saying.

8a. inside; 8b. The suspect said he wasn't involved in the recent spate of burglaries.

9a. inside; 9b. There is no sign so far that relations between the two countries are improving, but there may be in the future.

10a. inside; 10b. This untalented and boorish 'artist' should never be allowed in here again.

11a. outside – inside; 11b. There are some more applicants to see.

12a. outside – inside; 12b. It's not possible that the bus has arrived and none of the stranded passengers have been picked up.

Task five **

As I was looking for the fruit juice this morning, I found there was SCARCELY any left in the refrigerator. I wondered why there was so LITTLE of it so early in the week, but NEITHER Pam NOR Ruth could give a reasonable explanation. "Well," I sighed, "I suppose there's NOTHING to be done about it."

Going back to the refrigerator, I also found that there were very FEW oranges left. And as for grapefruits, there were NONE whatsoever. This was something that had NEVER happened before. I was about to ask Pam and Ruth again, but they were NOWHERE to be seen any more. As I had NOBODY to turn to now, I saw NO option but to hurry to the shop around the corner. RARELY had I felt so let down by my two roommates, sending me off to the grocer's on an empty stomach like this.

Task six **

As I was looking for the fruit juice this morning, I found there was VERY LITTLE left in the refrigerator. I wondered why there WASN'T MORE of it so early in the week, but Pam AND Ruth couldN'T give a reasonable explanation. "Well," I sighed, "I suppose there ISN'T ANYTHING to be done about it."

Going back to the refrigerator, I also found that there WEREN'T MANY oranges left. And as for grapefruits, there WEREN'T ANY AT ALL. This wasN'T something that had EVER happened before. I was about to ask Pam and Ruth again, but they WEREN'T ANYWHERE to be seen. As I hadN'T ANYONE to turn to now, I DIDN'T SEE ANY option but to hurry to the shop around the corner. I HADN'T OFTEN felt so let down by my two roommates, sending me off to the grocer's on an empty stomach like this.

13.9. Denial and affirmation 2

Section **263**; 586–587

Task one ***

1. NO news is good news.
2. Hubert gave me a NOT ENTIRELY CONVINCING reply.
3. NOT MANY of the students disliked their history teacher.
4. It is NOT UNUSUAL for tribespeople to behave in this extraordinary way.
5. A NOT UNIMPORTANT detail was overlooked by all those present.
6. Beatrice did sell her caravan, but NOT WITHOUT some regret.
7. Most observers agreed that the workers' demands were NOT (ENTIRELY) UNREASONABLE.
8. NO electricity means that people have to live in primitive circumstances.
9. In spite of everything, NOT ALL of these deprived children are UNHAPPY.
10. The President will visit South Korea in the NOT-TOO-DISTANT future.
11. Dyslexia in children NOT INFREQUENTLY goes unrecognized for years.
12. We can put off the scheme for some time, but NOT INDEFINTELY / NOT FOR (TOO) LONG.

Task two **

1. I tiptoed through the room (SO AS) NOT TO wake up the sleeping toddler.
2. NOT BEING ABLE TO tell the difference between the twins, I asked them both to wear name tags.
3. The ideal solution would be FOR DRIVERS NOT TO think of their vehicles as race cars.
4. NOT BEING rich doesn't necessarily mean that you are unhappy.
5. Mr Templar was the only person NOT TO drink a single drop of alcohol.
6. Laura was livid with rage AT NOT BEING invited to the wedding party.
7. The instructor began by telling us how NOT TO respond in an emergency situation.
8. One student objected to NOT HAVING access to the Internet.
9. Most observers expect THERE NOT TO be too many problems.
10. NOT KNOWING where to go, I simply decided to stay at home.

**Task three ** **

Amy: Boris, I DON'T think I'LL be coming to your party after all.

Boris: No problem. I DON'T suppose ANYBODY will miss you.

Amy: What a rude thing to say! I DON'T believe you REALISE how badly some of your guests behaved last month.

Boris: Well, I DON'T expect that bunch of lager louts WILL show up this time. They haven't been invited.

Amy: Oh, good. You see, I DIDN'T THINK I would have ANY chance at all of enjoying myself with them around.

Boris: Look, I'm sorry about what I said. I DON'T suppose you WOULD be willing to change your mind?

Amy: Hmm. I DON'T feel I SHOULD give in too easily. I can be very stubborn, you know.

Boris: Yes, I do know that. Still, I WOULDN'T expect you TO BE too stubborn, just for my sake.

Amy: Turning on the old charm again? OK, you win. I DON'T think I SHOULD make you feel miserable for the rest of your life.

Boris: Great! I DIDN'T believe I could EVER win you over. Thanks for proving me wrong.

13.10. Denial and affirmation 3

Sections **264–269**; **611–612**

**Task one ** **

1. There <u>will</u> be an inquiry (but it may not be held until next <u>month</u>).

2. It <u>is</u> going to be built (but not in <u>this</u> part of the city).

3. I <u>didn't</u> buy it (I found it in the <u>attic</u>).

4. They <u>didn't</u> arrive late (they were here in <u>time</u>).

5. I <u>can</u> lend a hand (if they are not <u>too</u> heavy).

6. It <u>doesn't</u> have secret funds (neither <u>here</u> nor <u>abroad</u>).

7. I <u>don't</u> keep refusing to learn a foreign language (I'm studying <u>Spanish</u>).

8. They <u>should</u> get upset (they don't want to encourage <u>truancy</u>.)

9. He <u>doesn't</u> deserve praise (his innovations are <u>worthless</u>).

10. They <u>aren't</u> coming over (they are staying at <u>home</u>).

11. She still <u>does</u> want to see you (but first you should ap<u>o</u>logise to her).

12. Someone <u>has</u> called an ambulance (but it collided with a <u>van</u>).

Task two **

Lynn: Mark, are YOU interested in history?

Mark: NO, I'M NOT, I think it's extremely boring.

Lynn: You are not being serious.

Mark: YES, I AM. People should be interested in the future, not in the past.

Lynn: I hope you understand that SOME people take an interest in the past.

Mark: YES, I DO. It's just that I've always disliked the subject.

Lynn: You probably had teachers who insisted on students remembering lots of dates.

Mark: NO, I DIDN'T, as a matter of fact. One of them even got the dates wrong himself.

Lynn: Well, he can't have been fully qualified for the job.

Mark: NO, HE WASN'T. He told us one day that Napoleon had died in 1812.

Lynn: Oh, he should have said 1821, of course.

Mark: YES, HE SHOULD. And he claimed that the Battle of Waterloo had taken place in 1805.

Lynn: That was an even more stupid thing to say.

Mark: YES, IT WAS. So I became convinced that history was a subject for nerds.

Lynn: And you didn't want to become a nerd yourself.

Mark: NO, I DIDN'T. That's why I started reading science fiction novels instead. They are the most interesting books I can think of.

Lynn: THEY ARE NOT. Nothing's more boring than sci-fi. Anyway, librarians will take such unscientific books off the shelves in the years to come.

Mark: NO, THEY WON'T. Some of those books are works of literature. You've never read Wells, Huxley . . . Orwell, I suppose.

Lynn: YES, I HAVE.

Mark: Well, there you are! We seem to agree at last.

Task three (suggested answers) **

1. ...., but he's done well in his job.

2. ...., but I've got a nice house.

3. ...., but the people feel free.

4. ...., but I'd like to go to Bali.

5. ...., but she should be told to behave better.

6. ...., but we found a ticket machine on the platform.

7. ...., but to a private TV station.

8. ...., but why it originally appealed to the people.

9. ...., but she DOES get on well with our foreign visitors.

10. ...., but he WAS a member of the gang.

Modifying

14.1. Restrictive and non-restrictive meaning

Sections 110–112

Task one **

1. the house for sale; 2. the business that went bankrupt; 3. the local history society; 4. a visitor from Latvia; 5. a heavy fall of snow; 6. the marketing manager; 7. the Hungarian president; 8. the delayed 6.45 train; 9. the woman who reported the crime; 10. the school on the hill

Task two **

1. R: only the animal parks that are large vs N-R: all the animal parks are large

2. R: only the houses that were old vs N-R: all the houses were old

3. R: only the train services that were unreliable vs N-R: all the train services were unreliable

4. R: only the Finnish students enjoyed the course vs N-R: all the students were Finnish

5. R: only the students who had worked hard vs N-R: all the students had worked hard

6. R: only the voters who were democratically sophisticated vs N-R: all the voters were democratically sophisticated

7. R: only the hospitals that are understaffed vs N-R: all the hospitals are understaffed

8. R: only the teachers who were/taught French vs N-R: all the teachers were French

9. R: only the students who were poor vs N-R: all the students were poor

10. R: only the portraits that were famous vs N-R: all the portraits were famous

Task three **

1a. French paintings are naïve. vs 1b. The naïve group of French paintings.

2a. It was the first time we'd had a sunny day. vs 2b. The first day also happened to be a sunny one.

3a. There had already been one disastrous game. vs 3b. Their second game, unlike their first, was disastrous.

4a. The best of typical Greek music. vs 4b. The Greek music which is classical music.

5a. The last romatic novel she wrote. vs 5b. Her last novel was romantic.

14.2. Post-modifiers

Sections **641–649**; 70; 106; 110 etc.

Task one ***

1. I'll always remember the moment when the lawyer realized he'd lost the case. (clause of time)

2. What you wrote in that article about the new laws offended people who had fought hard for changes in the law. (relative clause)

3. There's no reason why you should have to go there. (clause of reason)

4. There is no other way to do it but this one. (clause of manner)

5. It's next to the old building they are going to pull down. (relative clause)

6. The doctor will have time to see you. (clause of time)

7. I'll do it some time next week when I'm free. (clause of time)

8. That is just one reason why he should not be allowed to go. (clause of reason)

9. That's the best play to see. (appositive clause)

10. That was not the right time to do it. (clause of time)

Task two **

1. I shall be detailing the plans in a paper to be distributed next week.

2. Everyone working in that department was angered by the proposal.

3. The couple next door both work in the Social Studies department.

4. All those wary of walking too close to the edge of the cliff should stay near the leader.

5. Hillary and Tensing were the first men to get to the top of Everest.

6. I have nothing to do this afternoon.

7. People in the train delayed for three hours were given a full refund for the ticket.

8. There is no more for anyone to do.

9. I have nothing to say.

10. The train going to London will leave from platform 4.

14.3. Pre-modifiers

Sections **650–653**; 440; 459; 522

Task one **

1. *new*: adjective

2. *anorexic*: adjective

3. *sworn*: -ed participle

4. *published*: -ed participle

5. *very long*: degree adverb + adjective

6. *interesting*: -ing participle

7. *train*: noun – *great*: adjective

8. *government*: noun

9. *very exciting*: degree adverb + -ing participle

10. *punishment*: noun

Task two **

1. that Victorian terraced house; 2. a red lambswool jersey; 3. a successful self-made man; 4. the artistically designed oak table; 5. the self-financed institute; 6. the very old black-and-white television; 7. the three-door estate car; 8. the hard-working student; 9. that early-flowering rose; 10. the expiry date on the credit card

Task three ***

1. very wet English spring; 2. beautiful oriental; 3. strong German wheat; 4. long university summer; 5. strong blond Australian; 6. very small unknown French textile; 7. craggy south-facing Welsh; 8. cold snow-covered; 9. very kind patient old; 10. classic Hungarian dessert

Task four **

- *famous* (adjective) *Manchester* (noun) *flat* (classifying adjective); *new* (adjective); *Commonwealth* (noun)
- *northern* (adjective); *flat* (classifying adjective) *cap* (noun); *official* (adjective); *games* (noun)
- *cotton* (adjective); *no-nonsense* (compound noun) *northern* (classifying adjective); *squashy* (adjective); *all-conquering* (compound -*ing* participle) *baseball* (noun); *games* (noun)
- *tested* (-*ed* participle); *Yorkshire pudding* (compound noun); *Soviet* (noun); *Soviet worker's* (classifying genitive noun phrase); *homely* (adjective); *Manchester* (noun) *Asda* (classifying noun)
- *particularly* (degree adverb); *chief* (adjective); *supermarket* (noun); *11-day* (noun phrase)
- *nearest* (adjective); *traditional* (adjective); *snazzy* (adjective); *water* (noun)

14.4. Relative clauses

Sections **685–694**; 110–111; 371–372; 461; 595; 659; 747

Task one *

1. c; 2. f; 3. e; 4. a; 5. h; 6. i; 7. b; 8. j; 9. g; 10. d

Task two **

1. It is something (which/that) I'm expected to do.
2. She was a clever woman, who(m) the company exploited.
3. He was an actor (who/that) no-one had ever heard of.
4. I like being married to a chef whose sister owns a restaurant.
5. I enjoyed the production of 'No man's land' (which/that) Ian Holm starred in.
6. I've finished the book (which/that) you got as a prize.
7. How do you like living in the town (which/that) you work in/where you work.
8. It was a lovely day when we went to Brighton.
9. He's got a new computer, which he can't use.
10. He told me about it in the letter which/that came this morning.

Task three **

1. which/that; 2. who; 3. which; 4. who; 5. of whom; 6. of whose; 7. in which; 8. of which; 9. in which; 10. who

Task four **

1. The bike tethered to a tree . . . ; 2. The house in need of repair . . . . ;
3. The man driving too fast . . . ; 4. Any company hiding its accounts . . . ;
5. The article discussing the use of nuclear power . . .

Task five *

1. He's working very hard now, which is a good thing.

2. Jane's finished her thesis, which is amazing.

3. Jack's working in Tokyo for two years, after which he's hoping to go to Hong Kong.

4. The old lady died on her husband's birthday, which is sad.

5. The train was an hour late, which was not unusual.

14.5. Apposition

Sections **470–472**; 397; 589; 593; 646

Task one **

1. David Brown, owner of the garage across the road, has a good reputation.

2. Mrs Davies, a teacher at the local school, is loved by all the children.

3. Anne and Peter Austin, the executors of my aunt's will, have retired and gone to live in New Zealand.

4. I once knew James Kane, the star in last year's Oscar-winning movie.

5. John Williams, a writer of poetry, has won several prizes.

6. That building over there was designed by James Stirling, a celebrated architect in the 1970s and 80s.

7. The production is by Richard Jones, director of both opera and theatre.

8. I always book my holidays at Compston's, the travel agency opposite the bank.

9. Impact 92, a language consultancy, does a lot of work in Scandinavia.

10. Nokia, now a mobile phone company, started as a company selling rubber goods such as tyres.

Task two **

1. A: David James has bought the house next door to mine.

   B: Which David James? David James our school friend or David James the dentist? (R-R)

2. Hello. Is that Robert Hunt <u>the builder</u>? (R)

3. I was at university with the actor <u>James Marlow</u>. (R)

4. Barbara Castle, <u>the British socialist politician</u>, died on 2 May 2002. (N-R)

5. One of my oldest friends is Keith Godard, <u>the New York-based graphic designer</u>. (N-R)

6. Your doctor, <u>John Beasley</u>, is retiring next year. Did you know? (N-R)

Task three ***

1. such as; 2. especially; 3. for example; 4. in particular; 5. notably; 6. for instance

Modality

15.1. Agreement and disagreement

Sections 270–273

Task one **

1. Well, it WAS a rather silly story, but the actors seemed to believe in the parts they were playing.
2. I'm not so sure they made a big mistake: she is very young and may still grow in her job.
3. I would say it's undercooked MOST of the time, especially when there are too many customers to be served.
4. Aren't you being a little unfair? His latest idea may be provocative but it's also very innovative.
5. Yes, it's a rather unusual colour, but now the house will stand out from the rest.
6. I think I agree with you, but it's just his youthful enthusiasm that makes him say these things.
7. Well, it wasn't their best match to be sure, but in my opinion the game should at least have ended in a draw.
8. There are definitely people who are more suitable for such a job. On the other hand, he's a good communicator and that's an important asset too.
9. I would even say it had some EXCELLENT ideas, but not enough people are receptive to them.
10. Well, the average score was lower than last year, but half a dozen students got top marks this time.

Task two **

1. Yes, they should have won by a large margin.
2. I agree, in fact some people will be in for a nasty surprise.

3. Oh, it was a fantastic film! I could see it three or four times.

4. Oh, it's pure art, a real masterpiece!

5. Yes, he gets better and better all the time.

6. No, there aren't any at all. The real leaders are the CEOs of big corporations and they pull the strings in politics.

7. It was incredibly good. I'd do it again.

8. Absolutely. You must be out of your mind to travel by car these days.

9. If you ask me, he's definitely NOT going to be happy working under Alan. He's going to feel utterly miserable.

10. You can't imagine how much I enjoyed it. It was a terrific play.

Task three **

1. Oh, it wasn't too bad.

2. It's difficult to please ALL the voters, you know.

3. They may live to regret that.

4. She may not be very intelligent, but she's very generous.

5. Don't you think his work for the club deserved to be rewarded?

6. There may be better teachers but I rather like him.

7. I think some, not all, are quite good.

8. Well, perhaps he was rather technical. But he did make a number of points that were fairly clear to me.

9. I'm not so sure that this is the best time to invest.

10. Well, he IS very rich, but I know of at least half a dozen people who are richer.

15.2. Fact, hypothesis and neutrality

Sections **274–282**; 416; 493; 589; 609

Task one **

1. F; 2. H; 3. F; 4. N; 5. H; 6. H; 7. F; 8. H; 9. M; 10. N

Task two **

1. Should you get the job; 2. Do you know whether; 3. I'd be surprised if; 4. It's time; 5. Suppose; 6. Did you know that; 7. I'm glad; 8. Had you known; 9. They were surprised; 10. I doubt whether

Task three **

1b. It is (somewhat) less likely that he will come. (= more tentative)

2b. The very idea makes me feel angry. (= not just the fact / putative 'should')

3b. He assumes it will take place. (= somewhat less certain than 'will' used on its own)

4b. The very idea surprises me. (= not just the fact / putative 'should')

5b. The government has made a decision in principle, but could still be prevented from going ahead with its decision.

15.3. Degrees of likelihood

Sections **283–292**; **461–463**; **483**; **501**; **542**

Task one ***

1. hypothetical possibility; 2. tentative possibility; 3. certainty or logical necessity; 4. probability; 5. hypothetical necessity; 6. tentative possibility; 7. possibility of the fact; 8. hypothetical ability; 9. prediction and predictability; 10. certainty or logical necessity

Task two **

1. can't; 2. must; 3. should – may; 4. must; 5. can't; 6. can; 7. It is possible; 8. could; 9. can; 10. must

Task three ***

1. Well, it is possible that she will get the grades she needs for university entrance.

2. It is necessary for jobs to go. There is a need for the company to restructure itself.

3. Don't worry. They are certain to give in in the end.

4. It is (very) likely the play has started by now.

5. John would be able to make that business work if he wanted to.

6. It is just possible / There is a remote possibility that there was an accident. You don't know.

7. After all these years, it's impossible that she's still living in Brook Street.

8. I assume there will be a bus home after the concert. After all, the concert finishes at 9.30.

9. It is possible that she's not the best 400-metre runner in the world, but she deserves a place in the team.

10. I'm bound to be dreaming. It is impossible that it's you after all these years.

Task four **

1. Someone had to tell him to stop; otherwise we'd have had a lot of trouble from the management.

2. Right from the beginning, they couldn't have selected her for the team.

3. By mid-century people may be taking holidays on the moon.

4. The financial director must have been in deep trouble and must have chosen to disappear.

5. You don't have to finish the project by the end of the week. The boss told you . . .

6. It's a pity for the old people, but the bus service will have to be cancelled. Hardly anybody uses it.

7. Can you/are you able to increase the fonts available on this computer?

8. They can order a review of the way the money was spent.

9. They must have questioned her about the missing documents.

10. If you had to choose, would you want to do research or teach?

15.4. Attitudes to truth

Sections **293–297**; 508; 587; 733

Task one **

1. feeling of certainty (or: firm belief); 2. feeling of certainty, expressed by a double negative; 3. assumption; 4. certainty; 5. confident assumption

Task two **

1. take it; 2. it seems to me that; 3. in my view; 4. conviction; 5. presumably; 6 seems; 7. thought; 8. don't you think; 9. supposes; 10. don't believe

Task three **

1. In my opinion, the newspaper report suggested she had committed suicide. (belief or opinion)

2. He's convinced the world revolves around him. (belief or opinion)

3. Apparently, she never had the ring in the first place. (appearance)

4. Presumably you knew exactly what the results of such an action would be. (assumption)

5. I think we should give in now and take what we have. (belief or opinion)

6. It seems he's not coming. (appearance)

7. I'm of the opinion that during this century overhead cables will disappear . . . (belief or opinion)

8. You do know, presumably, that this work must be completed within two weeks. (assumption)

9. I think you behaved rather stupidly. Telling him . . . (belief or opinion)

10. He should have got there by now. (assumption)

15.5. Volition

Sections 319–324

Task one ***

1. The government is going to press ahead with the new security bill in spite of strong opposition.

   (prediction ⇒ intention or speaker's feeling of certainty)

2. Are we going to work together on this new project?

   (mild exhortation ⇒ more neutral question about (possibly) shared intention)

3. She'd rather not spend time watching programmes like *Coronation Street*. She considers them to be trivial and no more than a fantasy world.

   (purely hypothetical 'would' ⇒ preference)

4. The chairman isn't going to postpone the shareholders' meeting just because the venue is considered to be too small.

   (prediction ⇒ intention or speaker's feeling of certainty)

5. They are going to help you in the garden. They enjoy doing that.

   (prediction ⇒ intention or speaker's feeling of certainty)

6. I'd be willing/prepared to put money into it if they could guarantee a minimum return for the investment.

   (purely hypothetical 'would' ⇒ hypothetical 'would' in combination with explicit willingness)

7. Do you want to be rich and famous like Cliff Richard?

(more tentative ⇒ more direct)

8. I hope she succeeds. She's worked very hard.

(tentative wish ⇒ even more tentative wish or preference / hypothetical)

9. The minister refuses (or: is unwilling) to admit he was wrong about the Sports stadium.

(very little difference)

10. Ivan wants Tim to teach with him in Hungary.

(more tentative ⇒ more direct)

Task two **

1. 'll; 2. intends to; 3. want; 4. would like; 5. wish; 6. I wish; 7. want; 8. shall; 9. are going to; 10. always WILL

15.6. Permission and obligation

Sections 325–329; 483

Task one **

– Permission: 2, 8
– Hypothetical permission: 1
– Obligation or compulsion: 3, 4
– Hypothetical obligation: 5
– Prohibition: 6, 7, 10
– Exemption: 9

Task two **

1. C; 2. F; 3. E; 4. A; 5. C; 6. E; 7. C; 8. A; 9. E; 10. F; 11. C; 12. C

Task three **

1. You should write to the head teacher of a school at once.

2. You will have to pay your travelling costs to Britain.

3. You don't need to register with the police.

4. You mustn't take any disciplinary action yourself against unruly pupils.

5. You can take your car to Britain if you want.

6. You may (or: are allowed to) contact anyone who has done this before.

7. You must arrive in Britain at least three weeks before the beginning of the term.

8. You mustn't live more than four miles from the school.

9. You don't need to attend any special induction courses.

10. You mustn't take pupils out of school without special permission.

15.7. Influencing people 1

Sections 330–335 & 339; 417

Task one **

1. request: *lunch*
2. request: *doing*
3. invitation: *down*
4. command: *home – home(work)*
5. advice: *out*
6. suggestion: *(A)ca(demy)*
7. warning: *care(ful)*
8. promise: *post – morn(ing)*
9. warning/threat: *(a)gain – (re)gret*
10. threat: *shoot*

Task two **

1. (Be) careful! . . .
2. . . . or I'll send the bailiff.
3. Would you be kind enough to . . .
4. You must (definitely) . . .
5. Could you . . .
6. You should (go and) see *A Midsummer Night's Dream*. . . .
7. . . . You may/can depend on it.
8. Shall we go . . .
9. If I were you, I would have . . .
10. Would/Will you join . . .

Task three **

SITUATION 1: (a) Could we discuss it some other time?

(b) I must ask you to go.

(c) Well, let's discuss it some other time . . . , shall we?

SITUATION 2: (a) Would you please not testify in this particular case.

(b) I'm afraid you simply can't testify in this particular case

(c) It would be better if you agree not to testify . . .

(d) If I were you, I wouldn't testify . . .

(e) If you do testify, you and your family will be facing grave consequences.

(f) Testifying . . . could harm your career in the Civil Service.

SITUATION 3: (a) . . . the currents in the middle of the river are very dangerous.

(b) . . . you should stay close to the river bank.

(c) . . . you'd better stay close to the river bank.

SITUATION 4: (a) If you don't accept them, we won't have a garage.

(b) Why not put them behind the garden shed and cover them with tarpaulin?

(c) If I were you, I'd put them behind the garden shed and cover them with tarpaulin.

(d) Would you please keep some in your garden.

15.8. Influencing people 2

Sections **336–338 & 340**; 608; 730

Task one *

1. E; 2. J; 3. G; 4. A; 5. H; 6. I; 7. F; 8. C; 9. B; 10. D

Task two **

1. Mary, let's invest in the new company (together). (or: Why don't we invest . . . ?)

2. David, don't go near the station after dark. (or: It's not at all safe to go . . .)

3. Mrs Johnson, would you please stand for President of the society? (or: Mrs J., we invite you to . . .)

4. Jane, you should do more exercise. (or: I strongly advise you to do more exercise.)

5. I won't support this government on the matter of lowering taxes. (I refuse to support . . .)

6. We are going to sue the newspaper (or: you) if you don't publish an apology.

7. I promise to give back all the money I('ve) borrowed by March. (or: I will give back all the money . . .)

8. You mustn't come into the club until you've paid your debts. (or:You are not to enter the club . . .)

9. You should spend at least four weeks travelling round Australia. (If I were you, I would spend . . .)

10. Flights will be delayed because of a strike in France.

Task three ***

1. Staff were told (by management) there would have to be some redundancies.

2. My boss promised me I was definitely being considered for promotion.

3. Rob suggested finishing the work that evening/night so as to be able to have the next day off.

4. Shirley asked Mary if she could possibly lend her £50.

5. I advised X not to invest in a dot com company.

6. I was told to finish this by nine o'clock.

7. We were told to finish this quickly or else we would have to stay here/there all night. (or: . . . if we were not to stay here/there all night.)

8. The club rules prohibit(ed) members from introducing anyone under the age of eighteen into the club.

9. The secretary promised the manager the report would be on his desk the next/following morning.

10. She asked me to get the tickets for her.

Addressing

16.1. Vocatives

Sections **349–350**

Task *

1. Dear Sarah; 2. Mr President; 3. Eric; 4. Operator; 5. grandma; 6. Ladies and Gentlemen; 7. Your Honour; 8. darling; 9. Slocombe; 10. Dad; 11. Doctor; 12. Your Excellency

16.2. Commands

Sections **497–498**

Task one *

Leave; make; Take; Be; Bear; turn; Cross; climb; Beware; Keep

Task two *

1. Let me give you another example.

2. Let's go for a drink.

3. Somebody move that stuff out of the way.

4. Let them eat cake.

5. Let's not pretend we support the idea. / Let's not pretend to support the idea.

6. Let me warn you just one more time.

7. Let's settle the problem once and for all.

8. Let there be no doubt at all about our resolve.

9. Let's move as fast as we can.

10. Don't let me detain you any longer.

Focusing

17.1. Focusing information

Sections **396–401**; **744**

Task one **

1. I like Kent, // but I prefer Sussex.

2. I find / that with so many of these problems – // marriage, // sex education – // as soon as you try to make it a sort of formal lesson, // the whole thing falls flat.

3. The fact that Burti feels only bruised and battered / after the accident with Schumacher // is a measure of the progress we have made on the safety measure / over the past two seasons.

4. We had our breakfast in the kitchen // and then we sort of did what we liked.

5. We took some children / to the environmental study centre the other day, // and they have various animals around there.

6. And the thing is / that the journalists – // I mean I've met some of these people – // they know nothing about the country at all.

7. Spectator sports are dying out. // I think people are getting choosy. // There's more to do, of course. // More choice.

8. Sundays in London. // If we're all working / or cooking / or things like that, // it can get fearfully dull.

9. Dave rang me about this business / of changing the groups.

10. Of course / the children have their own inhibitions / about talking about sex. // They're just not frank about it.

Task two ***

1. f; 2. a – b – g – g – g; 3. g – a – g; 4. f; 5. g – f; 6. g – c – g; 7. g – g – g – g; 8. g – g – g – a; 9. g; 10. d – g – g

Task three ***

1. *She's been painting that <u>door</u> / for <u>three</u> days now.* (rising – falling)
2. *Sue teaches at the school in <u>Queen</u> Street.* (falling)
3. *<u>No</u>. // Sue <u>teaches</u> at the school. // She's not the social <u>secretary</u>.* (falling – falling – fall-rise)
4. A: *That's a fine <u>penguin</u>. // Are you taking it to the <u>zoo</u>?* (fall-rise – rising)

   B: *<u>No</u>, // I took it to the zoo <u>yesterday</u>. // I'm taking it to the <u>cinema</u> today.* (falling – fall-rise – falling)
5. *I saw that film at the <u>Duke's</u>.* (falling)
6. *It was the film version of <u>Orlando</u> that I saw at the <u>Duke's</u>.* (fall-rise)
7. *The <u>phone's</u> ringing.* (falling)
8. *Ivan lives in <u>London</u> / in <u>King</u> Street.* (falling – falling)

   He lives in <u>London</u>, // but he also has an apartment in <u>Cambridge</u>. (fall-rise – falling)
9. *Can you understand all <u>that</u>? // If you <u>can't</u>, // just phone <u>again</u>.* (rising – rising – falling)
10. *I want more <u>time</u>, // more <u>money</u> // and more <u>coffee</u>.* (rising – rising – falling)
11. *The editor was John <u>Wrigley</u>.* (falling)
12. *Studio production was by Paul <u>Moore</u>; // the editor was John <u>Wrigley</u>.* (rising – falling)

Task four **

1. *<u>No</u>, // it was the summer be<u>fore</u> last.*
2. *Yes, I <u>have</u>, // I've been several <u>times</u>.*
3. *. . . but only <u>forty</u>-six per cent of the voters / replied on <u>time</u>.*
4. *. . . , but he's not a very good <u>actor</u>.*
5. *<u>I</u> say / he's just an oppor<u>tunist</u> / who arrived at the right <u>time</u>.*
6. *<u>Yes</u>. // And it still drives <u>well</u>.*
7. *I <u>haven't</u>. // The one I <u>gave</u> you / was in<u>correct</u>.*
8. *. . . , but the time will <u>fly</u> past.*
9. *I have to be hands-<u>on</u>.*
10. *He's had four al<u>ready</u>.*

Task five **

1. For me perfect happiness is a good meal with good friends.
2. What I fear most is drowning.

3. The most obvious one is Queen Victoria, a small lady.

4. Something I hate is an inability to laugh at yourself.

5. The only one I have is a car.

6. Something I love to spend money on is shopping.

7. My greatest regret is that life is too short.

8. I hope it will be suddenly and painlessly.

9. A great form of relaxation is crossword puzzles.

10. The most important thing I've learned is to take each day as it comes.

17.2. Organising information – Given and new information

Sections **402–407**

Task one **

1. *"Did they enjoy Sin<u>ga</u>pore?" "<u>No</u>, it was raining all the <u>time</u>."*

2. *"That's a <u>lovely</u> vase Anne gave you." "<u>Joan</u> gave it to me, not Anne."*

3. *The driver wasn't going very <u>fast</u> when he crashed through <u>the</u> <u>barrier</u>.*

4. *I know you find the noise from the trains dis<u>turb</u>ing, but here the <u>planes</u> are <u>worse</u>.*

5. *I took my holiday in <u>Hun</u>gary.*

6. *There's someone at the <u>door</u>.*

7. *Can I speak to <u>Alison</u>, please?*

8. *Tell her it's <u>Mike</u>.*

9. *I went to Berlin in <u>February</u> because the U-Bahn was a <u>hundred</u> years old.*

10. *It's <u>true</u>. He won the <u>lottery</u>.*

Task two **

1. The outbreak of foot and mouth disease was detected in England on 20 February.

2. Since then it has spread in the UK in an explosive manner.

3. By 2 March the disease was found in England, Wales, Scotland and Northern Ireland.

4. The virus causes foot and mouth disease only in hoofed animals but may cause a transient infection in horses and people.

5. Hoofed animal species include cattle, pigs, sheep, goats, deer, reindeer and elks.

6. The disease causes no risk for humans.

7. As a disinfectant you may use diluted citric acid available from pharmacies.

8. If you bring animals to Finland from the risk areas, wash them thoroughly with shampoo after arrival as pets may transport the virus.

9. As the situation in the UK is critical, it is the duty of travellers to be cautious.

10. Do not visit premises where animals are kept for at least 48 hours.

17.3. Organising information – Order and emphasis

Sections 411–414

Task one **

1. *Some awful films*: E

2. *Poor*: C

3. *Most of this work*: S

4. *Some days*: C – *others*: C

5. *Hard work*: E

6. *new houses in a traditional style*: C

7. *Stupid*: C

8. *Romantic novels*: C – *serious works*: C

9. *This*: S

10. *Street names*: C

Task two **

1. That cat they just don't look after properly. (S)

2. These new working conditions the company has already put into practice. (S)

3. Some foreign films they show, but the really important ones they don't show. (C – C)

4. Very clever he may be, but practical he isn't. (C – C)

5. In a very strange way she behaved at the meeting. (E)

6. Didn't they paint the house an awful colour? (S)

7. A lot of people his speech at the funeral offended. (S)

8. The reason for this celebration I don't understand. (S)

9. They gave the money to her; but to him they gave the painting. (C)

10. The problems you're speaking about the management looked into last week. (S)

Task three ***

Dear Edward,

Many thanks for giving me a chance to read your story. I think it is of importance to all people like us and most will find it reflects their own experience. The structure of the story is something I was very impressed by. The way the story shifted back and forth between the two protagonists and, because of this, shifted between the seasons to show the development of the main character are things I liked. I was a bit frightened by the introductory monologue. I think this was because I am shy of exposing myself and you had written this in the first person. When I discovered you had called the character Tim, I was relieved. The way the characters moved in and out of the story reflecting the parallels of experience was to my liking.

The way you described the town, the sea and the vineyard I also liked. I could imagine myself there, especially by the sea and in the vineyard. The philosophy underpinning the story I found interesting. There is never a beginning. Where we think there is a beginning, it is really a development of ideas and events that have gone before. You conveyed this brilliantly.

Well done, Edward. Many thanks again for letting me read this. Others will have this opportunity, I hope. Your story has a lot to say.

Yours,

Ivan

17.4. Organising information – Inversion

Sections **415–417; 584–585; 590–594; 681–684**

Task one **

1. There by the fence is John.

2. Over there is the house for sale.

3. Look; there is the person you want.

4. On the left is Rick; on the right is Nick.

5. Down the road, laughing and shouting, came Janet and Paul.

6. Up into the sky flew the kite.

7. Here lies John Nehemiah – looking up at his friends.

8. Outside the house stood the car of his dreams.

9. On the hill stood a city, proud surveyor of the valley below.

10. As the storm raged, down crashed an enormous tree.

Task two **

1. Only if the managing director quit would the government agree to bail out the company.

2. Never has England played better than with its new manager.

3. In no way (or: Not in any way) does your proposal touch on the real problem.

4. Not even the smallest concession did the Prime Minister make to the opposition.

5. Not only did their son fail his exam; he also refused the chance to repeat it.

6. Not a penny were they left in their mother's will. All the money went to charity.

7. Hardly had she had time to take in the new rules for welfare payments when she was put in charge of the office.

8. Little could the head of department do to stop the erosion of confidence in any future developments.

9. Little did he give away about his own future plans.

10. Rarely have I seen such a poor display of sportsmanship.

Task three ***

(Not far from Manchester is Eccles.) Not only is it famous for its special cake; it also has the world's only swinging aqueduct, carrying water from the Manchester Ship Canal. Now the people of Eccles are afraid that no-one will come to experience these jewels. Why?

Nowhere on the new ordnance survey map is there a town called Eccles.

"We're very sorry about this. Rarely do we make such mistakes," confessed a spokesman for the ordnance survey team.

"Little do they understand about how we feel," said a town councillor. "Hardly had I sat down at my desk this morning when the phone started ringing with complaints. When we are back on the map, only then shall I be satisfied."

Unfortunately, in no way can that happen until the next edition of the map.

Another mistake is that the map shows Ladywell and Salford Royal hospitals. No longer do these hospitals exist.

Seldom have residents of Eccles felt so confused and angry. "In no way can strangers to the region find us now," sighed one resident.

17.5. Organising information – Fronting with 'so/neither'

Section 418

Task one *

1. So did Miles.
2. Neither have Sara and Rowan.
3. So is Marc.
4. So is Rowan.
5. So did Rowan.
6. So does Miles.
7. Neither do Marc and Sara.
8. So did Helen.
9. So will David, Miles and Helen.
10. So does Marc.

Task two **

So catastrophic was the event that most people couldn't take in the enormity of the disaster. In reality, so small was the area covered that the majority of the world could only look on in disbelief. However, so enormous was the building that, as it crumbled, it brought others down in its wake.

"We have seen the end of an era," claimed one commentator.

"So we have," replied the politician.

"I had friends in there."

"In fact, so did we all."

"The world will never be the same again."

So extraordinary were the messages that flashed round the world that only pictures could help people understand what had happened. So often did commentators describe the scene as if it were from a Hollywood movie that the comparison became devoid of meaning.

"I saw that film 'Independence Day'".

"So did we all."

"It had scenes like this."

"So it did."

And so shocked and frightened were the people that they went home and left an eerie silence on the streets.

17.6. Organising information – Cleft sentences

Sections **419–423**; 496; 592

Task one **

1. It was in Sweden that I spent last week, not Switzerland.
2. No, it was Shakespeare who wrote *Much Ado about Nothing*, not Marlowe.
3. It was the lower interest rate that she supported at the meeting of the fiscal committee.
4. It was by our camera crew that the prince was filmed.
5. It's the 1960s that nobody will ever forget.
6. It was in 1969 that my sister got married, not 1970.
7. It wasn't I who told them and I don't know who did.
8. It's a global recession that we now face.
9. It was as an investment that they bought the house, not to live in it.
10. It was the movie Michael Apted directed I liked.

Task two **

1. What we now face is a global recession.
2. What I was working with was the army, not the navy.
3. What isn't known is when he will get there.
4. What Emily Dickinson wrote was poetry not plays.
5. What attracts the over fifties is cybereconomics.
6. What is on the increase is E-crime.
7. What the head of department needs tomorrow morning are the annual turnover figures.
8. What delayed him was a last minute error.
9. What the streets of London are covered with is concrete, not gold.
10. What Mick Jagger has become is a film producer.

17.7. Organising information – Postponement

Sections **424–429**

Task one **

1. It's lovely to be here.
2. It's expected they will soon attack.

3. It isn't clear why the government is being so cautious.

4. It's disappointing that he failed his exams so badly.

5. It's amazing how long elephants live.

6. It's very gratifying to be proved right in this case.

7. It's stupid to walk all the way to the university.

8. It's a problem if you always refuse.

9. It's hard to predict what will finally happen.

10. It's important for him to win the prize.

Task two **

1. A place has been found for him to stay.

2. The train was late coming from Berlin.

3. What a problem it has been finding this address!

4. How serious are you about resigning?

5. The commander gave the order to shoot himself.

6. The manager paid for the breakages himself.

7. Footballers have more status as celebrities than they used to.

8. All the bills have been paid except the one for the new computer system.

9. He's earned more money in a year writing that one novel than his father earned in his whole life.

10. What a story she had to tell about her adventures in Thailand.

Task three **

It is thought that the British National Health Service is badly run, when it is generally known that it is underfunded. You hear tales of vastly over-crowded hospitals, and it is frequently reported that people have had to wait months, if not years for minor surgery. Set against this, however, is the fact that the British people value the principle of the National Health Service, and it is acknowledged that no government would dare try to dismantle it. When it is suggested by politicians that there could be some kind of private investment, there is strong opposition, but on the other hand there is equally strong opposition when it is said that there will have to be tax increases to fund the service properly. Most analysts ac-knowledge that, in many ways, the service is the most efficient in Europe and that with more investment, it could be one of the best. It is assumed that it will always be there, but it is also feared that it will disappear because of lack of financial support. It isn't appreciated how determined the government is to see it survive.

17.8. Organising information – Other choices

Sections **430–432**; **488**; **608**; **613–618**; **730**; **740**

Task one **

1. How could he afford such a large house?
   He was given the money by his parents.
2. They have proved false the reasons he gave for meeting that woman.
3. How did such a successful company collapse like that?
   Some poor decisions were made by the Chief Executive.
4. In 2001, they gave the prize for the second time to Peter Carey.
5. The writer carefully checked the samples he'd been sent.
6. Don't leave to the last minute work for the exam!
7. His father was finally pleased that he'd done so well in his career.
8. Marc's girl friend was irritated because he insisted on spelling his name with a 'c' instead of a 'k'.
9. Ivan often failed for months to contact his friends.
10. Cathie asked for a second time if she could leave early.

Task two **

More than fifty years after the event, it is instructive to look at how honestly the civilian population was treated by Second World War leaders. Were we regarded as delicate flowers? Were we given all the truth and nothing but the truth compatible with security?

(. . .)

They are revisionist historians, these beady-eyed people who have second thoughts about mighty events. (. . .) Sometimes we are forced to face freshly revealed unpalatable truths by burrowers and snufflers through the once-secret archives: in the war, there was the usual tarnished brass – the military geniuses, heroes, yeomen who were worthy of their country were supported by cowards, deserters, psychopaths and black marketeers.

17.9. Organising information – Avoiding intransitive verbs

Sections **433–434**

Task **

I paid her a visit.; . . . Christine goes for a swim.; . . . , she takes a rest.; They do very little work.; Well, Tom was having a shower.; Suddenly he gave a shout.; I gave the door a hard kick.; Will you have dinner with me tonight?

Bibliography

1. Books

- 2001 *Britannica Book of the Year: Events of 2000* (2001). Encyclopaedia Britannica, Inc.: Chicago, etc. [10.1]
- Carroll, Lewis (1966 edn.). *Alice's Adventures in Wonderland and Through the Looking-Glass.* MacMillan: London (Pocket Papermacs, MacMillan: London-Melbourne; St Martin's Press: New York). [2.1]
- Carter, R. & McCarthy, M. (1997). *Exploring Spoken English.* Cambridge University Press. [1.1; 1.2]
- *Chester Cathedral and City* (1987). Jarrold Publishing. [7.7]
- Conduit, Brian & Brooks, John (1989). *(Pathfinder Guide:) Dartmoor Walks.* Ordnance Survey and Jarrold Publishing. [16.2]
- Crystal, David & Davy, Derek (1975). *Advanced Conversational English.* Longman. [17.1]
- Cunningham, Hilary (ed.) (1996, 6th ed.). *(Insight Guides:) Canada.* Houghton Mifflin. [7.2]
- Dalrymple, W. (1997). *From the Holy Mountain.* Harper Collins. [4.3]
- Dibdin, M. (2000). *Thanksgiving.* Faber & Faber. [4.3]
- *The Highway Code* (1999). The Stationery Office. [7.14; 10.1]
- James, P.D. (1980). *Innocent Blood.* Penguin Books. [5.9; 7.8]
- Morris, Jan (1985). *Among the Cities.* Penguin Books. [4.1]
- *National Statistics* – Social Trends – 2001 ed., The Stationery Office. [4.2]
- O'Driscoll, James (1995). *Britain.* Oxford University Press. [7.1; 7.2]
- Palin, Michael (1992 ⇒ 1996). *Pole to Pole.* Penguin Books. [7.3; 7.17]
- Palin, Michael (1995). *Hemingway's Chair.* BCA: London, etc. [5.1]
- Palin, Michael (1997). *Full Circle.* BBC Books. [7.7; 7.14]
- Raban, Jonathan (1990). *Hunting Mister Heartbreak.* Picador. [7.17]
- *Royal Mail's Code of Practice* (August 2000). [4.3]
- Vine, Barbara (1995). *The Brimstone Wedding.* Penguin Books. [5.9; 5.11]

– Wolfe, Tom (1988). *The Bonfire of the Vanities*. Bantam Books: New York, etc. [2.1]

2. Newspapers
– *Coventry Evening Telegraph* [5.6]
– Finland: Ministry of Agriculture and Forestry, Food and Health Department – Press Release [4.3]
– *Metro* [4.3]
– *New Statesman* [4.3]
– *Newsweek* [5.4; 5.7; 5.11; 6.1; 7.1; 7.2; 11.1]
– *SAGA Magazine* [7.15; 8.1]
– *Sandwell Chronicle* [4.3]
– *The Guardian* [5.8; 14.3]
– *The Independent* [5.6; 5.11]
– *The National Trust Magazine* [14.4]
– *Woman's Weekly* [5.7; 5.9; 5.11]
– *World Cancer Research Fund, Newsletter* [8.1]

3. Websites
– www.news.bbc.co.uk [13.1; 13.6]
– www.pbcountyclerk.com [1.8]
– www.rainforest.amazon.net [5.11]
– www.sydneyexpresstravel.com.au [5.11]